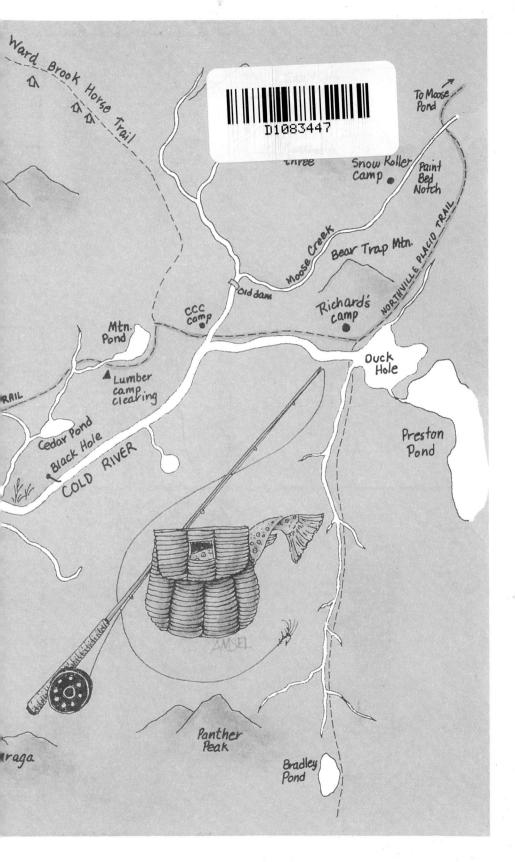

Ward Brook Horse Trail

To Moose Pond

Three

Snow Koller Camp

Paint Bed Notch

Moose Creek

Bear Trap Mtn.

NORTHVILLE PLACID TRAIL

Old dam

CCC Camp

Richard's camp

Mtn. Pond

Duck Hole

Lumber camp clearing

TRAIL

Cedar Pond

Black Hole

COLD RIVER

Preston Pond

AMSEL

Panther Peak

Bradley Pond

raga

LIFE WITH NOAH

Stories and Adventures of
Richard Smith with Noah John Rondeau
as told to
William J. O'Hern

North Country Books, Inc.
Utica, New York

LIFE WITH NOAH

Copyright © 1997
by
William J. O'Hern

ISBN 0-925168-61-0

First Printing 1997
Second Printing 1998

Cover photo courtesy of Richard Smith.

For permission to reprint the following material by Richard Smith, grateful
acknowledgment is made to *Adirondack Life* for:
"Roaming and Trapping," March/April 1985
"Paths to the Past," May/June 1985
"Mosquito Madness," July/August 1985
"The Trapper's Ghost," September/October 1985
"I Shot My Lat Bea . . . ," November/December 1985
"Lost . . . Lost . . . Lost," January/February 1986

Library of Congress Cataloging-in-Publication Data

Smith, Richard, d. 1993
  Life with Noah : stories & adventures of Richard Smith with Noah John
Rondeau / as told to William J. O'Hern.
    p. cm.
  Includes bibliographical references (p. 275).
  1. Rondeau, Noah John, 1883-1967—Anecdotes. 2. Smith, Richard, d. 1993—
Anecdotes. 3. Pioneers—New York (State) —Adirondack Mountains—
Biography—Anecdotes. 4. Hermits —New York (State)—Adirondack Moun-
tains—Biography— Anecdotes. 5. Mountain Life—New York (State)—
Adirondack Mountains—Anecdotes. 6. Adirondack Mountains (New York)—
Biography—Anecdotes. I. O'Hern, William J., 1944-   . II. Title.
F127.A2S65   1997
974.7'504'0922—dc21
[B]   97-15663
                                                                                CIP

Published by
North Country Books, Inc.
311 Turner Street
Utica, New York 13501

Dedication

Contents

Preface

Old friends called him "Red," the Boy Scouts affectionately called their scout master, "Red Beard," still others simply called him Richard. His hermit friend, Noah John Rondeau, kiddingly referred to him as "Quack" because he hailed from Duck Hole, the headwaters of the Cold River.

For his entire life Richard had a love affair with the Cold River in the Adirondack Mountains.

He was an industrious individual, a tinker of all trades, one of Lake Placid's most reliable camp caretakers. A teller in the old-time style, his experiences are a credible history of what it was like to be a woodsman. He was a true friend.

Pursuing the life of a solitary trapper and roaming the woods his entire life, he developed a great understanding of the workings of nature, surpassing the knowledge of the ordinary outdoors person. He most wanted to live with one foot in the Adirondacks of the 1930's and 1940's (Richard's favorite years of his life), and the other firmly resting in an even earlier decade, but he was also realistic.

An unassuming man, Richard explored his human spirit and shaped his life in order to stand up and survive in relation to the technological and industrial universe that surrounded him and created social changes he preferred to resist.

He gained personal satisfaction from recording everyday experiences in a journal. He never considered himself a writer; just someone who enjoyed writing. His writings about living in the wilds of the Adirondacks expressed thoughts, impressions and feelings in a language of a woodsman devoid of all the philosophical nomenclature associated with a polished professional outdoors writer.

He found his greatest joy in the natural world. In the weather. Cold, often punishing winters. Hot summer days filled with insects. Or, the beauty of autumn. Nature. The plants and all the animals were central in his experience. Much like his friend, Noah Rondeau, whom he tried to emulate, Richard found he could live easily with solitude. That type of life experience was inordinately affected by the weather. His sensitive descriptions often romantically personified the universe. Hence the reason hardened woodsmen refer to nature in the feminine gender: "She."

He dabbled in mental exploration of the planet Earth and, while he didn't pretend to begin to unravel the mysteries of nature, he recognized a deepened sense of his earthly dwelling place. He found that man and nature could not, should not, be on opposite sides. It was enough to know that from the carefully scattered ashes of his campfires, the plants of tomorrow would grow.

Acknowledgments

Developing an amateur interest in Adirondack folklore and history is one thing, but to actually see the fruition of one's research take print takes an entirely different set of skills.

I am particularly indebted to Richard Smith, in my view, the last of the Adirondack woodsmen, for his voluminous correspondence over the recent years; to Maitland DeSormo who was positive Richard and I would become great friends; to C.V. Latimer, Jr., M.D., Anthony Okie and Clarence Whiteman who supplied memories, correspondence of Richard's and photographs; to Inez Wood Buis who donated her father's complete Adirondack photographic collection to me; to William Wilkins, long-time friend of Richard's; to Adolph Dittmar and Peggy and Wayne Byrnes for the use of the photographs and memories; to Clarence Petty for his valuable details; to David Greene and Ted Comstock for their reading and commenting on my rough manuscript. David also wrote a short story revealing Noah John Rondeau's code. Ted's initial commentaries helped me to modify my initial focus and pointed me in the right direction; to Sheri Amsel, Adirondack Illustrator for her wonderful map; to Edward and Lloyd Blankman, Harvey Carr, Ted Hillman, Ruth King, Leigh Portner, Sr., George Shaughnessy, Peter Reeves Sperry and Frank R. Studer for the use of photographs; to William F. Palmer for his expertise needed in a pinch; to the Adirondack Museum and librarian Jerry Pepper; to the North Elba-Lake Placid Historical Society; to Jeff Kelly, former editor of *Adirondack Life*, I am deeply indebted for his belief in this project and his editorial work. Without his interest, encouragement and belief in Richard's memories, this book might not have been written.

Introduction

Richard Smith's stories are a firsthand history of the Adirondack woodsmen and hermits who lived back in the mountains and off the land in the 1930's and 1940's, out of choice, love or necessity. A dying breed, to be sure.

I was editor of *Adirondack Life* magazine in 1984, when I received a packet of letters addressed to a friend, Tony, in California, from his childhood buddy, Richard Smith. Tony thought the story-like letters might be worthy of a wider audience.

The letters revealed a shy man, an Adirondack native, who cherished the excitement of the deep woods and who was a genuine friend of the legendary hermit of Cold River, Noah John Rondeau. Richard's writing was folksy and honest. I believed the stories were a valuable historical glimpse into a way of life gone forever.

I chose six stories and made them into a separate department in the magazine which I called "A Woodsman Writes." The title was unassuming, the same way Richard was. "A Woodsman Writes" ran for six consecutive issues from March 1985 to January 1986.

The stories captured the romantic spell of the woods as Richard talked about finding the remains of an old trapper's cabin which had a hidden trap door that opened to a babbling spring of water and a pearl-white, sandy bottom. In one story, Richard played a game of chance with two mountain lions in 1944, long after they were thought to be gone from the Adirondacks. In another, Richard and Noah walked along the overgrown, corduroy logging roads, while they imagined what the life of the logger must have been like in the 1890's.

The stories captured the Adirondacker's cherished spirit of adventure. Richard calmly spent the night out in thirty-degrees-below-zero weather on a remote ledge with only a fire for survival, or bushwhacked in raging blizzards, ending up stumbling into a cave and finding a rusted muzzleloader rifle leaning against a wall next to the scrawled words, "I shot my last bea . . . "

I met Richard just one time. He was then a caretaker for a Lake Placid estate, and he came to visit in my office in Jay. I found him to be a quiet man. I think he just wanted to see for himself where his letters were being published from; wanted to see this editor who had pulled his letters from a stack of submissions, and decided they were a real treasure worthy of publication. For him, seeing his stories in print may have been a revelation and an affirmation that his life in the woods, which he called his best years, meant something to others too.

William J. O'Hern's work here in this book is a lasting tribute to Richard and his vanished way of life. Credit O'Hern with befriending Richard, gathering and, in some cases, writing down Richard's marvelous stories, standing by him to the end, and persevering to publish this rare look at the life and times of a trapper, hunter, fisherman, and romantic hermit of the Adirondacks.

—Jeffrey G. Kelly

PART I

ROAD TO YESTERDAY

Author's Collection

Simple Beginnings

I do not expect anyone reading this to imagine how austere life was for my family living on a rock-bound farm in the township of North Elba, outside the village of Lake Placid during the infant days of the 1900's. No matter how many stones I picked up, more were always waiting. Some of the basic necessities taken for granted today had not yet been invented; others were beyond the reach of my father's meager wages. In contrast, my life today depends on my truck, snowblower, and chainsaw. Electricity is also nice. As a result, the independence rural families such as mine once possessed has vanished in the name of progress.

I consider myself fortunate to have grown up when a man living in the North Country could still provide a respectable income for himself by hunting and fishing, until the 1940's. In those days reputations were made by deeds, not by words. And, although I never sought out recognition from friends and neighbors regarding my prowess for woodcraft, I cannot help chuckling at how some of the younger generation looks upon me as the model of a vanishing breed. To think me, Red Beard, as the scouts in my troop called me, a model. I laugh at the notion.

I don't understand why my neighbors on River Road feel being a trapper and a woodsman is a thing of the past. Growing up in the Adirondack Mountains, we took it for granted that one could hunt and fish. I always wanted to live up to the reputation of Daniel Boone and the other frontiersmen. They were my heroes; their self-reliance was my inspiration.

I enjoyed growing up when people did not rely so much on technology as they do today to solve their problems. One of my greatest pleasures was reading about our country's early trappers, guides and pioneers. When I wasn't needed on the farm I roamed the surrounding forest and mountains, daydreaming of going into the wilderness with Daniel Boone or the Deerslayer of Leatherstocking fame.

My first adventure happened when I was nine. I went on a search in the great swamp behind our farm. Father warned me not to get distracted because I had to track down and drive back our prized yearling heifer which had wandered off after breaking through the fence. Armed with my toy rifle I called my coonhound, Blue, and we set out.

Approaching the swamp on the trail made by the heifer, I was confident I would soon have the animal headed home. Blue quickly picked up the scent, and shortly we sighted the calf grazing in a small clearing in the middle of the swamp. My dog closed in causing her to panic and she leapt in my direction. At that moment Father's words were forgotten and my imagination kicked in. I wasn't out on an errand, I was with Deerslayer and we were on an important hunting expedition. Hungry pioneers waited for our return to the settlement with much needed venison. Without a moment's hesitation I snapped the pine board rifle to my shoulder, gauged the speed of the animal and squeezed the trigger. I watched the black rubberband, cut from an inner tube, fly toward the target and witnessed the calf drop in a heap. As the animal fell, my mind snapped back to the present. Scared out of my wits, I ran toward her. Had she broken a leg? My eyes caught a red mark high on her ribcage. What had I done? Before I was able to reach her, she scrambled to her feet and went crashing through the balsams with Blue herding her back towards the barn.

Everything worked out fine in the end. The yearling, alarmed by the baying hound, had stumbled the moment I fired. What I thought was blood on her side turned out to be the red clay I had smeared on the rubber band. No matter how scared I had been I knew I was hooked on hunting. (The red clay was a youthful thing I did to promote realism, but I forgot all about the clay when I saw the animal drop.)

There was an old clearing grown-over with brambles where we used to chop wood about a half mile beyond our homestead. Everybody knew that during July and August this was the best spot to pick wild blueberries, red raspberries and blackberries. I remember the pleasant sound made by their clanking pails as locals walked down the dirt road toward the sunny cut-over. One man stood out. He was a barber and lived by himself in a small shack on Greenwood Street. Father was good friends with him and knew he enjoyed Mother's cooking, so whenever we spotted him we invited him in for lunch.

The after-lunch ritual always interested my brothers and me. Father would take down his old Marlin .30-.30, and he and the barber would walk out to the field for some target practice. Both were expert shots. We boys would climb up on the rail fence to watch and listen to the men deep in conversation as they fired at bottles and cans. I was amazed at Father's skill when one time a partridge was flushed out, and he actually shot the eye out of it. I didn't know it then, but this other man would be partly responsible for shaping my life in the years to come. He used to say matter-of-factly, "The best way to become known as a great hunter, fisherman and trapper is to do a lot more of it than anyone else, and sooner or later you are bound to be recognized as the best in the field." How true his comment was for he, Noah John Rondeau, later came to be known as the hermit of Cold River, the famous outdoors man.

Father said Rondeau was a storehouse of knowledge regarding woods lore. Just the opposite of what I expected of a barber. He had a reputation around Lake Placid as being rather odd, a bit of an outcast. His strong outspoken opinions about his fellow man and the law set him apart from others. He frequently talked about how times were not the best, and how he wanted a life free from government interference. At age thirty he contended that his hair cutting would never provide a decent income, and figured he was never going to amount to anything. He would gladly give up his trade for a life in the wilderness. He believed the woods had healing powers and that living alone in the wilderness would provide him a happier and more rewarding life.

My Wanderings on the Chubb River

As a boy the Chubb River fascinated me. It was only a short walk away through the fields from my backyard, along Old Military Road. Its waters held a special intrigue. I couldn't wait to be old enough to explore the wild country it drained.

In the 1930's I started my muskrat trapping career along it to keep coins jingling in my threadbare pockets. I felt like King Midas. Each muskrat I caught suddenly turned to gold. When I was fifteen, using only my two rat traps, I was able to save enough "shekels" to buy my first rifle. For three dollars, I became the owner of an old Stevens .22 with a pump action so tired that it operated as a single-shot. This forced me to make each bullet count so that eventually I could drop a rabbit or grouse with one shot.

Before long I decided to graduate to trapping red foxes. Each of their pelts would fetch a dollar and a half more than a rat pelt. I was fascinated with an advertisement that showed E.J. Dailey, a St. Lawrence Country trapper, standing next to a display of fox pelts closely hung on a sixty-foot wire. The ad appeared in *Fur News and Outdoor World*, a magazine I enjoyed reading. All I needed to do, I thought, was to purchase Dailey's custom scents, and fox were sure to walk into my traps. Dailey and a friend named Dick Wood, who was a professional photographer and outdoor writer, caught Cold River fever and had trapped the entire river basin from about 1916 to 1925. They wrote about their adventures in several sporting magazines of the day, the early articles which interested me. Sporting stories might not be the type of literature that appeals to a wide audience, but when I would begin one of their articles in which they described being separated from their main camp in the "inky black darkness of a stormy night," I couldn't put it down. They wrote about Big Dam, their headquarters at Duck Hole, trekking from Moose Pond into the Sawtooth Range, and of a particular fox in the Cold River Valley they dubbed Keen Nose—whose savvy assured its survival no matter how cleverly sets were prepared. Duck Hole and Cold River were approximately sixteen miles as the crow flies from our farm, but for me, at home doing chores most days, it could have just as well have been as far off as the Yukon.

The exploits Dailey wrote about hooked me. I couldn't move fast enough to place my order for his powerful inducements. By foregoing sweets and picture shows, I was able to save enough money to buy six fox traps—enough I thought to launch myself on a fox-trapping career. The first winter proved disappointing. I found wily red foxes deserved their reputation and I began to wonder about Dailey's testimonials. Each time I diligently followed his directions for applying the fox lure my luck got worse. Eventually I gave it up; the lure's ingredients seemed to repel not attract. I imagined a fox getting a whiff of my concoction and running away so fast that he would hit his head on Gibraltar before stopping.

Once I became more familiar with better techniques, I saw why the foxes must have laughed until their bellies ached at my feeble efforts to trap them. I made up my mind to erase those sly grins and place steel bracelets on a few of the less cagey ones next season. I bought more traps and began to dabble with my own scents and lures and found (contrary to the experts) that using a generous amount profited the maker not the trapper. Only a drop or two were needed. I likened scents to a woman's perfume—a trace being most effective. Then when everything about my set had been perfected, I used to imagine the animals fighting each other for the privilege of being the first to step into the steel jaws.

A New Friend Moves In

In 1934 I met Tony Okie who was to become one of my closest friends. He had been living with his mother and grandfather in Antwerp, Belgium, and for most of his youth had suffered from reoccurring respiratory infections. Home remedies of mustard plasters and suction cups "cures" had proved ineffectual. Concerned that he had tuberculosis, Tony's mother sent him to treatment centers at St. Gervais-les Bains and later to St. Moritz.

When he recovered his mother decided to relocate in America. New York City was to have been his new home, but soon after immigrating he once again became ill. This time his mother chose Lake Placid where the Adirondack mountain air made a difference. By the time Tony entered high school, his mother had decided they would stay in Lake Placid and had a small, rustic lodge, complete with a fishing pond, built on Bear Club Road, not far from the home of Jacques Suzanne, Lake Placid's famed sled-dog racer.

Tony enjoyed the freedom of the wide open countryside and roamed the surrounding woods. In high school he met Bill Wilkins, a classmate who one day promised to teach him to swim, something he had always wanted to learn. Tony accepted Bill's offer, although he admitted he was worried. He had almost drowned in two previous attempts. Bill took him to the banks of the Chubb River one day when I was there. In spite of its mucky shoreline the swimming hole was the most popular gathering spot in the neighborhood. I stood watching as Bill instructed this new boy to first peel off his clothes and then crawl on all fours right into the water up to his neck. It was obvious he was scared, so I went down to the water's edge and encouraged him. After he succeeded in swimming a little using the doggie paddle method, we celebrated his success by sharing a forbidden cigarette. Then we taught him how to use spittle from chewing tobacco—we kept a cache hidden in an old tin can nearby—to dislodge the suckers before we got dressed.

That was the summer Tony and I became fast friends. Although his home was a fair distance from mine, that never discouraged me from going over when I had time. How I loved his mother's special sauce with lamb chops and fresh sweet peas.

The Okies were not well off, but even during the Depression they were comfortable because of his late father's military pension. Mrs. Okie recognized our families had different backgrounds, but she was always kind and generous toward me. Whatever Tony had, even his rifle, he always shared with me. In return I taught him what I knew of woodcraft and told him stories of the deep woods.

On weekends we would venture into the fields and woods target shooting, or we would go fishing. We got pretty good at bagging wood-chucks and squirrels, and enjoyed eating what we killed. One spring day a city man—we assumed from his fancy clothes and his car—watched us as we fished from a bridge. After we had caught several trout he asked what our secret to success was. We both thought he was amusing and probably inexperienced, because he offered us a rod and a new creel if we would tell him. While Tony was speaking to him, I turned away from the stranger's view and swiftly cleared away the dirt that clung on a few worms, using my thumb and forefinger like a squeegee to clean them. Then, still keeping my actions from the two, I slipped them into my mouth and walked toward the man. Tony caught my glance and knew I was up to something when he saw my cheek bulging. Putting my hand to my mouth I spit the wigglers into my cupped hand and outstretched it open to the city man's great surprise. "There ya go, mister," I said, "no charge. When it's cold like today you have to keep the bait warm." His facial reaction was nothing less than dumfounded. It made our day.

We Try Bow Hunting

Bow hunting was not a popular sport or even well-known in the 1930's. Neither of us knew much about it. Our research at the local library provided us with some books that showed us step by step how to make and use archery equipment. In addition to the technical side, we also became interested in reading about medieval battles where English archers battled French knights in armor at Cre'cy, Poitiers, and Agincourt. We read all the history books we could find.

One day while Tony was getting his hair cut at the shop near school, he mentioned his interest in archery to the barber who told him that years ago there had been another barber in town who went off by himself to live in the wilds around Cold River. This man, he said, actually hunted with a bow. That was exciting news to us. We imagined ourselves walking through the forest with this hermit, bow and arrows in hand. We had all we could do to contain our excitement.

Our Wilderness Trek

Several days later we set out in the early morning to find this bow-hunting hermit. We had made homemade bows and arrows from designs and instructions in Saxton Pope's book, "Hunting with the Bow and Arrow." With these bows, my father's hand-me-down .30-.30, a few chocolate bars, raisins, oatmeal, sandwiches and blankets, we hiked toward Four Corners—a short distance beyond Lake Placid's railroad station and my home. As I think about it now, those few provisions seem so imprudent. We didn't consider carrying canteens since we could quench our thirst by drinking from streams. From the Four Corners we turned on to the Averyville road until we reached a farmhouse close to the Northville-Placid Trail, and a footpath we had never ventured down. The footpath was the first big project of the Adirondack Mountain Club in the early 1920's. The marked trail led first to Wanika Falls. A plunge in the pool looked inviting, but despite the warm day the mountain stream proved far too cold, so we passed it by. From there the trail continued towards Moose Pond, the outlet of which we followed until it joined Cold River. At that point we were on our own, because no one we talked to seemed to have a clear idea where along the river the hermit lived.

The first ten miles went quickly, but somewhere along the way I began to question whether this trek into the wilderness was worthwhile. Tony wouldn't hear of turning back. He insisted we "forge ahead," as he put it and I am forever grateful we did. My life would have been different if we hadn't. Beyond Moose Pond the trail narrowed as it passed the remains of an old dam on the pond's outlet to Cold River. This trail, I recall, passed through territory that had been lumbered. One section we hiked through contained a magnificent stand of old growth timber that towered over the trail. Our hike took most of the day as we lollygagged along, shot arrows and stopped to eat our chocolate and raisins.

A short distance beyond a virgin stand of hardwoods we came to a lean-to on the north bank of Cold River about a mile below Duck Hole. When we began our trip we had grand plans of living off the land, so I found it ironic that we would eat, with no hesitations, a can of sardines and some stale mice-nibbled doughnuts left on a shelf in a lean-to we happened upon by the river. While exploring around the log shelter we noticed the remains of a giant head of a trout on the picnic table. We learned later that Black Hole, a famed local fishing spot, was just down-river from the shelter. Once our wanderings had taken us beyond the sight of the cookie jar, we realized that our original thought of subsisting on wild food was pure poppycock. Gathering scrub apples and berries in logging clearings was time-consuming and unproductive, given the few handfuls of fruit the forest creatures had seen fit to leave us.

Tony had brought along a crude hand-drawn map the barber had given him. We didn't know enough to buy a USGS topographical map even though they were cheap and readily available. However, the painted disks nailed to trees made following trails easy and allowed us to stick to our route. Within sight of the Cold River lean-to we came across a sign-board nailed on a tree indicating Lake Placid was fifteen miles away. On a second sign which pointed to Mountain Pond, some considerate hiker had scratched, "To Rondeau's—Big Dam, 6 miles." We were on the right trail.

We kept on and crossed the outlet of Mountain Pond to a clearing, the site of an old logging camp. We investigated the ruins and found that the layout of the bunkhouse and cookhouse were still visible. The camp had consisted of a bunk and cookhouse, a barn, and a blacksmith shop. We picked through the rotting logs and found some old metal tools and con-tainers that were still usable. We feasted on the thumb-nail-sized raspber-ries eating them bear-style, that is, green ones, leaves and all. But hand-fuls of the sweet- tasting fruit really did little to change the gnawing in our stomachs. The afternoon temperatures had risen making us more inclined to refresh ourselves in the nearby water. We plunged in to one of the deeper swimming holes. We learned why someone had once chosen to name it Cold River! Refreshed, we were ready to venture on.

Judging by the sun, we estimated it was about four or five o'clock. Three hours of sunlight plus another two hours of twilight remained, cer-tainly enough time (we thought) for six miles. But before we had hiked that distance we decided to stop and make camp while it was still light. As we gathered firewood, Tony heard the sound of someone chopping wood in the distance. We repacked our supplies and followed the dull thuds and soon spotted what looked like a teepee silhouetted against the darkening sky. Then we saw a miniature one marking a path off to the left. This was, we later learned, "the Gate to the City."

Sparks popping in the clear sky led us up the slight rise as a cool breeze wafted pungent woodsmoke our way. We continued until we came upon what turned out to be cone-shaped log structures and two small cabins. What we had initially taken to be teepees were crudely engineered pole buildings. We walked straight toward the man swinging an ax into a block of wood. I waited until he straightened up and summoned a soft "Hello" so as not to alarm him. The thin figure turned and looked toward us as we approached. We then saw his long black beard and the deerskin overalls, and immediately guessed we were face to face with Lake Placid's barber-turned-hermit.

I began to speak but stopped myself when I realized the hermit was looking at the rifle I carried. He was obviously curious for he continued to study it as I drew closer to the fire where the brighter light afforded a better view. In a high tone he queried, "You must be George Smith's boy and if you're going to deny it, then explain why you have his old chicken hawk Marlin .30-.30 ?" I was astonished: this man knew my father! His revelation made our trek into the unknown seem like the world had just pulled in at the waist a wee bit. "I'll venture a guess your George's youngest and that you've got fiery red hair under that cap," he exclaimed.

By the time we had completed our introductions, I recalled he was the one who used to stop by our homestead and shoot with my father. I was overjoyed. It didn't take long for Noah John Rondeau to size us up. He remembered me as a four-year-old. To his way of thinking that made me an "old friend" now that I had made my way back into his acquaintance.

Sensing how hungry we were, he offered us some of the stew simmering in his iron pot. In addition he boiled a large turnip. Before long we were filling in the gap of years since he had last seen me at a distance by our pasture fence. Noah told us of the day he witnessed my father bring down a chicken hawk with the rifle I carried. As he congratulated father on such a fine shot, he said he remembered a shy red-haired boy peering through the rails of the fence. Surprised that he remembered, I announced that I still had red hair; it was so red my friends teased me about it. As I listened to the hermit talk about his life in Lake Placid, I couldn't help thinking how sharp his memory was and how delighted he was to reminisce.

In the glow of the firelight we ate and showed him our hunting equipment. We explained that we had followed instructions found in a book on archery. Noah reached out and took first Tony's bow, and then mine. He inspected them carefully and asked how we became interested in hunting with bow and arrows and why we chose to make our own equipment. His questions and comments conveyed to us the feeling that he actually was interested in what we had done.

We explained it was not possible for either of us to purchase the store-bought equipment. Besides, we liked the challenge of building our own outfits. We also enjoyed perfecting the gear and had became proficient enough to kill woodchucks, rabbits, grouse and squirrels. Tony had even shot a fox.

Enthusiastically, Tony explained we favored a flat short bow over the long narrow English style model because we thought it more suitable for hunting small game. After looking at our paraphernalia, Noah told us we did a fine job making the equipment. Naturally we were anxious to hear anything he said, but that one comment alone bolstered our self-esteem. He then disappeared into his tiny cabin and reemerged dressed in a deer-skin jacket with fringe. As he approached us with his bow in hand, I remember thinking how he fit the archetypal stereotype of a hermit. His black beard, felt hat made waterproof by painting it with green paint, and the rawhide fringe swishing as he walked, cast an appearance of a genuine mountain-man. His bow looked more to be the conventional English style. It was as tall as he was and was wrapped in leather. He said the bow had a seventy-five pound pull. The arrows had razor sharp home-made points, made from old crosscut sawteeth mounted on brass rifle cartridges. "I gave up hunting with a rifle a few years ago," he volunteered. "Too unfair to wildlife." Then he laughed and admitted he was exaggerating. While he had brought down partridge and deer with his bow, he had actually killed more with his rifles. "You see," he continued, "I got a .22 Remington pump-action for small game and camp prowlers like coon and porcupine. Them rifles are a big, practical thing you know."

Noah didn't ask us many questions but when he did, we gave a careful and probably longer response than necessary. We were delighted he appeared interested in our bow hunting. When we mentioned we had studied the history of archery in the library, he said he had too.

As a youngster growing up in a rural environment, he had made many of his own toys. As a boy, a bow and arrow were essential to him. With his whittling knife and a small bow saw, he would leave his Jackson Hill home and go off in search of just the right ash sapling. When he found one with the arch he wanted, he would cut it, then notch a circular groove an inch below each end and string it with butcher's twine for a bow string.

For arrow shafts he used the long straight stems of cattails. With a notch on the string end of the arrow, he could set the thread into the space and hold the arrow on the string as he drew it back. In this way he could hit most targets if he "stood close enough." As he grew older he continued to refine his homemade equipment trying different woods, strings, arrow heads and bird feathers to improve the flight. After drawing a target on the side of the family's barn, he got to be pretty good at hitting "big things." "I was born to a woodsman's life," he said. "Hunting came as naturally as slipping on a pair of trousers."

I learned later that Noah wrote down words exactly as they sounded. Some of his words made me chuckle. For instance an old friend lived on Park Drive in Lake Placid, which he pronounced "Porxide." Sometimes he would use words I didn't know. But each time I asked, he would explain their meaning. Back home I would look up some of those terms in a dictionary just out of curiosity and would find his definitions nearly always correct. His speech and wisdom were homespun, and I felt his learning was above that of many who had the advantage of a formal education.

Noah liked to read and write. He often consumed weeks, even months of uninterrupted time between visitors, laboring over how to link rambling thoughts together in poems written only for himself. Decades later he gave me a large package of his handwritten "scrawls" as he called them. He had been promised by a mountain climber that his poems would be printed in the Forty-Sixers of Troy's publication. They never were; he was greatly disappointed.

I wonder just how long it did take him to organize those scribbles? One titled the "The Barefoot Girl" attempted to advise one to enjoy one's childhood. For once the colorful quilts, dolls and mud pies were set aside there was only " . . . war, taxes, gods and stovepipe hats." And he rambled on:

> ". . . don't be good for rewards after your earthly life.
> White Robes, Harps of Gold and Crowned with Stars
> Fall short for dead women and dead men,
> As for dead tomcats and old dead hens.
> And beware of all creatures of Bible lies
> Or you'll believe a man lived in tripe three days in the deep
> Then came back alive to reveal mysteries of myths called god.

> Don't be a hero worshiper of Roman collars.
> They are not your friend; they are liars.

Myths are not to know to gods or mystic men,
Now or in the end of the world without end.
Beware of the preachers of Democracy,
Without enough in practice for a mockery.

Beware of politicians speech in war time,
   And hope for pillage on blood-soaked ground.

Beware of blabbers of equal born rights,
Which is not true for the most part.
And for the few possible equal rights
Everything's been done to hither and retard.

Beware of politicians who stream popular votes
When their election costs billions in the hole
Beware of modern new deals of democracy;
   It's the same old crooked deal advanced in robbery.

Don't buy liberty from labors holy robbers.
Liberty bought at a price for work
Is bondage of itself from the start.
And the holy robbers are never satisfied.
Beware of 'The Land of the Free and the Home of the Brave'.
It's the Land of the Thieves and the Home of the Slaves.
Beware of radios that pretend to entertain with advertising blab on pills
   for belly-ache."

Leaning back in a homemade wooden chair, book resting on the top of his crossed leg, was Noah's reading position. This way he could gently rock as he read, his attention occasionally diverted by the sounds and movements of wildlife. A keen observer of nature, he enjoyed the entertaining antics of the local "Clan of Knaw-It-Runabout-Us." Pesky field mice abounded. It was a challenge to catch them, and true to Noah's character he'd make some of the most hag-ridden devices for traps. Scampering around the pansies that ringed the base log of the Town Hall, they "raised mischief" collecting seeds from fallen flowers. "They're a lot like the mayor," Noah would say as they darted about like thieves, further illustrating the connection between the mice and himself. "Victuals are not bountiful back here. The law, you know, is pretty strict—so you have to look out for danger. Just like those little critters that get caught in my back breaker traps. I always played that game very cautiously." I knew he meant illegal hunting and trapping. "It wasn't unusual to hear some people counsel I had nothing to be concerned with since I lived so far back in the wild. I knew better; that's dangerous talk. A mistake could jeopardize my security, so I always played the game guardedly. I've bamboozled the law and have never been convicted. Never will be either!"

A logging chain held the kettle we had earlier taken stew from. During the course of the evening Noah remarked that rangers had come by recently and questioned him about the kind of meat cooking in the pot. "Is it deer meat?" they had asked. He said he'd invited them to sample it, but they declined and let the matter drop. The pitch of his voice rose as he told us how he'd like to part any ranger's hair with an arrow, a remark he punctuated with a great burst of laughter.

"I've got no use at all for dishonesty," he frankly admitted. It was obvious from his accounts that he'd had his share of dealings with game wardens. "There's so much of life I don't care for, and I seemed to find it in every town I worked in," he reflected.

His complex of buildings, which Noah referred to as his "City," made an interesting scene. There were two crude cabins opposite the outdoor fireplace over which we were cooking breakfast. They were about ten feet long and eight feet wide. Both were crudely built out of old logs and boards. The roof and sides were covered with bits of canvas and tar paper held in place by rocks, poles and nails. Signs above the doorways identified them as the Town Hall and Hall of Records. The exterior walls had the most exotic decorating I had ever seen. Tacked to the wood and canvas siding was a large assortment of animals bones: chalk-colored shoulder blades of beaver, deer antlers, and a number of bear skulls. When the wind blew the bones rattled like wind chimes.

Wigwams, Noah's word to describe the teepees, lined the riverside bluff beyond the fireplace. They were made of logs of a manageable size so they could be carried or dragged to his hilltop. Each log had been part way cut through into segments before being placed upright against a frame that was held together by a heavy logging chain. When the fire needed feeding all that was necessary was to pull off a pole and strike a healthy blow where it had been already nearly cut through. In a few minutes a number of chunks of stove and fireplace-length wood was ready for the fire. "You see, they welcome visitors to my city," he replied to my inquiry of the wigwams. "I got the idea from when I was a child. Children would often make a playhouse by stacking poles and cornstalks in such a way as to create a room inside." The collection of wigwams and little huts were all that made up his Cold River "bailiwick" which boasted a population of one: "The mayor, justice of the peace and dog catcher."

Earlier that evening Tony had mentioned that a barber in Lake Placid had put us on to him. After inquiring who the man was, Noah said he had always tried to look behind the face of the person he shaved. "Man is forever a stranger and alone," he commented solemnly. After that declaration he must have thought his statement a tad too perplexing for teenagers since he qualified it with a bit of humor by saying crowds were okay, but he liked them best "when they were going the other way."

As the hours elapsed into late evening Noah talked about the stars, moon, animals of the forest and life away from civilization. He asked about our schooling and counseled about the benefits of a good education. It hadn't been easy for him, he said. He had little formal education but tried to make up for it by reading everything he could get his hands on. "I got my learning back here among these lofty peaks, but the mathematics is hard to get alone." While in the fifth grade his teacher had confronted him and asked a perplexing mathematics question. "Noah, how would you divide twelve apples among fourteen people?" He told us he thought on it for a minute before coming up with a solution. "I'd make applesauce."

He explained, "Some learning's were harder than others but if people would just give new and difficult material a chance they'd see it won't be all that difficult." He was convinced that more students could become scholarly in the many disciplines if they would accept the struggle and at least try harder to learn their lessons.

One of the many things he would do for enjoyment those days was to take a mock college course "just on my own authority." He often carried a book back in from his trips to the "outside" and read cover to cover other volumes friends would bring him. He particularly liked those on creation, philosophy, geology and astronomy. Each time he would know more than when he started. "I would have a lot of fun laughing at myself, going through that stuff."

Going without a radio or phonograph meant nothing to Noah. In the late 1920's, after he had moved permanently to Big Dam, he was given a violin, "my Stradivarius," he called it. Along with his books, it became the provider of hours of diversion. We were not prepared to believe our hermit was a virtuoso musician. Any notion that he might actually be accomplished disappeared within the first minute. As he drew the frayed bow across the strings, we knew Noah's fiddle playing was not going to be the sound of soothing melodies. Yet, we did enjoy his "entertainment hour." In addition to several folk tunes, he took the greatest pride in playing two of his favorites: "Pop Goes the Weasel" and "The Irish Woman's Washboard."

When his playing ended, Noah, still seated in his plank rocker with its bearskin cover, put aside the fiddle and began to draw deeply on his "goose egg" pipe—a great meerschaum given to him years ago by his friend Billy Burger. During his musical I had noticed a sign slightly illuminated by a reflecting metal object that picked up light from the fire. The words "The Beauty Parlor" were painted on a cloth nailed over the opening to one of the wigwams. I was surprised I hadn't seen it earlier in the evening, but there were so many things to see. I wondered what it meant, but didn't want Noah to feel I was prying. Ultimately my curiosity got the best of me and I asked. "Oh, that's just a hermit's joke," he laughed. "I have names for all of them. There's 'Mrs. Rondeau's Kitchenette' where I do my summer cooking and then there's the 'Pyramid of Giza,' my meat wigwam. Each fall I hang and cure a deer and a bear carcass there. Hang them right in full sight so any game warden that comes a-snooping sees what I got. Of course the lady mountain climbers who visit my city have to stop at the Beauty Parlor," he said as he pointed to it. "I got me a tin wash basin in a hollowed-out cedar stump there for freshening up. Even got eyebrow pencils for the fancy women! You see, I remind folks that although my name is Noah, I didn't build the Ark; I'm the one who builds wigwams!"

The six wigwams were uniform in size about twenty-five feet tall and were made from poles that were deeply notched every thirty inches. Each were designed with an entrance to the interior that allowed the inside cavity to be used for storage. Cultivated flowers grew around the perimeter of the cabins; he even had an official flower bed and vegetable garden in the clearing where the plants could receive the most hours of sunlight. There were several pole tripods with heavy iron kettles hanging from chains by which he suspended his cooking pot over the fire. Out of them grew a mixture of colorful flowers, many of which had long stems that hung over the sides giving the old kettles a touch of beauty.

When I brought up the subject of survival hunting and fishing, Noah began musing again about the game laws and the game wardens. "Ain't any government that's good, " he informed me. "The devil has had a running controversy against Jehovah for over six thousand years and it's going to be coming to an end soon." I assumed his harsh reaction was in reference to a run-in he had with the law. The topic appeared to be a sensitive one, so I steered the conversation to a related one. I mentioned that I knew of an old fellow who lived in a cabin on the side of the Sentinal Range in Lake Placid who was plagued by the game protectors. He perked right up at the mention of that. "How so, Richard?" he asked. I had gotten his mind off religion, so I resumed as if I had first-hand knowledge of the situation.

My brothers had told me about him. He was supposed to have been a guide in his younger days and even now folks thought he was a darn good trapper despite his advancing years. He had himself a little cabin in the woods between the Ausable River and the South Notch in the Sentinal Range. People around there said he had constant problems with the local law enforcement officer. Noah looked interested. The game protector believed the old woodsman was breaking the law by hunting out of season. He might have been, but locals held he was only trying to provide for himself. Anyhow, people said the protector was one of those so-called reformed game offenders the state occasionally hired to patrol the woods. The protector was determined to impress his superiors and get a feather in his hat, so he placed the old man high on his list of law breakers to catch.

The man's activities had been scrutinized for several years but he was never arrested. Eventually the warden was replaced by a younger man who boasted that he'd catch the old fellow with ease. Yet, he too, spent several fruitless years dogging the man off and on. Then because he was tormented by the fact he was becoming the laughing stock of the community, or because he had yet to uncover any evidence, he decided to resort to a round-the-clock tactic.

His first fall night in the field was a particularly frosty one. Chilled, sore from sleeping on the ground and hungry, he awoke to see the woodsman come out on the back porch, cup his hands to his mouth and holler, "Hey, Mr. Game Protector! You must be cold and hungry. Why don't you come in and get a hot cup of coffee?"

The young warden remained out of sight. He was later observed making his way down the mountainside to his vehicle. Word spread quickly about his defeat. The thought of being the butt of local jokes was more that he could bear. The warden made up his mind he would hike to his watch undetected that night, even if it meant walking many miles.

Another night spent in the woods ended the next morning with the old trapper again appearing on the back porch to shout out the same invitation, "Hey, Mr. Game Protector! You must be cold and hungry. Why don't you come in and get a hot cup of coffee?"

The warden was more perplexed than ever. He was sure he hadn't been detected, yet here he was being mocked. With great reluctance he decided to accept the man's offer. As he climbed the porch steps the woodsman greeted him. Once inside the snug cabin he felt warm and the old man seemed friendly. Perhaps all the stories he had heard about this fellow were unsubstantiated.

Following a cup of very black coffee, the old-timer placed fried pork and flapjacks on the table. As they ate, the inexperienced warden inquired what he had done to be detected.

"Well son, you didn't do nothin," the woodsman replied. "I didn't know you was out there. For more years than I can remember I've gone out on my porch every morning and as a kind of ritual and shouted something like, 'Hey, Mr. Game Protector! You must be cold and hungry. Why don't you come inside and have a cup of coffee?' Darn if it didn't work on the other warden too. Don't worry, I won't mention this embarrassing incident to a soul if you don't want me to. By the way, how did you like my coffee?"

I could tell Noah was amused at my tale. "You see there, Richard, the government just ain't no good and it never will be! There's no better remedy for it than a revolt. It has got to be overthrown. Course actually ever being able to turn the government out will be a slow thing at best, but I do believe it 'll happen in due time."

Little did I realize my story would only serve to fuel his distaste for government. He didn't hold back at all, as he told about how he had been hounded by the law. The last straw came when he was found guilty and fined for a brush fire that got out of hand behind his Greenwood Street house in Lake Placid. He paid the fine because he was "railroaded" by officers, left with no way to prove he didn't cause the blaze. He gave no hint he actually was at fault. But I could not help thinking why else would he have buckled under to the charge?

"I finally decided I was sick of civilization and all it represented. That was back in 1913," he said. "I never thought the country was any good. I sweated for small wages all through my twenties and never got anywhere. I didn't have much education, but I was a pretty good carpenter, painter and finally a barber." He considered his meager income "insufficient" and the work unrewarding. He didn't need to convince himself. One day he got up and quit . . . quit on life, as he put it.

Blue smoke rose from his pipe. "A person can just take so much of the world and its tendencies in one lifetime. Mind you the common work didn't bother me so much. It's just that good wages never accompanied all my hard labor. After I'd pay my board and all, it was about impossible for me to get ahead. I got to taking a narrow view of life, and I didn't care for what I saw."

"Yeah, I headed out, I did. Went to the forest. I was familiar with the old so-called government trail that lead from North Elba to Duck Hole. I'd known all about that country for quite a while. Even when I held a job, I'd get out into the woods with the rabbits and deer. As a youngster I was born and raised to that kind of life. It was as a grown-up that I strayed from it."

"I also knew about the big woods around Coreys. In the teens the population consisted of a few summer camp owners, and about a half-dozen families who were full-time residents. Catherine Petty ran the small post office. The Petty's and Hathaway's, old-time families in the area, were guides and caretakers. In time we came to be good friends."

Tupper Lake was ten miles away and Saranac Lake sixteen by the old road. A stagecoach would come in from Tupper Lake carrying mail and supplies. During the winter, on the few occasions snowdrifts in the farm clearings east of Tupper blocked the road, a four-horse team pulling a sled was used to tote provisions in. There was no store although practical supplies could be purchased from the remote Santa Clara lumber camp. Pelcher's, or Camp 4, was a typical Adirondack camp along the lumbermen's road that ran southeast from Ampersand Pond. It paralleled Ward Brook that flowed in the wide valley between the Sawtooth and Seward Mountain ranges. Hundreds of deer trails seemed to crisscross that roadway. In the vicinity of Ampersand Pond, Noah mentioned he would often notice signs of mink, fox, otter and beaver. It was also from that camp that he would hitch a ride with a teamster who would drop him off at Mountain Pond.

"I did a lot of thrashing around in there. I was pretty good with a gun, a fish pole, and everything else. I didn't get lonely either like a lot of the people in Coreys figured I would; I didn't have time to! There was so much to do just to survive. Besides, what would I have to miss? I hate Big Government and Jackass Democrats. And Big Business, you know, it's crooked too. The world itself is like that. It's no good and it'll never be any different. I came to the woods to get away from it all mainly because I hated it all. I still do and always will!

"In the beginning I did a little guiding for a hotel. Following my arrest in '24 on trumped up game law violations—charges that proved to be false—the government denied me a guide's license. I still guided though—not much of course—and all unofficial. In time I found ways to teach those wardens a thing or two.

"The furbearers got pretty numerous in those isolated pockets among the mountain peaks after the loggers had left. I had me a canvas wall tent down on the Raquette River first and then I rented a camp at Coreys. When it burned I made a little cabin around Calkins Creek near a place I called Peek-A-Boo Hill; I referred to it as my Jungle Camp. It was located to avoid the likes of the noisy game protectors who used to steal from my traps I laid down along the Raquette River. I made it so that someone would feel more like a mouse proceeding in the jungle. And then, I had another one or two cabins—nothing much—here and there around the woods. It was a natural thing for me to live in the mountains. In time I worked my way back to Cold River, even stayed a season with the crew at the camp at Big Dam that was here then. I suppose you could say I went at it like a wild man in those days."

My First Morning at Big Dam

Tony and I woke up well after sunrise. Before leaving the wigwam we peered out and surveyed the hermit's city. By the fire where we sat for hours was Noah's plank rocker with his special brand of upholstery. Humorously, he had declared he pitied any hermit who didn't own a bearskin covered rocker. I didn't pinch myself as we walked out into the yard, but in some ways I felt as if I were in a dream. The bright morning light felt soothing to our faces as we walked the top of the bank behind Noah's cabins that overlooked Cold River. A thin veil of fog, fast dissipating in the morning warmth, was suspended over the water. We saw our host standing at the base of the dam casting a line towards a hole beneath the dilapidated spillway. He caught our good-morning wave and responded with a nod.

With that we descended to the river via what Noah called his "Golden Stairway"—a log crib fitted into the gravel bank so one could walk up and down the slope easily. Downstream a ways we completed our bathing with a few handfuls of cold water splashed onto sensitive skin. Returning to camp we took a survey of our spare provisions. We began to prepare our oatmeal before Noah returned. We knew a host customarily offered food to visitors in his camp, but we were uninvited guests. We certainly did not want draw upon his store of provisions.

We were both surprised at how comfortable we felt at the hermitage. Our original plans were to find the hermit, ask for some pointers on archery and leave; we figured our stay should not take longer than a day. As we warmed towards Noah, he gave Tony and I a number of clues that made us relax enough to realize he wouldn't think it rude of us to ask more questions. Tony thought it all quite quaint, but I was beginning to sense this visit would be a special experience for me. I wished we had prepared for a longer stay. I was definitely becoming hooked on his backwoods style of living.

As Noah climbed the last stair, our oatmeal began to boil. In one hand he held a string of seven-inch trout; I recognized them as speckled trout based on the black markings on top, red spots on the belly and the square tails. The waters must have had a multitude of them this time of year, I thought as I eyed his interesting homemade rig.

We didn't hesitate to accept his offer of pan-fried trout and boiled coffee. In return we shared our oatmeal to which he added his own home-made brand of maple syrup from an old ketchup bottle that was caked with dried tomato paste. Over breakfast we learned that the mountain climbers who frequented his hermitage on their way to climb the neighboring summits had often kidded him about being the mayor of Cold River. "I figured I couldn't be a mayor without a town hall, " he chuckled as he pointed out the sign over his cabin. "Yes sir, and them mountain climbers found the mayor's coffee was better than any ten-mile hike." Neither of us was used to drinking coffee although we couldn't help but note the pleasant aroma it added to the morning air. Adding a generous splash of canned milk, we found the coffee tasted quite good in spite of the fact that a tablespoon could stand upright on its own in all the grounds at the bottom of the pot.

During breakfast, Noah seemed less animated than the previous evening. I thought he might be talked out or tired of us. As he had chosen the forest, lakes and streams, we assumed he prized solitude.

Just before falling asleep last night, I had listened to a forest creature—probably a raccoon—outside the wigwam. I mentioned the commotion I had heard and asked if he had ever kept a dog or cat. I thought each might have added some company or at the least would serve a useful purpose—dogs to ward off unwanted prowlers—cats, to catch mice of which there was a large population. "Yes, I get me some night callers," was all he said but then added, "Mostly I got the deer, skunks, raccoons, squirrels, porcupine and rabbits who come a-visiting and of course I've got lots of birds, song birds and such. You could say I've got all kinds of wild animals, but no pets."

"The deer and rabbits tiptoe into my garden over there when I'm not looking," he said as he pointed to his garden spot beyond the Old Ladies' Wigwam. "They eat up the tender stems just about as fast as they shoot up from the ground. I have experimented with all kinds of tricks like ringing the perimeter with bear droppings and cultivating small garden spaces in the lumber camp clearings. I even tried planting a small potato patch down by the Big Eddy once, but nothing ever worked."

"Of course the animals of the forest, my friends, are also garden ma-rauders. If they would let me harvest every bit of my crops just once, I'd have quite a winter larder."

"Wouldn't a dog help?" I asked.

"I don't care for them. They're a bother. They can't take care of them-selves and besides they'd bark from morning to night. Then, they'd chase all the animals for miles around. There would be no forest creatures left at all. The deer especially enjoy my fiddle playing," he chortled. This was an understatement. Four years later I observed several resident deer standing only yards away from Noah as he played. It was as if they were hypnotized, although Noah assured me they enjoyed it and seemed to give him high marks for his rendition of "Pop Goes the Weasel."

"I thought hard once when it came to cats. I had owned one when I was barbering in Lake Placid, but up here a cat would only kill just enough mice to amuse itself leaving me with a few breeders who'd catch up the population in jig time.

"About the only pet I enjoyed was a young fox. I used to keep it in the hollow cedar stump that holds the washbowl over by the Beauty Parlor wigwam. But I had to get rid of it. Gave it to the Petty boys in Corey's in '24 when I was arrested and hauled off to jail."

From my experience I said raccoons could be altogether destructive as well as entertaining, and Noah seemed to agree.

"They sure are inquisitive. Occasionally I'd leave corn in an open tin can for them. I wouldn't serve them though; they had to work for their supper." With a laugh that showed he enjoyed the animals, Noah recalled their frustration when the can wouldn't tip because it was tacked to the surface of the table. "I'd get me a flashlight and watch their nighttime antics. They'd stand up on their hind legs and study the light beam. The biggest bother was when they'd get out on the limbs of the cherry trees that hung over the Town Hall. Things generally got rather messy; that's where I drew the line. Under those circumstances we parted friendship, and I felt it was necessary to shoot them. Of course, they're good to eat and their skin fetches a fair price."

I wanted to show Noah that I shared many of his interests, so I figured now was a good time to ask him if he had heard this coon-trapping story.

I fired up my tall tale delivery. "My neighbors told me about a local man who reputedly was a full-time hunter-trapper, quite experienced when it came to chasing 'masked bandits' with his hound." Encouraging me to continue he asked, "How so, Richard?"

"When I announced I planned to get into trapping, I was encouraged to talk with this fellow to see if he would share his skills, especially making stretching boards. He put great pride in his craft and considered his boards superior to anyone elses." I had noticed a few of Noah's crude stretchers pegged to the side of his cabin. They were obviously cut from boards taken from aging lumber camps. His design lacked the expertise of old Hank's, but I was sensitive not to cast any aspersions on their condition. "He was an artist, custom fitting each and every board to the size of the raccoons he'd catch."

"Well, he started to notice that when it was time to go coon hunting, his dog would go around the side of the woodshed and study the boards, especially new ones the woodsman had added to the collection. It looked like the dog was surveying the various sizes. After this routine they would go hunting. In the woods the canine picked up a lot of raccoon scents, but appeared to only track down selected ones. Peculiar behavior he thought, but as time went on it was obvious his hound was ferreting out raccoons whose pelts would match one of the boards the hunter owned. Of course word spread around Lake Placid and the hunter and coonhound became famous.

"Famous that was, until one day, when the two were preparing to go into the woods, the hunter's wife appeared at the back door carrying her wooden ironing board. The hound took one look at the size of that ironing board and his eyes bulged three inches out of their sockets. He turned on his heels, emitted several deep, long howls—not his usual yelps—and fled into the forest.

"Although the hunter searched for days he never saw him again. His hound's disappearance led to much speculation. But to this day no one knows for sure whether the coon hound met a superior masked bandit in the woods, or that the hunter's wife had just plumb scared the gee whizzes out of it."

Noah thought my story an admirable effort. "Yes Richard, it sounds like that fellow's dog might have run into a Cold River coon. I've relished a few of their carcasses. That's why all my prized food possessions are kept in garbage cans suspended inside the meat wigwam."

At the story's conclusion our conversation dropped off, but the quiet did not bother me because I noticed a twinkle in Noah's eyes. I interpreted it as a sign of acceptance. It was wonderful to be at Cold River. I liked the solitude; it seemed to go hand-in-hand with being alone with your thoughts. As I learned later when I was able to make frequent trips to The City, it was perfectly normal for Noah and I to have a lull in conversation for days; the only words we spoke were of necessity. If you didn't know him well, you might think he was angry or batty, sometimes Noah simply talked himself out. I've since come to realize that if you like someone, you don't have to always make conversation. This was certainly true of Noah.

Following our leisurely breakfast, Noah suggested Tony and I show him how well our archery equipment worked. Our target was a crude burlap deer silhouette and the outline of a game warden's hat traced on a large wooden board he had set up by the vegetable garden. We exchanged equipment. His bow was stored in a blackened, aged buckskin sheath fashioned during the first years he lived at Cold River. Noah demonstrated just how good his homemade bow and arrows were. As a form of sport he mentioned that if he were hunting wildlife with this equipment and the game happened to move out of the arrow's range, the he would compromise with a more lackluster meal, settling for old fashioned "pan-e-cakes" with syrup. The hat outline was a curious target; he explained it helped him to practice his "sweetest dream," which was to someday nail the game protector's hat to a tree with one of his well-placed arrows. As he pulled the bowstring back to demonstrate his deadly marksmanship with the longbow he cautioned us, "If the shot happens to strike a bit low that will be too bad. Nothing planned or deliberate of course. The weather affects a bows performance, you know." Then he released the arrow. When it struck just slightly below the brim I thought it was a shame he missed, but it didn't faze him. Rather he cried out gleefully, "Oh, oh! Poor shot. Too bad." Then he danced a little jig around the grassy yard. We had come to seek advice, which we acquired.

But never had I anticipated I'd be regaled by alluring stories, enchanted by his primitive conditions of living, dazzled by the view from the bluff overlooking Cold River and captivated by the solitary existence of the hermit. My original impression of a hermit included an individual whose hair was greasy and tangled, whose beard was long and unkempt, whose fingernails were incredibly dirt encrusted, whose clothes were fashioned from animal skins, whose ability to communicate was minimal and whose aroma prompted one to stay upwind.

Noah on the other hand was clean and careful of his appearance; he combed his long hair and beard twice a day. His quarters, while cramped and filled with years of clutter, were about what one might expect from a bachelor who didn't care for tidiness. I was taken by his artistic and musical interests. His refined handwriting could have graced the United States Constitution. And, he was articulate.

His voice had a distinct timbre. I vividly recall how soft spoken he was as he responded to our questions. The only time his voice rose to a shrill was when he talked about the game protector, "the all-American son-of-a-bitch" whom he identified as the main source of all his trouble with the Conservation Department. I was also impressed by his living as comfortably as he did, in spite of the lack of creature comforts. His buildings looked like they had been continually repaired using the crudest methods. Smoke stains, dirt and spills were abundant. But The City, as he called it, suited him just fine. Some people held Noah in low esteem, even ridiculing him. Tony and I thought, as the wise old lady once said when she kissed the cow, "Everyone is different. We best not judge each other."

Time to Depart

The hour was approaching when we had planned to depart, but Noah suggested a fish fry "Cold River style" was in order before we left. Tony and I decided to fish from an old log raft tethered to a stake by the old dam. We poled out onto the flow to try our luck with the equipment Noah loaned us. The hermit fished his favorite holes below the dam's spillway using lures he had made from bear skull bone, vertebrae and teeth of small animals, and feathers from birds. As we returned to shore and started the campfire within a circle of stones ringed on the gravel shoreline, we watched Noah below us. He was so fortunate to have Cold River right at his front door, and I'll bet he used to warn the fish, "Look out, trout, the Mayor of Cold River is hungry."

As we dined on native trout we looked upstream where we saw that the flow narrowed before the bend in the river. Marshy areas along its edges added to the tranquil scene. Noah pointed out surrounding landmarks and talked about "Adirondack clears," an atmospheric condition he named. He explained it was the "hours when the air appears to depart and only the limited vision of our eyes prevents us from reading a newspaper a mile away."

"I had this notion in me," he said as he pointed out Panther Peak to the south, "that I'd do something once and for all about the clears and sunsets. I got me some canvas and oils and began to put those visions on canvas, but the tubes of paint dried out before I could master the proper technique of transferring the images fittingly. Mind you, I wasn't an expert or anything, but I could produce a fair resemblance."

How many boys, I thought, have had an opportunity like this. Our farewell lunch wouldn't be complete without another of Noah's tales. After telling us about a hunting experience that took place in Belly Ache Swamp, a short distance beyond The Finger, Noah's term for the point of land that jutted into the flow opposite his hermitage, he invited us to return when there was more time available—perhaps we would fish the whiz-bang Black Hole a few miles upstream. He told us the rocky, steep banks and boulder strewn waters made it difficult to reach, but the big trout made the effort worthwhile.

Before we left, Tony gave Noah several store-bought arrows. Waving good-bye, we turned toward his footpath that led toward his spur trail and the gateway that marked the junction with the Northville-Lake Placid Trail. We had advanced only several yards when he once again urged us to come back whenever we were able.

Just beyond Mountain Pond we veered off the Northville-Lake Placid Trail and picked up the outlet of Moose Pond Creek where Noah had told us about a shortcut around an old dam that retained the snowmelt from this sizable Cold River tributary. Once we circumvented the swampy section around the perimeter of an old flow, we found firm ground all the way to Moose Pond. Half way there we came across the remnants of another former logging camp. The blacksmith shop was the only building that remained standing. A large snowroller, covered by witchhopple, stood in the clearing. I found a horseshoe which I kept as a good luck souvenir. I still have it tacked up on the wall of my Handsome Hill cabin. I thought the campsite would provide ideal shelter if I were ever to establish a trapline in this territory and marked it in my mind for possible future reference. Maybe I'd even like to try living like Noah someday.

Reaching Moose Pond, the end of our trip was near. My feet would carry me the remaining miles home, but my thoughts wandered back to Noah. I wondered if he was gathering poles to add to the wigwam; Adirondack winters are long and cold and require a large supply of firewood. Or perhaps he could be cultivating his garden. That was an activity he enjoyed. "I do a lot to thinking as I tend my planting," he told us. "Helps 'em grow big; I've got a vegetable pit to fill each fall you know." The turnips Tony and I ate were the product of good storage.

Then again, Noah might be making some minor repairs to his home-made telescope—an instrument he constructed himself. It consisted of two fixed lenses inserted in a cardboard mailing tube attached to a sawed-off birch stump in his clearing. On clear nights, the self-taught astronomer would view the heavens.

As I covered the final miles toward home, I knew part of my heart remained back at Cold River.

Along My River

I was restless following Tony's and my adventure to Cold River. My spirit of exploration was whetted and I longed to be somewhere else other than where I was—home on the farm. The winding path of the upper Chubb River ran by our back pasture. Upstream, along the shoreline were dry banks, good places to swim and fish. The Chubb was the neighborhood children's gathering place. Like Huck Finn and Tom Sawyer, we'd built our share of crude rafts. On lazy summer days it was a challenge to pile as many of us on to the lashed logs and see just how long it took to either tip or submerge the craft, flooding the surface. Noah had the Cold River. I had the Chubb. Having your own river is quite important!

A log lay outstretched from the bank into the water. The far end bobbed as I made my way out along its mossy top. It afforded me a favorable standing-place from which to scan upstream. As I stood there, alone,

I looked upon the scene and pondered what lay beyond, far in the distance —to the river's top, the source, or at least to the head of navigation.

The Chubb offered my best hope to break out, to experience carefree adventure. In those days it was not the popular course for recreational paddlers as it is today. By rowing and polling I moved my boat, navigating the narrow stream against an almost invisible current.

In the first stretch of stillwater I found the banks were fuller than I had expected. Where beaver dams spanned the river, the banks on both sides were often impassable on account of dense and matted underbrush. The mass of interlocking branches of bushes and trees lining the sides obstructed my way making it darn right challenging to disembark, or to pull my plank bottom boat around or over the dam to reach the open water beyond.

Leisurely advancing, I noted wide patches of tall, savanna-like grass around the outlets of mountain-rills and the paths deer made through the dense brake to the water's edge. Those shallow pastures were their feeding grounds. Eyeing the broad surface of the floating water lilies of a small cove, I poled into a patch just to hear the sound of the leaves scrunch along the bottom of the boat. Often crowned with a white or yellow flower, they basked in the summer sun, their aromatic fragrance refreshing to inhale. I found that the long, slender stems that stretched from their roots fastened deep in the mucky bottom were quite elastic when I tried to pluck a flower. And, not once was I able to slip up to an occasional frog sitting on a pad before it would make a remark and dive underwater.

I am not a highfalutin type of person, but I am consciously affected by the beauty I perceive around me. It's satisfying just to view it, to be part of the scenery, but I must say the river's unblemished solitude profoundly affected me. I suppose that is why I have always enjoyed reading poetry. Where I can appreciate my inner feelings toward nature, poets express their feelings in ways I cannot.

I was completely alone in sole possession of my river. Unlike Noah's rocky, sometimes boulder strewn, fast-flowing waters, mine never had so much as a boulder's head poke above the water's surface. The swamp grass had a luxuriant shade of green, and here and there colorful flowers shone their reds, purples and yellows clear down to the waters edge.

I felt no part of the wilderness could be more attractive than this bold scenery I viewed. The river seemed to welcome me as I glided. There was beauty and peace.

Reaching the carry, a place I called Pine Tree Meadow, I would have no way of knowing on that summer day in 1934 that in four years I would keep two boats there, using them to collect muskrats along the upper and lower stillwaters. The Chubb was a regular muskrat factory with its vast open marshes and bays. In the distance was a jutting, ledgy rise I named Lookout Mountain. I would build my first cabin there. It was high enough for me to survey the whole upper stillwater in the spring, waiting for the day the ice had left the river. I would set April first as the date to get my old flat bottom boats caulked and painted. I stored them in a thicket near the head of the rapids. How my heart jumped for joy when I could see the sun sparkle on the open water like a chest of jewels. It marked the end of winter and a forward jump to trapping muskrats and fishing for the browns and speckled trout that were so abundant in the Chubb at that time.

Each and every time I reached the upper water, above the rapids, I felt the same flow of feeling as I did the first day I viewed the scene. There God had unfolded unparalleled beauty. High summits far from the waters edge stretched upward off in the distance. They welcomed me upriver where, from tree tops, an unseen bird caught my ear with a pleasant harmonious call.

The reflection of the trees on the water's surface and the cloud forms framed a wondrous picture of a grand water and forest scene. Often nothing stirred. The trees were still. The water calm. The mountains motionless. Only my boat made a very slight ripple as it advanced on the water.

The water was clear allowing me to peer below the surface and see large fish in pursuit of smaller ones or fish-hunting flies. Cranes, their long slender necks and far-reaching wings with legs thrust backward, would circle overhead and then land, setting down in the shallows to wade for fish and frogs. A crane could stand statue-like, patient and still, until an opportunity for a strike occurred. Then, with lightning speed, it would strike the water, poking its head under and coming up victorious. Motherly brown ducks floated on the surface. With easy graceful motion, their heads erect, as they paddled their offspring about with their quick dark eyes rapidly moving, watching for danger. Circling hawks soared high on the wind, watching, ever ready to swoop down on swift wings to snatch prey in their hooked beak or sharp talons. On occasion my silent thoughts would be broken, when I would hear the distant toot of the whistle from the old coal burning locomotive hauling railroad cars from Utica.

When the stream narrowed so much that my boat could no longer move forward, I had finally reached the head of navigation. I was surprised at that point to find a footpath. Out of curiosity I followed it a short distance coming upon an old lumber shanty. As I began to approach a man with a long black beard and shoulder length hair stepped out of the door. Just seeing someone there took me back, but what really got my complete attention was the wicked looking hunting knife he held in his outstretched hand. My heart instantly jumped into my mouth; if I had not the foresight to close my jaws tightly I would have lost it.

I think he, too, was startled at my arrival. He wasn't your typical looking neighbor. I wondered if he had any quantity of the milk of human kindness within him. That was my first and most lasting impression of him. But I was to shortly change my initial feeling after we exchanged some words. I figured he was a true native woodsman when he extended his free-hearted hospitality and invited me into his cabin for something to eat and drink.

Once inside I saw, hanging from the overhead rafters, about four dozen animal pelts. He told me they were "black squirrels," but I had seen pictures of pine martin so I surmised he was taking them illegally. I figured it was trouble enough just to make a living during the Depression, so I behaved as if his trapping was none of my business.

Needless to say I didn't overstay my welcome. Upon leaving, he shook my hand and told me he liked young lads who could keep their mouths shut. Yet I also left with an invitation to visit again if I wanted to. I never did!

The trapper I met at the head of the Chubb was a bit before my enthusiasm for the wilderness had much of a hold on me. At fourteen years old I never even imagined I would one day pursue and dedicate a part of my life to woodlore: hunting, trapping, fishing and camping. The dream was strong enough but I had yet to find the means.

Next Summer's Return

The following summer I managed to make one visit to Rondeau's in order to deliver some staples I hoped he would find useful. It was my way of thanking him for his generosity and kindness the previous year. My only other contact that year was an occasional letter. In them Noah never failed to tell me I would be welcome. "I'm glad to get word from you . . . when you do find time to visit the City you should plan on staying about a week; it's only the same effort for a week as for a day. Happy Living Among the Mountains. Sincerely, Noah John Rondeau."

During my last two years in high school I was able to free up time and return to Noah's for more than an overnight. Visits were satisfying, but always shorter than I would have liked. Each encounter increased my resolve to some day do as Noah had done. By 1937 I was developing into a competent teenager. I honed my woodsmanship skills while on adventures exploring the upper Chubb River drainage basin. Between my 1937 and 1938 sojourns Noah began calling me "son," which made me feel close to him. Without being conscious of it, we had developed a relationship akin to that of a father and son.

The dark side of our lives—something we held in common—solidified our friendship. During subsequent visits Noah sensed my fear of and hostility toward my father. I had been able to contain my anger until the day I left home; Noah, on the other hand had been rebellious. Fed up with unwarranted beatings, he left home in 1898 at the age of fifteen. No wonder this kind, gentle man tried to make me so comfortable in his presence. He understood what I tolerated. He was trying to make up for the abuses I experienced.

The Civilian Conservation Corps established a seasonal camp near the Cold River lean-to during my junior year. One friend, Phil McCalvin, who worked at the camp, also became a very good friend of Noah's. The three C's camp, as some called it, was only a few miles east of Noah's hermitage and a hangout for a number of the enrollees during the weekend. This was a temporary boom to Noah's larder because he became the beneficiary of much surplus food from the mess kitchen. I would have loved to have joined the Corps assuming I had been assigned the Cold River camp, but that was only a fleeting thought. My goal was to graduate from high school. I was determined to earn a diploma.

I viewed my home situation as akin to that of a hired hand, and I didn't care for a position like that. After my brothers left home, Father found a job away from the farm and the majority of the chores fell to me. Cows, pigs, goats, sheep, chickens, and our few turkeys needed tending daily. And, there was always the field work. Cutting hay was a big job. I spent endless hours hoeing long rows of potatoes and spraying potato bugs with a mixture of Paris green and arsenate of lead, a popular homemade pesticide of the time, that always made me sick. Though I used the farm wagon and team of horses, potatoes, a staple, were harvested by hand by hooking them out of the ground. Drying, bagging and hauling the spud sacks to our cellar storage bin was also hard work.

Chores did not end once school started either. My father demanded I complete the farm work before I began my school assignments. Most evenings I was busy with homework until eleven o'clock, if I hadn't fallen asleep before. The best part of school was the extra time several of my teachers invested in me. Their faith in my ability and understanding of my family circumstances pulled me through the final years. I graduated in June 1939 and that summer left home for good.

The Call of the Woods

While graduation released me, the magnetic attraction of living in the wilderness tugged at my heartstrings. Although I had more work experience than most my age, I quickly found there was a lack of well-paying, permanent jobs around Lake Placid. By the end of summer, I was disappointed to have only secured a month of steady employment. What was in my future? If I only knew. I felt I was a practical thinking teenager. I had to give up the small scholarship I won for postgraduate industrial arts because Father had no funds to round out the balance of expenses. I mulled over the typical philosophical questions many youths-turning-adults think about. What about happiness? How important was money going to be? Did I want a steady job just for the financial security? Did I want to leave my Adirondack Mountains? And, where did I see myself in society? These were weighty questions, and I realized I could end up living a rather dull, unrewarding life if I didn't choose carefully.

In the short run life in the woods had more appeal. It's true that I had thought about it as an option ever since first meeting Noah. His influence was a pivotal experience in my life. Yes, like Noah, it looked like I was going to choose the less traveled path.

Once I revealed my plans to pursue my dreams of youth, some friends politely called me a castle-builder-in-the-air while others were not so diplomatic. One by one, my boyhood friends drifted into the adult world of work, marriage and family. Some, like Tony, moved away from Lake Placid and chose the Army as a career, while I was going to be a hunter and professional trapper. Was I a dreamer? Perhaps, but I'd enjoyed the thought of the freedom I'd have.

Living frugally, I knew I could survive on the basics a limited income would provide. Market prices for fur were still firm. Working part-time, all I needed to do was earn enough shekels for a stake. Trapping would provide the rest. And for a few years the idea worked.

During my junior year of high school I had constructed a small cabin on a ridge opposite the second set of stillwaters overlooking the Chubb River. The twisting stream was only a ten-minute hike away. It was not difficult for a resourceful person to salvage cast-aside building materials and to put up a weather tight structure complete with a snugly furnished interior for next to nothing. The main ingredient was hard work because materials were readily available for the taking from abandoned lumber camps.

For almost eight years I lived a life similar to Noah John's whose backwoods wisdom and interest in me had first stirred my senses. My Chubb River base camp was built on state land but officers who enforced conservation laws did not seek out an "outlaw" camp unless they knew of its actual location. I made sure mine remained a well-kept secret. Using the traps purchased with cash from my last season's take of furs, I staked out a trapline that I hoped was capable of generating all the money I would need to live on for an entire year.

I worked at odd jobs, hiking out each morning at five in order to arrive at work by seven. By early evening I'd be back trolling the stillwaters for supper. Life was carefree. I had my rifle, a 16-gauge shotgun and a good bluetick hound. From late fall until spring there wasn't much work to be had in town. For the most part I stayed in the woods, hunting rabbits, grouse and deer in the swamps along the river. To be sure, I had to stretch what money I had at times, for it was often as scarce as hen's teeth. I enjoyed my new found freedom and independence; it was a challenge to use my experience to solve problems I encountered. My favorite times were many. But rowing contentedly on the second stillwater as the softly whispering waters flowed beneath my boat was one moment of contentment I will never forget.

My pioneer life could not last forever. Neither would Noah's. We were treading on the very fringe of an era—the transition years; the period between the Great Depression and the U.S. entry into World War II.

Fur prices plummeted. A blanket beaver worth eighty dollars dropped to ten. New York State acquired vast logged-over tracts adding them to the Forest Preserve. Noah foresaw these changes and warned me that, "soon the yoke of civilization would be in place. All that was lacking would be the ring in my nose!"

For six years I managed to balance part-time work with my wilderness wanderings. I knew the ways of the animals I trapped and hunted. My requirements were few. Noah would tell me, "Too many people have too many laws to make everything work, so everyone can get at least half-a-chance to grab the brass ring. But as more people try for it, the faster the merry-go-round spins. In the end only a few are able to grab it. The vast majority just get trampled underfoot." His comments might not make a lot of sense to most people, but it was how he saw life.

Our views coincided. Life is too short to get mixed up in the 'rat race,' the way to the good life. My answer to Noah's observation about society's scramble dealt with people placing too much emphasis on the almighty dollar and not enough emphasis on the real treasures of life such as friendship, nature and leisure. I joked that if I worked long, hard and invented the perfect mouse trap, I'd be too old to enjoy the fruits of my labor.

Phil's Duck Hole Cabin

In 1938 Phil McCalvin and another friend named Vince built a crude cabin at the base of a bump of a mountain we called Beartrap Mountain, about a half mile from Duck Hole. Like I had, they scrounged building material from the old logging camps in the vicinity of the former CCC camp. The owners of an old, private hunting camp located off the Bradley Pond trail donated a few windows.

Phil and Vince originally met Noah while serving in the Civilian Conservation Corps. Both were outdoors men, loved life in the woods and got along well with Noah. Once the Corps' main project of rebuilding the dam at Duck Hole and upgrading the lumber camp tote road along Ward Brook for motorized vehicles was completed, the camp was closed.

A camp such as this one was temporary and generally consisted of large, military-issue wall tents. Choosing a well-hidden site, Phil and Vince cut green logs for cabin walls and relied on cast-offs to outfit the rest of the building. Vince, who had a fondness for the bottle, set a bear trap in a cubby somewhere on the mountain.

Somewhere was the key word, because he placed it during a bender and couldn't remember its location. After sobering up and realizing somewhere on the mountain lay an illegal steel jawed-toothed trap, they both agreed it would be safer to stay off the mountain than to accidentally step into it. A short time later Vince drifted away from Lake Placid, and in 1940 Phil joined the Air Force after turning the cabin over to me.

I had occasionally stayed at Phil's during the beaver trapping season; I had also hunted with him from Duck Hole camp. I thought of his camp as similar to Noah's Jungle camp, an early trapline bivouac concealed in a thicket of spruce.

My standard route to Phil's cabin followed the Northville-Lake Placid Trail to the outlet on Moose Pond. From there I followed the creek a short distance and then veered easterly through a wall of rock I called Paint Bed Notch. From there I'd proceed to Roaring Brook and then southwesterly toward Duck Hole. When I wanted to stop by Noah's first, I used an alternative route that followed Moose Creek outlet, but with a twist of my own beyond the old lumber camp clearing I called the "Snowroller Camp."

I spent many days with Noah once I moved from my cabin above the Chubb River to Duck Hole. We roamed the wilderness, he teaching me about the network of old logging roads, well defined thirty years earlier, that were routes to his favorite hunting, fishing and trapping sites. I soon got caught up in my new lifestyle. Here I was, Richard Smith, with a camp near the site of the old Duck Hole Headquarters Camp, the wilderness shanty of Dick Wood and E.J. Dailey, writers and trappers whom I read about in sporting magazines during my youth. I was to find out Noah knew E.J. although he didn't hold him in the highest standing.

Once I told Noah about my early frustrations with fox-trapping and, half expecting him to laugh good naturedly at my naiveté of being duped by a tale, quickly asked if he had heard of the so-called legendary fox E.J. Dailey called Keen Nose. To my surprise he had, but not from the writer "EJ." He had heard from Joe Dishaw who was once a log-jobber around Coreys.

He had first met Joe, a wiry French Canadian, near Peek-A-Boo Hill in the Calkins Creek country. He had listened to him talk about an elusive fox. Joe thought he might meet up with it someday as he tended his trapline along the Raquette River. Once Noah became familiar with the wilderness around Corey's, he'd see Joe during the guiding season at Camp Four's company store along Ward Brook. This lumber camp was a popular gathering place for local guides to buy food and trail goods when guiding sportsmen on hunting trips into the Sawtooth and Seward Mountain ranges. Joe, a colorful storyteller, often entertained a congregation of men in his broken English. After listening to several versions of Joe's fox stories over the years, Noah came to believe Keen Nose was nothing more than a tale himself.

Noah was amused to hear of how I swallowed Dailey's advertisements for scent lures. He never said E.J. was a sham, but led me to believe he had little respect for the man's woodcraft. Noah felt Dailey fancied himself an expert woodsman and trapper. I suspect a falling out between the two came about over an incident in 1919, the year Noah worked at Big Dam lumber camp. E.J. had stayed overnight there, one of the last years it operated. Following a big snowstorm, Dailey, who was unfamiliar with the territory, lost his bearings and asked Noah if he would help him find a canvas bag of traps he had hidden along the winter road to Mountain Pond. Noah concluded Dailey had more "thunder than skills" just because of this innocent blunder. "If E.J. Dailey sold enough of his special scent around the North Country," he quipped, "foxes might migrate all the way to Ogdensburg where they might blunder into his sets. That's the only way I can see him trapping anything!"

Although Phil turned his camp over to me in the spring of 1940, I didn't have all my possessions moved until after Memorial Day. I remember the last load well because I had help from a friend named Don who wanted to meet Noah. The loads I moved had become routine by the time he offered to help. To shorten the trip, I had carried everything upstream in my boat to the landing which is a popular overnight destination for canoeists today. A short bushwhack along the outlet of Wanika Falls brought me close to the Northville-Lake Placid Trail where I set up a cache under a waterproof canvas.

Don was thrilled at the thought of meeting Noah and asked many questions about him as we carted my stores over the remaining ten miles of trail. After an overnight stay at camp we arrived at Cold River City just before noon on a clear, bright day. Noah wasn't home but it looked like he would be back soon. After mixing up some batter, I set up my reflector oven in an open area near his telescope stand and baked a couple dozen baking powder biscuits. Don's mother, Mrs. Beebe, had known Noah when he lived in Lake Placid and had sent him a quart of her strawberry preserves. Noah arrived shortly after the biscuits were cooked noting the plate piled high on his outdoors table. When his eyes spotted the jar of jam next to the plate they seemed to light up as wide as a motorcar's head-

lamps. He didn't need an invitation; he just sat down and ate. Each bis-
cuit was smothered with preserves, which we finished off along with
three-quarters of the jam. The next morning we went back at it again,
consuming the balance between sourdough pancakes. Don got a big kick
in Noah's saying, "Pass Mrs. Beebe's preserves this-a-way, Richard."

I like to think I was Noah's apprentice. He passed on to me tried and
true woodcraft skills he learned from Indian Joe, one of the few people in
Corey's beside the Petty family who had befriended him. I couldn't help
but admire Noah's wide range of interests. His formal education was
lacking, only having gone through the eighth grade, but he was one of the
smartest men I ever knew. His attempts at oil painting and poetry were
rough but personally satisfying to him. He was well read on a number of
subjects. His favorites being astronomy, religion, philosophy and history.
But political news appealed to him. I asked him once which major political party was the lesser of two evils. His response came immediately, "It
wouldn't be those Jack-Ass Democrats. I've got no use for them."

Noah's Chicken Scratching-Like Cipher

Rondeau's 1930's "license plate" code.

One extraordinary example of Noah's prowess is the code he developed by combining circles, squares, drawings, compass points, Zodiac
signs and French. He felt it was a system of writing no one would be
capable of deciphering because of all the false leads he included. Dr.
Adolph Dittmar, a long-time friend of Noah's, once referred to his code as
looking like the tracks of an "inebriated hen." While many people have
been intrigued, it had remained a mystery for almost seventy years. Recently a young man has worked at cracking the code. I helped by providing background information to help verify the validity of the decoded pas-
sages. It will only be a matter of time before he deciphers all of them.

Although Noah and I were of different generations, we enjoyed one another's company. Close friendships were not something he came by naturally. When Noah first lived in a tent in the woods near the Raquette River, most natives and summer residents around Corey's thought he was odd. People didn't live alone and away from everyone. Local gossips said he was running away or escaping from something. Neither was true.

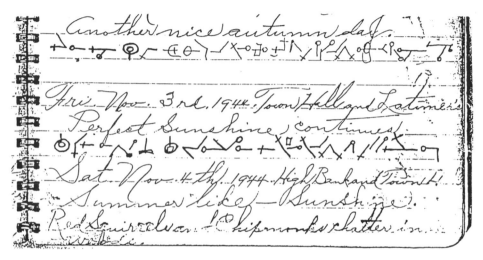

November 3, 1944—Greatly evolved 1940's code. Decoded entry reads: "1 haircut and 1 beard trim. PM. Walked to Lattimer's."

I often heard him tell about his "dozen points of failure." "Richard, from the time I was fifteen until I was thirty-three, I done the hard work and sweated for an education. I wanted a decent way to earn a living. After eighteen years, I took inventory of my intellectual stock and found I hadn't progressed much. I wanted to be a scholar but that wasn't going to be. It pained me to realize I would not reach my academic goals. I was a pretty good barber, mason, painter, and carpenter but eventually decided to give up the tools. I saw no great level of achievement by continuing. Let those who want to sweat for a lowly dollar and a half a day keep on sweating, I wasn't interested." (At the age of twenty-seven, Noah went back to school and completed the seventh and eighth grades in one week.)

Over time, Noah's negative perception of himself began to fade. Once he was established at Big Dam, rumor spread to the hotels at Corey's and Upper Saranac that a man who knew the woods like an Indian lived alone at Cold River. He was a successful trapper-hunter, unconventional in some ways. Soon hardy sportsmen became attracted to his knowledge of that part of the woods and sought him out as a guide. This positive rein-forcement was a fact that began to rebuild Noah's self image.

Climbing Time

By the 1930's climbing the High Peaks began to catch on. Adiron-dack Mountain Club members and a group calling itself the 46'ers began to use Noah's city as a base. Noah referred to them as the "highest caliber of people. You see, I'm so well hidden away here, the majority of the few folks I meet are mountain climbers. You've got to be a nice, clean-living person to climb mountains, so I meet the best of them." Unlike a few unsavory characters, natives, who would occasionally steal items from his camp, he felt the climbers presented no threat.

Noah's Christmas Season

Staying with Noah, or using his buildings for shelter when he wasn't around during the beaver trapping season, became a tradition with me during the eight years I balanced living in the woods with working part-time. Noah, too, kept a fairly regular tradition whereby he would leave Cold River just before Christmas to spend the season with his friends Roy and Violet Hathaway in Upper Saranac. Roy met Noah about 1920 when they both trapped along the Raquette River. Once Noah estab-lished himself at Big Dam, Roy frequently hiked in to fish during the spring and hunt with him during the fall. In time Roy took a care taking job at Pine Point Camp on Upper Saranac Lake which consumed most of his time. In the mid-1930's he began inviting Noah to Pine Point, an agreeable arrangement with Noah. Before that Noah had spent almost a decade of winters alone at Big Dam. The only time he did leave was to buy supplies at Tupper or Saranac Lake. Teamsters working for the Santa Clara Lumber Company usually offered to drop those supplies at a prearranged spot near Mountain Pond. From there Noah would spend the better part of those two weeks transporting his supplies to camp.

Noah looked forward to his yearly visits with the Hathaway's, who not only opened their quarters to him, but also included him when they drove to their house in Lewis, New York. Noah had a number of friends there as well as in nearby Elizabethtown and Westport who also invited him to be their house guest.

Long Winter Nights at the Hermitage

After I had been trapping from my Duck Hole cabin for two years, Noah invited me to put in with him along his line. Due to his age he had a short trapline, but he was willing to share his knowledge of it. I always knew in advance if he'd be at Cold River because he'd notify me by letter when he was planning to return. But as the 1940's arrived Noah stayed outside his digs more frequently, often months at a time.

Those years that I used Noah's cabins, I used to spend hours at night thumbing through his journals, which he had given me access to. He had prefaced every entry with a weather report for that day. For example:

January 1, 1943 Friday
Nice crispy winter day
At Lewis and Westport

I go from Lewis to Westport with Mr. and Mrs. Phil McPhail. Then I walk to Pipemakers (about 3 miles). I met Mr. Burger sliding on a sled near Camp Dudley. I had supper with Burger's at 6 P.M. At 8 P.M. the Pattisons and others arrived (at Pipemakers). Good Serene Visit. I slept for the night by Burger's lingering Christmas tree.

January 4, 1943 Monday
Cloudy, Snowed 2 inches
At Lewis, N.Y.

I'm staying at Roy Hathaway (Lewis). 8 to 12 P.M. at Fish and Game Club. At 10 P.M. I address the Club members. I gassed them with a storm of Adirondack yarns.

April 26, 1943   Monday
Sun Shine and clouds
At Pine Point Camp, Upper Saranac Lake

A. J. Hathaway fix broken Truck at Bartlett Club. I pack up to go to
Cold River.

April 29, 1943   Thursday
Cloudy morning followed by a day of perfect Sun Shine
At Pine Point Camp and Ampersand Park

I left Pine Point at 7:30 A.M., at Coreys at 8:30, at turn to Ampersand Pond in Ampersand Park at 2:30. Saw 4 Deer; I saw tracks of
two Bear, -several times from 3 -7 mile mark. After Sun Down 2 Deer
and a Rabbit feed a few feet from camp door. I put up for night at
Ampersand Pond turn.

May 2, 1943   Sunday
Nice day of Sun Shine
Ampersand Park and Cold River

A fresh Bear Track 300 ft. from camp. I took a 10 miles walk with
40 pound pack. From No. 4 to Mountain Pond (4 miles) snow is from 2
to 4 ft. Lots of Bear Tracks from 3 mile mark to the Cold River. I
reach Cold River after dark; Snow Shoed all the way.

In the course of our confabs I asked him about all the isolation—those
long years, the rainy days and evenings when he couldn't venture outside
and those winters when snowstorms would pile up the ground with deep
snow. His answer was in keeping with the homespun philosopher he was.
"I prefer to think of it all as solitude." And he was right when I thought
of it. There was a difference. He joked that he distanced himself from
Thoreau, because his Town Hall was "farther back from the cookie jar
than Walden Pond ever was."

It was an act of generosity on Noah's part to have taken me under his
wing. It meant so much to me that I wanted to thank him, but every time
I thought of saying something, it just never seemed to be the right opportunity—until one particular evening following a delicious meal of fresh
venison. We had an exciting day hunting in Laughing Buck Swamp and
looked forward to relaxing by the fire. There was little conversation as
we gazed contentedly at Panther Peak looming over Cold River Flow.
The prospect was grand—Noah's name for it was "Hand-some View." He
would tell me, "That mountain's for sale. Would you like to buy it?"

Following an account about the antics of a particular pesky raccoon that had been "greasing its mustache" at Noah's expense, our conversation dropped off entirely. We sat for a long time enjoying the fire burn. When the embers had died down to a low red glow, Noah leaned over, poking the now smoldering hollow cedar stump to revive the campfire. I had been thinking of breaking the silence for a while and decided now was the time to take the opportunity to tell him how much I valued his companionship and all he had taught me. I began easily enough, but soon I was so overcome with emotion that I was wheezing and puffing like a locomotive with a boiler capacity for a mile grade straining on a five-mile climb. When I finally came to a sputtering stop, I thought I had overdone it for the hermit remained as silent as the night woods for a long time. So long in fact I wondered if I had said something to offend him. By this time the stump had taken hold and through its natural chimney came sparks of many colors not unlike the imaginary locomotive engine I had recently abandoned. As the fire brightened and the night pushed back the listening shadows, a glance at Noah revealed in the firelight, that old familiar twinkle in his eyes, and the unmistakable look of pleasure on his face.

Getting more and more anxious I waited for his reply. My ears must have been sticking out as big as catcher's mitts. I was so nervous and I didn't want to miss a single word. Edging back in his plank rocker he said, "I don't know if I can manufacture the correct words of response to such an oration of flattery. I'd sooner tackle an enraged bear with a hatchet. I'm not used to so much praise. I can't claim so much credit because you are a good student and love the wilderness as I do. Teaching you some of the ways of forest life has been a pleasure for me. Besides a good student can teach even an old master new ideas. We have learned from each other. There are many things about the wilds we may never learn. But don't we have grand, glorious hunts? Now let us stand in the cedar smoke for awhile so we can get our eyes full. Then if someone happens along we will have an excuse for the tears."

An Unlikely Twist for a Hermit

In 1945 when I visited Noah shortly before entering the army, he reminded me about the "many miles of trail we laid down together." He was right. They were some of the best of times. Following my discharge, I returned to find Noah's life had changed considerably. He was still living at Cold River, but no longer on a year-round basis. The Conservation Department had initially introduced him to the general populace through an eye-catching magazine article, then by arranging his appearance at sportsmen's shows. Noah, no one's fool, realized the very department that had tried to railroad him out of the woods on trumped-up charges was now popularizing him as a genuine Adirondack hermit. Most of what I knew of Noah remained unchanged, but there was a part of him that had changed. Recognizing the "golden egg" the Conservation Department had laid for him, he became a self-promoter and marketed his career by selling photographs and autographs, seeking paid appearances, giving speeches and generally enjoying the limelight.

He was sixty-eight years old in 1950, and that contributed to his decision to leave Cold River. The North Pole, a summer amusement park in Wilmington, New York, offered him a job as Santa that year. He readily accepted and worked there until the beginning of deer hunting season when he moved back to his city.

This visit turned out to be the autumn of the big blowdown. Early, on the morning of November 25, 1950, Noah left the Town Hall hiking toward Ampersand Lake. He was planning to stay with a friend who worked at Avery Rockefeller's woodland estate. Later in the day hurricane force winds hit the Adirondacks ripping apart ten thousand acres across the Cold River country. Noah's cabins and wigwams survived. They were not in the path of the storm, but fearing a disastrous fire the Conservation Department closed the woods for three years. Thus preventing Noah from returning to his beloved city.

Although Noah received some income during 1950, it was not enough to support him. He had applied for and was given assistance by the Essex County social services department. When his caseworker notified him that his monthly check from the county would be less because of the income he was making at the North Pole, he balked and decided not to return as Santa the following season. He then lived as a ward of the county for the next thirteen years, boarding in a variety of rented rooms and cabins in the Wilmington-Lake Placid area. By 1963 he had hit Adirondack bedrock. I remember seeing the despair in his eyes, and I knew how painful it was for him to endure living in the ramshackle rental cabin on River Road. I saw him often that year because the cabin was a short distance from my house on Handsome Hill along the same road. His circumstances were more than I could bear.

The memories of excursions, campfire chats following bear and venison chases, his sourdough pancakes, powerful coffee which could support a spoon upright and our enduring friendship motivated me to do something more for him. He was fiercely independent and didn't want to rely on handouts. It made him feel helpless as his pride and dignity were being chipped away.

I had always wanted a little hunting cabin, and so I bought an acre and a half of woodland in Wilmington and skidded an old chicken coop onto the property. On my off-hours from caretaking at several large camps around Lake Placid, I worked on converting the building into a weather-tight abode far from the tourist traffic along Route 86. When it was just about completed, I offered it to Noah telling him I preferred to have someone on the property watching over things since most of my time was spent caretaking or at my home on River Road. I told him he could live there for as long as he wanted and to treat it as his own.

His despair vanished within twenty-four hours of moving. I was delighted to see my friend happy again, with his dignity restored. I kidded him about his improved smile, but he assured me that it had to do with the new set of teeth Dr. Dittmar had presented him! Offering him this camp, which I had dubbed Singing Pines, was a modest gesture, but the cabin was comfortable and he had regained his independence. We resumed our laughing good times once a week. For the next four years he gardened, looked after a few fruit trees, chopped wood and entertained old friends regularly. I remember him commenting, "It's just like Cold River, but nearer to the grocery store and post office."

Cold River Longing

In 1965, almost fifteen years since I had last been in Cold River, I had a longing to revisit my wilderness haunts. I tried talking Noah into going back with me. But he was realistic telling me that, "If I was only a year younger you'd have to run to catch up with me. I always thought I'd go back to fish Cold River in June one last time, but as it stands now you'll have to go back for both of us."

As I trotted down the trail from Mountain Pond I saw how the route had remained mostly unchanged. I enjoyed the time alone. My caretaking jobs were caught up and while my employers and their families were enjoying the late summer, I was doing something I had wanted to do for some time.

As I passed familiar landmarks, I realized a lot of water had spilled over the dam since Tony Okie and I first followed this route. I visited the site of my old cabin and stayed overnight at Duck Hole. The next day I sat on the deacon log of the lean-to where Tony and I, over thirty years earlier, had eaten some cast-aside food. The water in Cold River was unusually low for that time of year which enabled me to follow a narrow strip of sand and graveled shoreline. In several hours time I reached the bank below where Big Dam logging camp once stood. I realized I had nearly gone by it. The huge logs that once spanned the river had become flood victims. Over the years the logs were undermined and torn loose. Tons of earth and rock which was once part of the dike on both sides washed away, making the river corridor appear more natural—much like it did before man had made his mark on the river.

Looking upwards I traced the path of Noah's Golden Stairway down the slope from Cold River Hill. I pictured Tony and me as we waved good morning to Noah. I held back tears of joy at the memory.

Casting my fly below the remaining logs toward the hole that had so often proved reliable, I found that it was still possible to fill my creel. As I reeled in a speckled trout, a doe with twin fawns stood motionless on the opposite bank eyeing me without fear. I wondered if I was the first human she had seen. The three of them watched the entire sequence: the first strike, the retrieve, the netting, and the final placement in the basket. With a nod I complimented Mrs. Deer on her family and how well she looked in her summer coat of red. She remained unafraid when I spoke. And, as I passed by, I looked back for a final glance and watched her disappear into the forest.

Cold River is now classified as a protected, wild river. Gone are the stately, old-growth yellow birches harvested during the mid-1950's as part of the clean-up operations following the horrific windstorm of November 1950, locally known as the Big Blow. Noah and I always enjoyed touching their trunks as we walked among them. The logging operations (the Oval Dish company still owned this small piece of land, the gore, and harvested the remaining marketable timber as part of the salvage operations that also cleared downed timber in the area) performed their final indignity to the forest by circling each nearby pond, dropping the once grand birches, and then cutting a log length or two from each tree, leaving the tops like so many butchered bodies in their haste to cut and run. The land was later sold to the state.

And if that irreverence was not enough, bulldozers and graders had carved out a road two trucks wide. Hardly a tree remains of what Noah called his Cathedral Walk, which wound across the rolling hills toward Ouluska Pass Brook and Seward Pond.

One of these logging roads began at the confluence of the Ouluska Pass Brook and Cold River and eventually joined the old tote road—last used nearly a century ago—that went through South Pass notch. The new road veered into the woods, followed Seward Pond outlet and circled Noah's trout pond. In the years following the clearing operations, runoff from the road filled the pond with silt.

Beaver, too, have come, built their houses and further changed the appearance of this lovely mountain pond where Noah used to reel in trout from his raft, and then scoop them up in his simple landing net made from an onion sack laced on to a crotched stick. Simplicity, yes indeed.

Saddened by all the changes that had taken place, I knew that this would be my last trip. A horse trail constructed during the 1960's when Rockefeller was governor ran parallel to the east side of the river near to places we hunted called The Finger, Belly-Ache and Laughing Buck Swamp. In the vicinity of Black Hole, a well-known caldron for trout, were two horse barns and a lean-to. There was even an interior ranger's cabin at Duck Hole at which Governor Rockefeller vacationed.

I now know I saw Cold River at its best. Its wonderful contributions to my life can never be duplicated and will never be erased from my remembrances. Even as I miss my old friend, I realize how lucky I've been.

Just Fiddlin' Around

"The hermit offered no apologies for his brand of mountain music. His violin playing was powerful—and never in tune."

There's a photograph that I have,
It was taken a long time ago.

When I'm asked, "Whose in the picture with you, Red?"
I answer, "An old friend, I used to know."
He's just an old time woodsman
I used to spend time with.
A man who took the time to care
And help a young boy grow.

We spent thirty-three years together
in camp, hunting, fishing spinning yarns and trapping
on the snow.
Wonderful days and nights.
He was a special man—
one who has never lost his glow.

He was an Adirondack hermit, I used to hang around with.
A good and trusted friend from long ago.
I don't often tell how much I miss his company.
I just say, he's an old friend from long ago.

The 1934 meeting that spawned a lifetime of friendship. Left, Richard "Red" Smith; right, Noah John Rondeau.

Noah demonstrating how to nail a game protector's hat to a tree.

Rondeau's Town Hall was farther back from the cookie jar than Thoreau's Walden Pond.

Noah notching wigwam poles.

Courtesy of Adolph Dittmar

Noah's beloved city was spared during the "Big Blow" of November 1950.

Courtesy of Richard Smith

Cold River City. A wilderness lifestyle, like friend Noah's, tugged at Richard's heartstrings.

Cold River style fish fry.

Homemade raft Noah used on the stillwater.

Richard Smith's boat on the Chubb River, 1938.

Red "Robin Hood" Smith.

Guests, armed with pistol-fingers, aiming with the hermit.

Living among Noah's mountains was Richard's dream.

Phil McCalvin in front of his Duck Hole cabin.

Cold River Metropolis; Red Smith and Noah Rondeau, 1941.

Noah's buildings looked like they had been continually repaired.

Two views of a trapper's cabin near the headwaters of the Chubb River.

Smith chose the less-traveled path.

Rondeau's private trout pond in Ouluska Pass. A coded tally recorded the number of trout caught in one year.

Look out trout, the Mayor of Cold River is hungry!

Noah at North Pole in Wilmington, New York, 1950.

Teamsters hauled logs over tote roads to Cold River Flow.

PART II

TALES THE HERMIT TOLD ME

Courtesy of Adolph Dittmar

Confabs With the Hermit

Oh, the many times I made myself comfortable against the Leaning Stump, or sat around the campfire in Noah's yard, or relaxed inside the Town Hall during some very cold winter days, swapping stories with the hermit of Cold River City. If someone had drawn me, my ears would have looked as big as catchers mitts, since I was always intent when listening to Noah, never wanting to miss a single word. What made each confab session extra special was Noah's reciprocal interest. He was as good a listener as he was a teller of tales.

Before the black flies in late spring, when leaves were the size of mice ears, Noah and I allowed ourselves the leisure to bask idly in the warm, comforting rays of the sun. Generally we were waiting until the freshly spaded red wigglers absorbed a bit of heat and would be comfortable enough to sing the "Springtime Trout" song.

Relaxing, without a care in the world, we'd delight our creative bent and invent pictures from the billowy white clouds that slowly floated overhead against a clear atmospheric blue. One particular cloud formation inspired Noah to invent a marvelous tale he called "At St. Peter's Gate." Noah would exclaim, "It's a scream."

The central part of the story revolved around his passage into Heaven through the pearly gates while the "beggared" game protectors looked in from the outside. They were clinging on to the bars, pleading Noah's forgiveness, while "angel" Noah reminded them of their misdeeds from a scroll he let droop from his hand. The tale was one of his favorites, and he continued to refine it over the years.

During the fall hunting season Noah's friend, Oscar Burguiere, occasionally Dr. Latimer Sr. and I were often his sole audience as he rocked and exhaled blue smoke—as he called it—a sensation we could never get enough of—kept us close to the fire long into the night.

If during the day one of us had risen from the lowly rank of 'bloody bugger'—Noah's term for one who hadn't bagged a buck—the occasion would be an historic event to be celebrated with a nip from Noah's "Trophy Bottle." The bottle of scotch had a long strip of adhesive tape stuck from the neck to the base. On the tape, in his secret code, he recorded all his legal and illegal kills of deer and bear as well as historic events he shared with others. Of course any new registering required a celebration which naturally led to the retelling of past hunts.

When winter's snow piled four to five feet on the level, with morning temperatures often as low as 40 degrees below zero, I preferred to remain comfortable absorbing the radiant heat thrown from Noah's drum stove (and later box stove). Beaver trapping was allowed to wait a bit longer on those days. I placed more importance on a leisurely breakfast of delicious corn cake muffins and flapjacks, washed down with several cups of his "better than a ten mile hike" coffee. Our confabs were more important than facing the fierce elements outside the tiny cabin's log and rough-cut board walls. Those moments are very precious to me. What I once took for granted, now, in the scheme of time, I realize were some of the most interesting years I ever experienced. Noah was a proficient teller of tales, a master story teller. His true-to-life incidents peppered with true-enough stories and some legendary tall tales were a fantastic archive of his personal experiences honed from years of living in the wilderness. Even his variations of the typical tried and true old guides stories were most amusing just because they were his.

While I have always retained a fair share of the accounts he told, many had receded from my conscious memory. Over the last few years I began to make notes whenever a particular activity or topic, tiny as it might be, triggered a mental process which revived the remembrance of a long forgotten story my old friend once told.

The hermit's exact wording, timing and emphasis have been lost in the passage of time, save for the few tape recordings he made. Recognizing his tales have always meant a lot to me, I rationalized they might also be of interest to others. For that reason I've endeavored to pen some of Noah's tales as accurately as possible. They are my interpretations as I recalled hearing them. I leave it up to you to decide which contain kernels of facts rather than renderings of the standard guide's tales of the day. I wish I had recorded more.

Noah felt that the only thing of "corporal real store" he would leave behind would be "a little bit of dust that was dust before." Perhaps his stories, while they represent only a token of him, will preserve a little more history about a hermit's life that once was.

Mr. Bear

Richard was always taken with the tales Noah told. He said the hermit of Cold River claimed the Little John story was authentic, occurring during the time he cut hair in Lake Placid. Richard's recollection of the day he heard Noah tell this tale follows.

It is impossible to duplicate Noah's style and delivery, yet this rendition closely replicates the hermit's original version. Somewhere, within the narrative, is a true hunting experience.

The late fall sun had been a welcome addition to the day. I knew from experience the daytime warmth was only a temporary interlude against nippy evenings, when the probing fingers of Jack Frost would remind me that Indian summer was rapidly retreating before the overpowering onslaught of winter.

Autumn in the peaceful Cold River Valley is special. Long shadows tend to darken the cedar, hemlock and spruce swamps, while in the distance a mantle of velvety purple wraps the crests of Panther Peak, Santanoni and Couchsachraga.

This week I had been sharing the 'guest' cabin (the Hall of Records) with one of Noah's closest friends. I had heard about Oscar for quite some time prior to meeting him. Now, a few years after our first meeting, he (who was not known for his prowess in the woods) and I were helping Noah prepare his bear traps in accordance with his redundant custom.

On previous days we had drawn out the heavy traps Noah kept concealed, hauled them, built some 'cubbys' in the woods, and cooked a huge iron pot of bear chowder. Our tramping over some mountainous territory today was the final leg in the preparation that invariably insured Noah his annual bear.

For this season, we planned to sprinkle a bear chowder bait trail through the woods on the slopes of Seymour and Emmons Mountains. Getting away from Big Dam early, we carried the chowder in covered pails, with the help of homemade yokes, to a pre-established dump site near the 'Devil's Caldron' in Ouluska Pass Brook (Noah always called it Seward Brook). While Oscar and I made several hauls from camp, Noah began to work the lure toward his traps. When we had finished the grunt work, we donned old rubber boots that were also well lathered in the special concoction, and worked the remainder of the day on the scent trails.

We generously garnished the undersides of little spruce and balsam boughs along the way. It was certainly our hope that any bruin plodding through the woods on an ancestral runway would be lured by the odor, and recklessly close in on the steel bracelet, whereupon, he would plunge his foot into the middle of the opened jaws. The steel-toothed traps were strong, but Noah had learned from experience that a bear would get mighty angry when the powerful jaws closed around one of its legs.

His wisdom, drawn from previous experiences, seemed a mite humorous, but every word ushered caution. Noah was deadly serious when it came to capturing a bear properly. He knew that when a big bear stepped into a trap, one of its paws would first depress the pan against the frame. Immediately the jaws would clamp around the animal's leg, the teeth would quickly penetrate the shaggy coat, then bite into the flesh. Bruin was trapped, but not completely immobile.

It was at that stage that Noah had once upon a time come on to a bear. "The animal was awfully angry," he told me. "Mr. Bear stared at me, real mean-looking. It was obvious he was mad. There was circles of rage around its eyes and froth dripped from its chin, as its foot long tongue dangled from a gaping mouth." Noah said he tried to draw his rifle into firing position as the bear rose on his hind legs and emitted a loud, angry "woof," but once the weapon was raised, the big bear started toward him with the trap dangling from one of its forepaws. Instead of tugging on the trigger, the sight momentarily caused him to take his finger off it. Knowing the bear wasn't about to clasp its paws heaven-ward to pray, Noah let out a shrill yawl. The sharp, unexpected noise startled the bear and threw him off rhythm. Taken off balance, he dropped to all fours, but in doing so, the suspended trap glanced against the gun, knocking it out of Noah's hands.

For a moment, the two were only a short distance apart. They could have collided! He thought of his hunting knife at his belt, but it didn't seem the best alternative. His next option was to simply look the other way. He thought that if he avoided the bear's glance that would calm its rage. But the bear emitted a deep growl that made the hair on the back of Noah's neck stand right up "pretty much to the moon."

The bear's behavior gave Noah a tremendous scare, so he said. He was without a weapon that could dispatch the animal, and at any moment he might have been clawed, lacerated, bitten, or even chewed. It was high time to teach the bear "Who-Was-Boss." Noah considered grabbing onto one ear to steady the big, furry head, while reaching around and curling its mustache with the other hand. But he never got the opportunity to test that theory, for the bear turned in fear and headed into the underbrush. It was reacting in the way every experienced bear hunter would expect. The maxim: If an avenue of escape exists, a black bear will normally hightail it faster in the opposite direction, than the person can run, who chances upon it.

Following the bear in retreat would be a cinch. The trap had not been secured well, so the bear had no difficulty dragging it and the small log to which it was attached, along. As the bruin bolted down the mountainside through the brush and trees, he tore up a trail that would be easy to trace. The 'road signs' gave Noah hope that he might yet capture the bear.

Feeling somewhat jarred from the episode, however, Noah decided the wisest move would be to sit down, rest, and smoke a bowl of tobacco before following the bear down the mountain until he had an opportunity to shoot it. That proved to be the best choice. Within an hour's time, after finishing his smoke, he resumed the hunt. The bear, by that time, had come to a small clearing and was in the process of puffing like a steam derrick as it pulled at its trapped paw thinking he might manage to tear off a few toes and escape with a little more time. Caring not to have another close brush with an ugly-tempered bear, Noah took careful aim and fired. The bullet killed the bear from a safe distance.

That experience had been a valuable lesson. From it, Noah learned to always fasten heavy logging chains to his traps, fixing the opposite end around a strong tree. That simple solution could keep a discontented bear secure. In order to steal off with the trap, it would first need to tear up the tree roots that held the trap fast.

I was happy when, toward the end of the afternoon Noah exclaimed, "We had better get a move on, or any bear hitting our trail will be at the 'cubby' before we get the trap set. I'd hate to meet him there waiting for us to hand over the rest of the chowder before he even contributes a toe nail." I was comfortably tired and ready to call it a day. During the heat of the afternoon, my olfactory senses had absorbed the strong odor of the chowder, and I became quite heady—to the point of becoming nauseous.

My affliction from the chowder not withstanding, I was glad to have been on the trail with Noah. It had been the kind of day I have always enjoyed: laughing good times, crisp comfortable temperatures, and a well-learned lesson taught by the grandmaster of woodsmen. Following a fine supper of bear steaks and onions, garden fresh potatoes and carrots, we spread ourselves around the yard to rest. Constant conversation was not necessary, nor did it occur. We respected each others' space and privacy. I believed then, and still do, that if friends could comfortably share long periods of silence side by side, their friendship would not only strengthen, but last forever.

Before sunset, Noah left his rocker and walked out of camp. I watched him walk slowly through the crispy leaves that carpeted the forest floor, and knew he was heading to a favorite point of land that overlooked the Cold River Flow. If he felt like company, he'd have made an invitation. I never asked to accompany him. I just figured he wanted to be alone.

I was familiar with this routine. Noah would sit on the slope overlooking the head of the flow. Nearby was his Ash Ground, a circle of stones laid exactly where he hoped his cremated remains would be placed when the time came. There he'd smoke his pipe and commune with nature. It was a pleasant spot to enjoy the natural beauty surrounding the river.

Oscar and I, meanwhile, felt a contentment that is hard to explain. All things eventually come to an end; I knew that and thought about it each time I was at Noah's hermitage. One impression that will always stick with me was the merry rattling made by the chalky white shoulder blades of bear and beaver that hung loosely on the siding of the tiny cabins, stirring subtly whenever a gentle breeze came up. Small things, such as that, added to the mood. Time seemed to suspend as I stared into the fire. Boy, that was some potent bear chowder, believe me!

As the dying coals of the campfire spread their warmth toward us, Noah, the genial hermit of Cold River, returned to camp. We'd been talking bear all week, so it seemed natural enough for our conversation to again drift in that direction. During our exchange, I was glad to hear Noah preparing to recount a familiar tale. I've always liked the story. It was one of the first Noah told me. It's typical of the many stories that would be told, retold and then circulated among his customers during the time Noah worked as a barber in Lake Placid. Everytime I heard him tell it, I noticed it lacked the embellishments and exaggeration he often embodied in other tales. Because he always stuck close to the original story line, I've always believed the basic incidents were a true telling of real life events in the genesis of the 1900's.

A Long Ago Hunt

A city gentleman came up from New York City during the summer a few years ago to hunt and to visit with his friend in Lake Placid. Upon his arrival, he made known his desire to shoot a deer. Although he had only learned the bare bones about woodscraft, he was overly anxious, and would not wait until a guide could be hired. He was loaned an old single shot .45-70 caliber Springfield rifle, and was assured the gun had enough fire power to bring down both deer and black bear. The gent received some operating instructions, and a sure-fire hunting plan that included a most promising place for the chance at a deer in return for the least amount of work. The sport then tramped off to find this well-known, nearby hunting area just outside Lake Placid.

The "slicker" had been instructed to follow the Military Road northwest until he came to its junction with the main Post Road. There he needed to turn left and continue west approximately two miles until he eyed a newly grubbed wagon road that entered on his right. He was to follow that narrow corridor through the forest until it ended in a large clearing several acres wide. There an industrious farmer had recently cut down the forest, creating an enormous opening. The farmer had visions of growing bushels of oats for horse feed. It was an ideal site for agricultural purposes because of the sandy loam and gently rolling plain. Natives came to call the spot the "Little John Clearing," after the name of the tallest mountain in the area. Most of the stumps had been removed, and the brush had been piled in mounds a dozen feet high, ready for burning.

Like local hunters, the visiting sportsman quickly recognized the value of those brush piles. With the aid of a sapling pole ladder he climbed to the top, made a comfortable nest, and used the elevated platform to survey the entire area. Deer were first drawn to the clearing by the salt residue left in the soil from the dynamite that had been used to loosen the larger stumps. Later on, salt licks—salt impregnated stumps— were maintained by hunters knowing the lure of sodium chloride, and the succulent grasses that took root and would continue to attract deer. If everything looked favorable, deer could be shot with very little effort.

Often hot arguments broke out as to who had actually killed a deer first. Many hunters nestled on top of the heaps, thinking they were alone, were astonished to observe, upon firing at a deer, several other heads popping from neighboring piles, like jack-in-the boxes. Upon examining the deer, the shooters would find not one, but several bullet holes. A disagreement would break out. Fist fights proceeded. And finally, with grumbling execution, the deer's carcass would be shared.

This situation was not entirely legal, but the game laws of the day were not always enforced. I knew one warden who would suddenly remember more pressing business elsewhere just to avoid catching his neighbors "red handed" at the Little John Clearing. The wardens knew venison was a staple that natives relied upon to feed their large hungry families. It was an unspoken rule that if you didn't overdo it, the game warden would leave you alone.

But I digress. As our city sportsman first came in sight of the newly cut turn that lead to the clearing, he had begun to feel somewhat leery as he proceeded through the dense forest growth on either side. It was as thick as one could find, and thoughts of a hungry bear crept into his mind.

By the time our sport had reached the opening, his fears had calmed and he proceeded to follow through with the original plan: sit on watch from one of the piles and wait for a deer to emerge from the surrounding forest.

The clock moved too slowly for one so anxious. In time, our hunter left his high lookout and began stalking the full length of the field. He noted a wide herd path which came in from the foothills. Positive the animal trail would lead him to deer, he changed his plan.

His thinking was that he was not an absolute newcomer when it came to deer hunting. Heck, he had read for years about hunting experiences in *Forest and Stream* magazine! Following this herd path would be the opportunity he needed to, once and for all, prove to himself he could at least handle the low bush and trees on the side of Little John Mountain. He plunged into the woods.

Avoiding the many side paths that intersected, he concentrated on the main runway. Without paying attention to where he was going, he worked his way over several step-like ledges until he came to an outcrop of bedrock. From there he surveyed the forest, and suddenly was seized by the certainty that he had lost his sense of direction. Knowing he shouldn't continue on, he stood, trying to reconstruct from whence he had come, when suddenly, without warning, the event that occurred next eliminated his need to fuss over such a little thing as being lost.

Taking him by surprise, a bear appeared upon the scene, and without uttering one amicable word of greeting, immediately assumed the right of way. About then, the big city sportsman gave some serious thought to leaving the immediate area. Thoughts of family, home, and fireside flashed through his mind until he remembered upon what he currently stood. Remaining on top seemed more reasonable. Images of attempting to escape by sliding downward with a bear in hot pursuit produced an uncomfortable thought. Our sport gathered himself together, sidestepped and tried to act as non-threatening as possible, but the huge bear moved closer and began to growl. The hunter noted an unusually heavy growth of hair around the beast's head and neck. This alarmed him more; he might be facing the bear of legend. Our gent had heard stories of this animal on previous trips north, but had assumed they were strongly steeped in lore. However, if true, he knew his would-be-opponent was cunning. The large bruin in question had a reputation for unnerving every horse that caught its scent or traveled along the highway. More than once an unsuspecting driver had had a wagon upset. The bear ravaged fields of grain, killed all hounds that ever attacked him and stole away with grazing sheep.

Frightened at what might occur within the next minute, the would-be hunter let out a terrifying yell, but that only made the bear move more swiftly toward him. Gracelessly he drew the Springfield, lickety-split, into firing position, attempted to fix the sights on the target, and fired. Quite by accident, the rifle discharged a well-placed shot, mortally wounding the bear. The sport had no way of knowing what an extraordinary shot it had been. He was also completely unprepared for the bear's reaction. In dying agony, the large animal began to put on quite a show: uprooting small balsams, clawing up rotted logs, and throwing clods of leaves and earth into the air, all the time spewing loud roars of anger.

This demonstration of awesome power was too terrifying to face. Overreacting, our sport dropped the rifle and bolted toward who knows where. He somehow managed to get back to Little John's Clearing. Pausing at the base of the closest brush pile to gasp a breath or two, he glanced along his backtrail. The bruin was nowhere to be seen. This should have calmed him, but it didn't. On top of a nearby watch station were some poachers—curiously amused. They saw no immediate danger that would explain the wild running they observed.

Climbing to the top of the brushpile, the runner—feeling a mite plucky for escaping danger—nervously taunted, "Mr. Bear, you can come as close as you dare, but if you can't catch me before I reach the state road, I'm a popinjay and you are a monkey's uncle." He then scrambled down and crossed the remaining ground about as fast as anything on two legs could travel, all the while emitting a pretty queer shriek. Evidently being a witness to the bear's death struggle had completely unglued the Nimrod.

Not stopping to rest again until he reached his friend's house, the out-of-towner's dash attracted some attention from the neighbors along the street. Out of breath, and in a quivering voice, he hollered his fool head off as he ran to the front door. Once there he told the story. His friend assured him there was nothing to fear. He was safe, and the bear must surely be dead, as the formidable old .45-70 was more than a match for any bear, regardless of its size.

Gathering some interested neighbors, a party was formed to investigate. They hitched a horse to a buckboard, carried some additional rifles, just in case, and proceeded out of town. News spread of the procession. Additional onlookers joined the curious to learn if the beast with the heavy hair growth that terrified both men and animals had indeed finally been killed. The horse was slowly led into the forest while some choppers worked ahead, clearing a birth for the width of the wagon. Others started up the mountain to locate the site of the confrontation. All converged upon the "pawed-up ground." It was immediately dubbed "Little John's Little Clearing."

"Great Aunt Agnes!" exclaimed one of the first men to arrive upon the scene. "What a terrible hole in that carcass." There, in a lifeless heap in the center of a newly excavated field made by the clawing of the huge animal during its final death struggle, lay the renowned bear. The first and only shot had penetrated the body, mortally wounding the bear. The head, being in good shape, would make a fine trophy. The shaggy hair on the head and neck was over a foot long, and gave the animal a most fearsome appearance. Everyone speculated about the bruin's age, agreeing only that it had to have been very, very old. It's body size and weight made an interesting problem to solve.

With the great bear of Lake Placid eventually loaded, the wagon procession headed back to town. That evening many spectators visited the bear's body that dangled on a rope suspended from a large tree branch out front of the house near the railroad station, to learn of how it had been finally laid low.

Although a hero to the local population, the hunter declined any form of praise, and even refused to look upon his trophy after it was hung for inspection.

Gladly donating the bear to his friend, our sport soon returned to New York City, where a less dangerous life could be pursued.

The hide was removed, and as the kill took place in the summer time, it was not stretched, but rather shrunk to make the fur as thick as possible.

On future visits, the New Yorker was fearful that the sight of the rug, complete with skull, would reactivate old fears. He never entered the den where the beast's tanned remains adorned a position on the hearth before the fireplace. And one other thing—our sport never again had any desire to go into the woods—surely not to bear hunt!

The farmer who had cleared the field finally burned the brush piles, much to the sorrow of many local hunters who had used them as an easy way to kill a deer. Peace came upon the opening. Oats and buckwheat were planted first but the tall surrounding trees allowed precious little sun except in the center. The vision of a bountiful harvest never quite materialized. In fact, oats were reported to be stunted, so short in height an observer remarked, "That the farmer had to get down on his knees to cut them."

Corn was tried next, but it too grew so short that deer mice had only to stand on tiptoes to eat the miniature ears that somehow matured.

Whatever the farmer lacked in harvests, he gained in recognition for his dogged efforts. Eventually he abandoned his agricultural endeavor and concentrated on cutting the marketable timber off the surrounding mountainside. Raspberry and blackberry bushes eventually choked the field. Little John's Clearing became a meeting place for both forest animals and people during the summer harvest.

"This is where I first met your parents, Richard," Noah would end when he told me this story. "Your mother would convert the heaping pails of large luscious berries into preserves, pies and shortcakes, which they shared with me on my occasional visits to the farm."

The Bear That Tried to Polish Noah Off

Richard used the voice of Noah in the following tale.

"I never tired of the tangy smell of wood and tobacco smoke mingling in the cool air as Noah and I would sit around his fire pit. For long periods of time we'd silently peer at the flickering colors and shapes of flames licking around the cedar and pine knots. But the greatest magic of the campfire came when Noah would begin to tell a tale."

You know Cold River's got a reputation for harboring some of the meanest bears in the Adirondacks. And I don't believe there ever lived a bigger animal or one half as ugly as the bear I met up with beyond the Devil's Caldron. The most appealing aspect about that bruin was his determination to teach me a lesson. Well, I finally got him but it was the most peculiar killing I was ever a party to. It all happened like this.

C.V. and me went out hunting for partridge one day. We started from Camp Seward climbing the back slope of Emmons on an old tote road. The doctor offered to help me move some bear traps I had stashed. So you might say we were mixing business with pleasure.

We hadn't gone very far when we struck onto a fresh bear trail. The number of prints indicated it had been worn down by several bears who had been entering this herd trail from different directions. This was somewhat unusual because when they search for food they travel singly.

We stopped to study the movements. The bears were surely on a migratory tromp. For the past few years there was a general scarcity of forage crops. Shack was not plentiful. The bears probably had not developed a full complement of body fat. They continued to search for food well into the season when they normally would be ready to den up.

The most interesting thing about those tracks, besides being good-sized, was that one set of prints indicated the bear was missing its toes on one paw. The missing toes was a point the doctor and I discussed.

The toeless bear appeared to be heading toward Boulder Brook, the same direction we were going. Curious about the bear, we followed its trail a short distance. But finding nothing interesting, we soon split off. I continued up the east side of Boulder Brook crossing on an old corduroy span, a remnant of a haul road that came over from Ouluska Pass. Nearby were several large boulders, Paul Bunyon sized. An opening between them was the portal to my cache of number 415X high grip Triumph bear traps.

After I brushed the leaves and twigs away from the concealed opening and skidded the heavy traps out, I sat down, leaned against a tree trunk, lit my pipe and commenced to smoke until the doctor came around. I hadn't sat longer than twenty minutes when I heard a noise, a sharp snapping, in the forest behind me. I listened for a minute trying to identify what was coming. I knew it wasn't the doctor for he never made noise like that. So I figured it must be a wild animal. Whatever it was, it was heading my way. I only had my .22 Remington pump action along for small game and a handy stub-handled hatchet.

Some animal was stirring up a dreadful amount of noise as it approached, crashing over dead branches lying about on the forest floor. As it came on I heard a "woof, woof" in between a clicking of teeth. I jumped to my feet and crouched behind the back side of a large spruce tree. A bear, a big bear was a-coming on, a-tearing through the woods. It probably had red circles around both eyes because it sounded mighty mad as it reached down with its flanges and tearin' up trees, roots an' all, making a regular road behind him as he plowed through the woods.

Well sir, when he came into full view he was an awfully big bear; perhaps the biggest I had ever seen and I've killed a hundred or more in my day. I could feel my whiskers rising straight up to meet my eyebrows. When I took a second, more careful look I noticed that bear was not only bigger than any other two bears, but was missing its toes on one forepaw and was heading directly toward me. I suspected he had recognized me as being the trapper who was responsible for the loss of those toes.

Well, I hadn't finished my smoke, but seeing the froth dripping off his chin and his tongue—it was running out a foot long—I decided it wasn't the proper time to just look in the opposite direction. Maybe I'd just finish my bowl of tobacco while I waited perched up on one of the big limbs of that old spruce. I didn't waste a lick of time shinning up that tree.

I had just gotten comfortable and relit my pipe when that devil bear made a beeline and leapt at the spot I had been setting at only a minute before. When he saw he hadn't gotten me, he looked puzzled. But his confusion only lasted momentarily. He looked one way, then another and growled and so forth. Twisting his head about he caught sight of me sitting on a branch above him. He was a determined bear and tried to reach me. I was out of reach, although he stood all of twenty feet tall when he hyperextended on his tiptoes.

"Ohhhh Mister Bear," I called down to him. "So you think you want to tickle my feet?" Well now he could see from my tone that I wasn't much scared of bears and that made him madder. He stamped and he shook the earth fiercely. I had all I could do to cling tight to that branch. His rude behavior forced me to clench my teeth around the pipe stem if I was ever going to finish that bowl of tobacco.

Then he let a beller out of him that could be heard clear to Ampersand Mountain. My, but was he infuriated! He lowered his head and butted that tree. Then he took to shaking it. I was positive that tree would eventually split or he'd tear it up by the roots. One thing was sure, I knew I had better do something before I was dislodged. Peering down I saw my rifle was still astride a tree stump near by. It surely wasn't going to do me any good. Then a notion came to me. The next time Mr. Bear ran under the limb I'd drop down on his backside, straddle him with my legs, wrap my arms around his head and grab him by the mustache. Well, I did just that and you never saw a more surprised Ursus Americanus!

His great body shook; he twisted his neck and gyrated his head. Then he jumped and reared, but I held on until he finely reached the conclusion there was going to be no gain. He just wasn't going to get me off his backside. Then he lowered his head, and made a stone-blind dash through the forest. Peering out just above the hair on his head I gripped each ear. Not only was I holding on for dear life, but I also managed to steer him down the slope keeping my head as low as possible to avoid having it knocked off my shoulders against one of the low lying branches he ran under. The noise was horrific. Sharp reports from broken branches echoed down the valley. I wasn't at all sure just what that bear had in store for me, but I knew it was about time for me to whisper a stern warning into his ear to confuse his thinking. Better yet, I decided right then and there I was going to put the fear of the she-devil in him.

Reigning him south we began to make a fast track straight for my Cold River metropolis, four miles distant. Panting and exhausted as he crossed the Northville-Lake Placid Trail, he dragged up hill and entered my yard. Letting go of his ears, I pulled my hatchet from the leather belt sheath and raised it high over his head, as I reached around with my left arm and grabbed him tightly around the neck. With a tremendous downward force I cracked him reasonless. The thud created such an echo that Dr. Latimer said he heard it clear past Seward Pond.

Even with all the power I had mustered, that bear had unusual grit and kept running on very wobbly legs straight toward the Town Hall door. He almost made it clear to the handle, but halted momentarily. I suspect he envisioned he was going to be coming to a real fast stop, so right about then I cracked him again and he dropped dead in front of my cabin.

Of course there were three things I'll always regret about that adventure. One was that the bear was so big his carcass blocked the entrance to the Town Hall. I almost stumbled trying to get in. The second was I never did get the doctor to help me move those traps and finally, adding insult to injury, I had to walk more than four miles back up the mountain to retrieve my Remington.

Oscar's Favorite Hermit's Story

Noah and I had a common friend named Oscar Burguiere. Oscar dreamed of being the best woodsman; the best hunter; the best rifle shot and the best at anything else that related to being in the out-of-doors. Unfortunately Oscar was not adroit at any of those things. Try as he may to talk, dress and use mannerisms like more successful outdoors men he knew, he continued to be rather mediocre in the area of woodcraft. Recognizing this nagging shortcoming, he persevered, trying to heed our counsel. We wanted him to develop more proficiency at something. Nevertheless, as long as I knew him, Oscar's behavior and actions—while always made in earnest—failed to transform him into the woodsman he would have liked to be.

One cool day late in Autumn, Oscar and I were helping Noah prepare a kettle of his renowned bear chowder. It was, as always, progressing into a delectable smelling concoction—so appealing that we joked that it might be a toss up whether we used this batch for garnishing the bait trail or serving it as a tasty meal.

As we diced trout and cut up plant parts Noah cautioned us about checking any of his bear traps. He emphasized there was "proper etiquette to follow." Approaching a bear requires great caution, he pointed out. "Mr. Bear will know immediately who the boss is if there's a slip-up."

Oscar listened, asked advice and babbled on about how much he wanted to bag a bruin. He really wanted to leave the woods with a bearskin rolled up in his pack.

He was entranced by the lessons, but I didn't think he actually thought he would kill a bear. I was wise enough to know Oscar wasn't up to the challenge of a bear hunt. Knowing that made his next suggestion all too humorous. He tried to broker a deal with Noah for one bear hide. I could detect a gleam of delight in Noah's eye as he cautioned the bloody bugger not to be too hasty. There were many things he knew nothing of. Bear hunting was one of them. Barring all caution, Oscar pressed Noah for a reply.

"So you'd gladly skin all the bear I bring in just for the sake of a hide for a rug?" our hermit friend chuckled. "I warn you. You shouldn't make promises you might not be able to keep."

Our host then launched into a tale concerning a hunter that he had guided in 1916 while active as a guide for the Forester Hotel in Coreys, New York.

Many years ago when I was trying my hand at guiding sportsmen who motored to Coreys during the fall hunting season, a young nimrod hired me to take him bear hunting. He was fresh behind the ears and drank a little more than he should have, but I judged him to be a decent sort once removed from the bottle.

He wanted to learn "all there was" and asked me to teach him.

Having tramped down Calkins Brook, staying at the abandoned lumber camp he offered to skin any bears brought into camp. He appeared to have the ambition, but I suspected he'd never seen a bear in his life outside of pictures in a magazine. Not wanting to dampen his enthusiasm I accepted his offer.

Early the next day I left camp before my young guest woke up. It wasn't long before I came upon fresh bear scat. I had only followed the tracks a short distance when I heard clawing not far away. Approaching causiously so as not to jangle Mr. Bear's nerves, I slowly lifted my rifle and steadied my aim. He was within range; I could have brought him down easily but suddenly I was seized by an urge to show Mr. Bear how much bear facing courage this hermit had.

Catching bruin's attention when I announced I intended to curl his mustache, I turned and ran back to the lumber shack—the bear in roaring pursuit. Reaching the door, I burst in leaving the entranceway wide open for my pursuer to follow. I startled the young upshot at the rough plank table sipping morning coffee. Still dashing to keep ahead of the chase, I noticed the young hunter was still sporting his long underwear; reaching the rear door just as the frothing bear came roaring in the front.

By this point in Noah's story Oscar had become very attentive. He might have suspected Noah was up to one of his exaggerated tales but he pressed Noah with, "What happened?"

I hollered to that shaking chawbacon, "Young feller, you best start skinning this one 'cause I'm going after another right now!"

Noah kept up a serious looking face after the telling. For the longest moment Oscar acted as if he didn't know whether to believe what he'd just heard or not! He had been party to several wild affairs concerning Noah and might have partly thought there could be some truth to this tale. Then, with a wide grin, he acknowledged he understood the broader lesson in the story and proclaimed he wasn't ready for Cold River bears . . . just yet.

As the day of brewing continued, we were treated to a fine lunch. Generous helpings of corn bread were baked fresh in Noah's reflector oven. We referred to the oven as his "Ace Woodsman" because his good friend, Dr. C.V. Latimer, Sr., had laboriously punched that title into the metal top with a nail and hammer before presenting the stove as a present. As we ate, the conversation turned to what I knew was one of Noah's best.

It didn't take long for me to realize the direction Noah's confabulation was headed. Many months earlier during the March beaver season he had set me up; now he was preparing to ensnare Oscar.

He told of going up on the Seward Range to hunt bear. On a craggy slope thick with a jungle of scrubby dwarfed spruce below the summit of Emmons Peak, he eyed a black bear running all out toward him. It was hardly a worthwhile target. He knew the bear's swift galloping would carry it past him very quickly. With his catlike swiftness he shouldered his rifle, but at that very moment the bear brushed by him knocking against his outstretched elbow. Because of the animal's speed and how Noah spun, the collision was minor. As the bear continued on in fright, Noah pointed his rifle from an awkward shooting position and pulled the trigger. Then, scrambling to his feet, he prepared for that moment when the bear might turn and attack. He was prepared to face sharp claws and frothy teeth but instead of handing out a mangling, it disappeared into the underbrush. Firing one last time he saw the bear lurch unsteadily. He's been hit at least once, but how seriously he could not tell.

Inspecting the rocks and brush, he found the wounded bear had left a strong blood trail to follow. He followed the injured animal for several hours. It first lead him over the summit ridge toward Donaldson and then down and around an arm of Seward toward the general direction of Ampersand Park.

As the day wore on, the dark, ominous clouds that enveloped the higher slopes brought snow—first in fluffy flakes, but switching to a mixture of sleet and rain. Small icicles formed on his beard. His eyebrows were coated white with frost. A layer of thin ice crusted to his green felt hat and his shoulders grew numb from the cold. His vision became somewhat obscured, but he continued ahead following the bloody trail. He was determined to overtake the wounded bear even it meant following him as far away as the Great Bear Lake in Canada!

Darkness was approaching when the bear finally laid down in a bog hole to administer first aid with poultices of mud. While this remedy offered some soothing properties, it had allowed Noah time to catch up.

As he moved in the bear growled and made an effort to rise on his hind feet, but tumbled backwards. Experience told him to avoid close encounters. It wasn't worth the risk of upsetting a wounded bear. They had a nasty habit of displaying a rather ugly, angry mood at that point. Taking careful aim he fired; the heavy bullet from his .35 Remington automatic rifle knocked the bear down.

He raced to field dress and skin the animal. The evening would be darker than usual with all the cloud cover making it difficult to set up a makeshift camp. Just as he was about to light a fire he heard what sounded like a cowbell in the distance. As he peered into the darkness, he saw a ray of light from what might have been a kerosene lantern. Noah had no idea where he was, but he surmised he might be looking at one of the camps in Ampersand Park. Going on that assumption, he carefully worked his way toward the light. He was well aquatinted with the watchman at the Park and knew he could be put up for the night. Oscar was baited. His complete attention focused on what the climax would reveal. Since I had heard it before I only had to wait a minute longer for the trap to spring. I let Noah finish the tale while I tried to keep a straight face.

> Now as I was saying; it was dark, mighty dark as I approached the light. I realized long before reaching the house that I had lost all direction. I had no idea where I was. I only had rapped on the door twice when a little girl of around seven or eight years of age swung wide the door. My appearance must have been frightful with the lamplight reflecting off the icicles that clung to my beard. In her young mind I could have been a hobgoblin of doom for she went screaming to her father's arms before I could say anything to lessen her fears. I certainly couldn't blame her for her reaction.
>
> Following an introduction I was invited in. As I dried by the fireplace picking brambles from my clothing and wiping the melting ice from my hair the man of the house looked over the bear skin. By now the little girl realized I was not a demon. The hide I had draped across my shoulders and my frozen looking appearance had taken her by surprise.
>
> Having cleaned up and changed into dry clothing I was invited to eat and spend the evening. It was a most welcome offer. Following a fireside conversation that included a telling of my chase my host showed me to a large attic room. It was like entering the eighteenth century. There was a high standing bureau, wash basin and water pitcher. The bed was an elegant four poster design with a deep thick down-filled mattress. Four tall, spiraled wooden posts twisted upward probably eight feet high. And overhead, covering the entire top and draped on all four sides

were curtains— an embroidered brocade of linen and lace. It was indeed beautiful; I questioned whether I'd even feel comfortable sleeping on it. But for the life of me, I've forgotten just what that kind of bed was called."

As if on cue, the unsuspecting Oscar stepped into the trap offering the one word needed to make the snap. "A canopy, Noah."

With twinkling eyes, Noah ended his story.

"Noooo, that was under the bed!"

Noah and I laughed as Oscar shook his head momentarily allowing the joke time to crystallize; then, he too joined in the fun.

"Oscar, if there was any moral to that," Noah added it might be, "the only thing that doesn't get caught in a well placed trap is the one that sets it." And then he qualified that remark with, "Hopefully!"

When we calmed down, Oscar asked if any of the story was authentic. With a ready smile Noah said the best part was the trap marks on Oscar, but there was some truth to the tale and continued the story. The hunting portion had been true. He never did say whether he tracked the bear towards Coreys or Ampersand Park, but I do know Avery Rockefeller had a long standing invitation allowing Noah passage through his preserve as well as allowing him to stay in a little cabin near the watchman's camp.

His friends at the Park helped him cart in the meat the next day. Accepting some as a gift from the hermit, the remaining meat was transported over the Ward Brook tote road and hung at the customary drop site near Mountain Pond. From there Noah would then work it down the Cold River trail to the hermitage.

Fishin' Bear At Millers Falls

"Yes sir, talking of big fish," remarked Noah as he addressed three friends he'd last seen in 1943 during their June fishing trip. "In 1923 I watched as a monster trout nabbed a bear cub and reeled downriver toward Long Lake and I suspect you'll want me to tell you about it soon as I finish polishing off Doc Latimer's fine cooking." With that said, he tucked away a final mouthful of venison—camp meat he had shot while tending bear traps behind the doctor's camp—and complimented the doctor on his cuisine.

According to custom Noah arrived at Camp Seward on the doctor's first night in. Doctor Latimer having first landed at Jim Plumley's camp located at the far end of Long Lake earlier that day. He hooked up with a teamster he had prearranged to tote his supplies needed for an entire month. How dry the fall season had been dictated how far beyond Shattuck Clearing the buckboard would be able to advance before they had to lash the cargo onto the horses' backs.

At camp, Noah was treated to a meal prepared by "C.V." (Doctor Latimer's nickname) that would be fit for royalty or hermit alike. It was Noah's pleasure to provide the main course. Upon arrival C.V. would always find stovewood cut, the yard spruced up, all branches removed from the roof, the stove pipe in place and perhaps a bouquet of colored leaves on his table and a glip—a young deer deemed not capable of surviving the winter—hanging out back near the cool, bubbling spring. (In the early twentieth century, gilpins (glips) were considred standard fare for camp meat. Conservation laws were passed outlawing this practice, but many backcountry hunters resented goverenment's intrusion and continued this long-standing tradition in open defiance of the law.) C.V. and other men were long time friends of Noah's; they were also in a financial position to provide the aging hermit with staples he was not able to personally afford. In addition the younger member, Oscar, always helped Noah shoulder heavy packboards that often weighed sixty pounds up river to Big Dam. Numerous trips were generally necessary to cart all the supplies over the narrow, rocky, often muddy Northville-Lake Placid foot trail. The most precarious section was the High Banks area between the Big Eddy and Miller's Falls.

Noah patted his belly commenting that as soon as the last mouthful reached his stomach, his belly button might just expand far enough to pop a suspender button. Jay Gregory, Oscar Burguiere and C.V. all agreed it was good to be all together once again sitting around the plank table as they had been doing for almost twenty years.

Camp Seward was their second home, a place in their heart and mind they often thought of when the pressures of work mounted. Trout fishing in the spring and deer hunting in the fall were the times they were able to go to Cold River. This time of year was made extra special because of the autumn scenery. The doctor's camp was built in the 1920's by the state ranger at Shattuck's Clearing on his time off. It was assembled from green timber and salvaged materials from an abandoned river driver's camp. It was well concealed, being tucked away in a grove of spruce several hundred yards off the hiking trail that ran on the north side of the Cold River beyond the Big Eddy. Traces of an old corduroy road led across a marsh behind the camp and split into two directions. The main route led across a major drainage and proceeded to run toward Boulder Brook. The other route wound northeast keeping pretty much between the steep slopes of Seward and a series of small ponds eventually hooking east where it intersected Ouluska Pass Brook. Almost two decades had passed since C.V. first hunted out of a rustic hunting shanty near Calkins Creek. It was there that he had first heard of Noah from hunters out of Coreys. There were so many deer then they seemed to play and frolic; Camp Seward's backyard was still that way. For the last month each of the men had been edgy, having packed in advance, longing for the time when they could head for the deep wilderness where only the crack of their rifles could be heard.

As the full course dinner diminished from the china platters, the men continued telling tales as they sat warmed by the radiant woodstove that heated the aging board and tarpaper camp. Noah continued his story.

> You might of heard of some big lunkers from old Albert Hathaway when you were at Camp Pine Point over yonder in the Saranac's, but I know of an unusual fish, longer, heavier and smarter than the biggest lake trout Albert ever saw and it occupied the waters right here in Cold River. Yes sir, and I'm here to tell you that I once saw that fish snatch a bear cub right before my eyes and get away with it.

Hearing that kind of exaggeration the men quieted, focusing their attention on Noah. The build up had all the trimmings of a classic tall tale. Not wanting to hear anything else they waited for their old hermit friend to continue.

> The air was soft and balmy, yet there was an autumn tang in the atmosphere that heralded the time when the feathered creatures would begin to migrate to the warmer climate of the sunny Southland. Soon the hare and weasel would don their coats of white. The majority of the leaves were still clinging to the trees, a wondrous riot of yellow, brown, scarlet and pink. The forest abounded with scampering chipmunks and squirrels dashing at a frantic pace, gathering seeds and nuts. They chattered at me as if they were scolding me for intruding on their shopping. In the distance loomed the lofty Mount Emmons. It would have made a perfect subject for my oil canvas, rising high above the river valley with a back-

drop of deep atmospheric blue.

Since the tramping was fairly easy, I had been making good time until
I reached Laughing Buck Swamp.

Noah gave Oscar a wink about then for it was last year that Oscar's
buck had escaped his imperfect shooting and ran into the swamp. Somebody in the party reported hearing the buck begin to laugh once it eluded
poor Oscar.

Instead of circling wide around the perimeter, I picked a shorter route
aiming to place me on the tuffs of marsh grass and small hummocks. I
was hauling out some old equipment from a trapline shelter I used near
the base of 'Couchee.' Reaching the far end of the swamp, I worked
myself through a rough section damaged by a windstorm. It had up-
rooted trees, cripple brush and brambles intermingled with the yawning
limbs of the downed trees. Partridge flapped up or strutted away in the
underbrush. One brood even stood in line and watched me pass. I
though I might clip the head from the next plump one I saw. It would
have made a tempting dish with some strops of crispy saltpork but my
shoulders were aching from the heavy pack. I'd been using a tump line
to offset the weight but the rope threatened to blister my hands since I
hadn't wrapped them with a rag.

Sighting a convenient log I backed up to it and rested my pack on top,
then removed my shoulders from the straps. While I rested I ate a lunch
of pancakes I had rolled with jelly that morning. Suddenly I heard a
curious splashing in the river nearby. Making my way through the
spruce and occasional white birches that fringed the river's edge, I
caught the sound of water flowing over the short falls at Natural Dam,
what you call Miller's Falls. In fact it was just about where I met you
sitting today on that log that had washed downstream becoming beached
on Boulder Island.

The men all nodded, they knew Noah was describing the rock out-
cropping just below the cascade. It was the first place attorney Gregory
liked to hike to once he had helped settle things in camp. The site was
restful and relaxing and so far from the hectic professional life the men
had left back in the city. A similar expansive bare rock in the middle of
the Big Eddy was also a destination the men would occasionally gather to
sit and smoke in the early evening hours watching the sun until it dropped
over the horizon.

I moved closer to the bank of the river and, peering through the
bushes, I saw a long spruce log that reached out from the shore clear to

the deepest part of the pool. The trunk's end was held fast, ensnared on the shore between a pile of entangled driftwood and two boulders that kept it from being dislodged by the current and drifting downstream. Out on the far end bobbing up and down in the water was a bear cub. Behind it, padding ever so carefully out to the end was a big she-bear. I crouched down wondering what in the Sam Dickens those two were up to.

The log was about twenty-five feet away from where I was hunched in the bushes. Slipping ever so quietly forward to reach a better vantage point, I moved another five feet and secured a good look-out from which I could scrutinize the situation. The cub was stretching out, head down, paws draped over the log's side studying it's mama's every movement. The old she-bear, by then, had carefully edged her several hundred pounds along the incline and was smeared flat to the log with her right fore paw dangling in the water along side the log.

I hadn't watched for more than five minutes when the matriarch jerked her paw up and out of the water in a smooth swish and there hanging off her long claws were three, six-inch trout. As sure as black flies bite, that bear was fishing using her curved flangees as fishhooks. That was surely a new trick. I watched as she removed the fish, dividing them with the cub. But then she did something that completely benumbed me.

Just in front of the bear on the top of the log was a depression where a limb had once grown; having been rotted and then ripped out, a hollow was created. Well, low and behold that bear lowered her paw into the hole and dug out a worm, almost as big as a night crawler. Taking hold of it with the nails on her other paw she yanked the worm into fragments and proceeded to bait every one of her nails on her right paw. Then she dipped the paw and arm back into the river. It appeared she was using the hole in the log as a bait can. There was no mistaking it. She was out there in the middle of Cold River fishing.

Of course if anybody had told me they'd seen a fishing bear doing what she was up to I wouldn't have believed it. I suppose nobody would.

I watched carefully studying her movements. Everytime she sensed she might be getting a nibble she would twitch her hind foot against the cub's backside until he got the message that mammy wanted him to settle down and keep from pacing back and forth along the log. Once everything was calmed down she extended her long paw until she could not reach any farther. Just like you'd let a fish run with the line. Then with a lightning quick jerk she'd pull toward her and up out of the water she'd reel in several more trout hooked onto her fishing claws.

About the time when the she-bear had just pulled in her fifteenth fish the little cub ran completely out of patience. Consuming the last fish tossed to him, he reached over his mother's head and picked up the flopping trout the mother had saved for herself in the bait bucket. Coming out with her meal attached to his claws, the cub laid down on the log and hyperextended his arm out into the swirling current.

I'll be galldarned but that cub was going to fish with live bait, upping his mother. I was thinking about how I could keep these bears around Big Dam—I might even learn a thing or two from them when all of a sudden there was a great turbulence in the pool. It all happened so quickly but as near as I can recall there was a huge splash throwing a curtain of water four feet into the air and clear over the log. The mother, she was a-holding on with her claws as the log rocked from side to side, but in the confusion of the splashing water, the cub was flipped off and pulled underwater. All I saw of him were a few air bubbles where he'd gone under.

Turning quickly to her side the mother bear scooped into the water trying to locate her cub, but he was nowhere to be seen. There was a quick flashing movement and in an instant I saw a fin of the biggest trout I'd ever seen. It was pulling the cub down the chute and dragging it downstream to deeper water. The mother, all consumed in agony by now at the loss of her young'n, bleated one long heart-wrenching moan and climbed up onto the far bank making her way into the nearby woods. She was grieving beyond imagination, knowing there wasn't any way she could get her offspring back.

"So Noah," piped up Oscar, "just what happened to the cub do you figure?"

As near as I can figure, that cub was taken by one of those giant trout that lived upstream in the Black Hole. You know I've heard that there's a particular strain of Cold River trout in them big holes that's bigger, more powerful, with more fight, spit and vinegar than any other trout in the world. Why, say, even Albert Hathaway had to admit that of all the fish he'd ever caught in his guiding days on the Saranacs, this fish I saw was far bigger than any he'd ever heard of in the Adirondacks.

Silence fell around the supper table for a moment, broken only when Gregory mentioned he was going to have second thoughts before he ever dangled his toes in the water off Boulder Island.

Run-in With the DA

Tupper Lake Herald - Friday, May 23, 1924

Rondeau is Held for Grand Jury

Noah J. Rondeau, odd woods character, arrested at Coreys in connection with a shot at Protector Earl A. Vosburgh, was held for the Franklin County grand jury when arraigned before Justice M. H. Burno at Malone on a charge of second degree assault. Rondeau waived examination. He was confined in the county jail pending a decision by Judge Paddock as to the amount of bail to be required.

Since moving to Coreys, Noah had kept a daily journal that was described by one of his early clients, John Meyers, as being "a fabulous diary that describes all the birds, all the animals, all the flowers, all the seasons; everything he saw." Noah's diaries were written in a style that was half code, half script. Before he was hauled off to jail, he instructed Bill and Clarence Petty to take the proper steps to safeguard those journals as well as care for his pet fox. In addition, Clarence was also to guide two of Noah's annual clients to Cold River for a week of fishing. Reluctantly Clarence also agreed, upon his return, to tote out a heavy bear skin Noah didn't want left at the Dam camp.

Case No. *183*

Rondeau, Noah J. Address

Charge *Assault, 2 nd Degree*

Held by *M. H. Burns*

Date Held *May 13, 1924*

Bail Fixed

Undertaking Given

Presented to Grand Jury *June 4, 1924*

Defendant Arraigned Before Judge

Plea of   Guilty entered *No*

Case Sent to County Court   *indictment*

Disposition in   Court   *returned*

(a) Adjournments

Courtesy of Franklin County Court House

Convinced his diaries might, if they landed in the wrong hands (the game protectors) be used against him in a court of law, Noah experimented with a variety of methods to code his observations. As he told his long-time friends Peggy and Wayne Byrnes, "My diaries are like my poems. Poor scribble—no more." He indicated his coded comments contained no earthshaking revelations about the poor hermit. But he knew there were a handful of people just waiting for the opportunity to get some goods on him. "Their guns are already loaded with powder and they are gathering bullets to be ready to be fired."

The Cryptic Code

I often arrived at Noah's hut a week or more prior to the beaver trapping season in March, so I could enjoy some leisure time with my friend. Invariably I found Noah deeply engrossed in writing, reading, or clipping and pasting snippets of personal interest from old newspapers into his journal and scrapbook.

He sat for hours on a comfortable bearskin cushion that was draped over the top log of his bunk which served as a bench for a small table that was hinged to the side wall. When the table top was lowered a hinged pedestal leg unfolded on the underside steadying the horizontal surface.

There he sat shifting clippings into organized piles of interest. Flower and vegetable drawings, animal pictures, news articles, political stories, labels from canned foods; all were cataloged, then reshuffled and prioritized once again until he was satisfied with the arrangement. The next step involved gluing, followed by a hand written notation that expressed an opinion or simply recorded something he needed to remember, such as how many seeds he might have ordered from a mail order company. The majority of the notes in the journal were merely daily observations of animal movements, the weather and temperature, and where he had gone or what had happened.

Over the years he even developed an elaborate cryptic looking code to write in. While the code was an academic exercise that helped to dawdle away the idle hours, it did serve a useful function. He used the code to keep an accurate accounting of all his legal and illegal kills—the deer, bear and fish he caught. Noah was wary of the game protectors and that may have promoted him to create the code. As far as I know, it was never used to conceal any dark secrets.

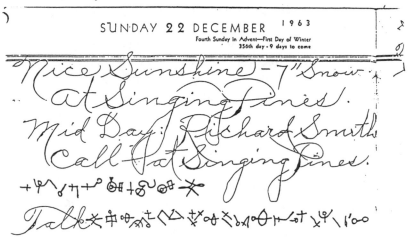

SUNDAY 22 DECEMBER 1963
Fourth Sunday In Advent—First Day of Winter
356th day - 9 days to come

Decoded:

Good visit. 10 hours.
Prs [presented] book. Fraisers. Lumber Mil. Dead. Abe Fuller.

Courtesy of North Elba-Lake Placid Historical Society

His yearly journals also helped to keep track of the day and date. Occasionally he left Cold River to spend the Christmas holidays with friends. Upon returning he experienced months of total isolation before seeing another human. A visitor would be a red-letter day.

Hermit Hieroglyphics

The following story, written by David Greene, is historical fiction. The events recounted in the story did occur. David constructed the narrative based on facts supplied by Richard Smith.

David cracked Noah's code in 1992. He plans to decipher all of Noah's coded journals. Richard was one of three close confidants Noah revealed his code to. What these people knew of the code they kept to themselves. It was confidential.

I dropped in on the Hermit of Cold River one bright day in September and discovered him sunning himself in his old makeshift rocker outside his cabin door and writing busily in his journal. I called out a cheery "Hooty-Hoot" greeting as I approached.

"Be with you in a minute," the Mayor said, glancing up. "Just let me finish updating the City records." He rapidly added another line or two to a page of scrawled symbols. I had long known, of course, that Noah used some kind of code in his journals, but this time I happened to glance at the page. It was covered with lines and crosses and strange hieroglyphic symbols—nothing I could even begin to recognize.

"I hope those Government Officials never have to go over *your* records, Noah," I joked. "I declare, your handwriting's even worse than usual. I recall I used to be able to make out letters and numbers in your code, when you showed me a sample of it a few years back, even if I couldn't exactly make out their meaning but now I can't recognize a darn thing. If I didn't know that Cold River City was population one, I'd swear you were letting a muddy-footed chicken or two run loose across that document there."

Noah let out a chuckle. "Glad to hear it, Richard, " he said. "These are top-secret records, you know, and I write 'em this way particularly to keep away the Big Fool Government Bureaucrats. I decided my old numbers-and-letters code was too easy to figure out, so I cooked up this new one a while back—even the experts would have a tough time making any sense of it. I've put in enough tricks to keep 'em guessing for ten years of Thursdays."

"What kind of tricks, Noah?" I inquired, not quite sure what he was talking about and a little curious to know more, though I resolved to back off the subject if it seemed Noah didn't want to talk about it. I recalled a story Noah had told me recently about an inquisitive stranger who had seen his code and wanted to know the secret of it. After considerable pestering, Noah gave in and wrote out a code key and a sample of the code. But when the nosy hiker painstakingly deciphered it, he found that it said "I AM A SILLY JACKASS TO THINK THE HERMIT WOULD GIVE ME HIS SECRETS!" Noah had invented a fake code on the spot, that looked similar to the original one, to fool his unwelcome questioner —and he never did give him the key to the real code. That wasn't exactly a position I wanted to be in, myself.

Noah looked at me solemnly for a moment or two; I got the feeling that he had a hankering to tell somebody about his cleverness in inventing that code and all the "tricks" he was talking about—but it went against the grain to let anyone else in on the secret. "You won't let on to anyone, will you, Richard?" he asked, then gave a little chuckle. "Course you won't. And it's not like an old hermit really has a lot of secrets to hide. It's just a little mental exercise for me, you know, to while away a rainy day and keep those confounded Game Protectors off my back. We-e-ll . . . " He rose and disappeared into his little cabin, and soon returned carefully peeling the label off a can of peaches. "Don't guess I'll forget what's in this," he laughed, "and if I do it'll just be a pleasant dinnertime surprise like the rest of the cans I keep soaking in Cold River all winter." He settled himself comfortably in his rocker again and began to write on the back of the label. "Guess I'd best start at the beginning—'less you're in a big hurry?" he inquired, glancing up at me.

"Not at all, Professor," I laughed, as I hauled over a chunk of firewood for a seat and settled down for a lecture.

"Years ago," Noah began, "I used to write a lot of pictures into my journals, just simple things like sun, moon, clouds, fish, bear, deer, whatever I was writing about. As time went on I had a little fun inventing pictures for other words—I'd draw a hand when I wanted to write 'and,' or as part of 'Handsome View' and so forth . . . But most of those journals burned up in that big fire I had awhile back, and about that time I was having a lot of trouble with the Consternation Department. So I just got to thinking: with all the Official Busybodies poking their noses into my business and trying to make out I was breaking the law, I didn't want anybody grabbing my journals and hauling them into a courtroom for all sorts of lawyers and judges to paw through. Not that I was writing anything that'd get me convicted, mind you," he added with a quick wink in my direction. "But the idea just rubbed me the wrong way, somehow and I figured it'd do the snoops good if they came sneaking into my camp to get an eyeful of my journals and found out they couldn't read a word of it! And I bet that's exactly what happened, too, once or twice over the years.

"Well, one day I was looking over a map in a book, and I got to looking at the direction indicator in the corner of the map." He drew a figure:

"Right then I had my idea. I could use a circle like that as a base for my code, and the four compass points, lines out of the circle like that you know, would stand for four letters of the alphabet: N, E, S, and W. And I'd modify the compass points various ways to account for other letters and numbers.

"I used exactly the same system when I wanted to write numbers—the marker for a number is another small circle in the center of the base circle, with the line pointing out from it: numbers 1 through 8 are lines pointing north, east, south, west, northeast, southeast, southwest, and northwest in that order. Clockwise from the top, see? First the straight compass points, then the diagonals."

"What about zero and nine?" I asked, "And bigger numbers?"

"Zero and nine don't have a direction; they can point any which way. The line for a zero has a rectangle marker—looks like a Z—and nine has a circle marker. For bigger numbers you just write the digits in a row as usual, or you can combine them with the 'clockwise' rule, like this: here's this year, 1943, in code."

The hermit wrote out:

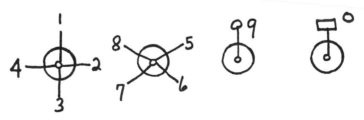

Followed by:

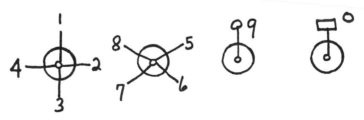

As an afterthought he added numbers to his code key:

"Both of those say '1943'?" I said. "Those first four digits—okay, I can see that, but that funny-looking critter on the right . . . I see a '1' and a '9' I guess, but what's that squiggle on the east side?"

"That wavy line tells me to skip the next number-symbol, and read it the next time around," said Noah cheerfully. "So, look, you read 1—9—skip the 3—4—and then keep going clockwise again until you get back to the 3, to read what you skipped on the first round. Without the squiggle that would read '1934,' because of the ordering rule; I invented the wavy line so I could squeeze a bigger number like a year onto one base circle —make it look more complicated and mysterious, you might say. Sometimes you have to read three times around the circle to get the whole number: the year 1876 would be—" He drew another symbol:

"Now if a fellow looks at that he's not likely to see the Centennial of Independence right off, now, is he?" said Noah with a chuckle. "But it's pretty easy to read. See the two extra arms on the eastern squiggle? That just means that that symbol counts double—you read it twice, so the number is 1, skip 6, skip 7 and 8, skip 6, 7, 6, reading clockwise from the top. 1876. You can add two arms to double a number, too: 1776 looks like this." He drew a new figure:

I shook my head in wonderment. "Noah, you've surely done a good job of disguising that number. Why, even a mathematics professor would think your 1943 was a turtle skeleton or some such. And 1776 looks more like a flying dinosaur hatching out of an egg than anything else."

That drew a laugh from Noah. "Well, I suppose that's appropriate enough. American Fool Government has grown up to resemble a Monster Pterodactyl in some ways . . . But I suppose that's a different lecture." He started drawing more circular hieroglyphics, this time without the small circle in the center. "Of course all of this I just showed you applies to the letters, too, not just the numbers. You can write a whole word on one circle if you're lucky—but usually even with the wavy-line skip-a-letter rule and adding two arms to double letters and so forth, the directions of the different letter symbols get in the way of each other and it's easier to use several separate base circles." He waved a hand at the sign over the door of one of his low-ceilinged shacks. "See, written normally, here's HALL OF RECORDS, and below it I've packed the letters as tight as I can onto just three circles." He pointed to where he'd written. Under that was:

I stared for several minutes at the scrawled symbols, glancing back and forth at the code key that Noah had written out, and finally figured out more or less how they both translated to HALL OF RECORDS.

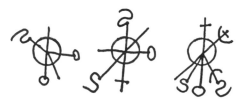

I sat back and looked at Noah in amazement. "And you keep all this in your head," I exclaimed, "and write your journals in it? Seems as if it would take forever and a day just to figure out how to write down what you had for breakfast. But I guess I saw how fast you can write . . ." I gestured at his journal, still lying open nearby to that day's entry—then did a double-take as I saw that the symbols I'd just been studying *still* looked hardly anything like the code in the journal! There were lines marked with crosses and circles and rectangles, yes, but there was not a single big "base circle" or wavy line on the entire page! Was Noah tricking me into learning some elaborate fake code, as he had done with that other visitor? I shifted uncomfortably as the phrase Noah had coded ran through my head: *I AM A SILLY JACKASS TO THINK THE HERMIT WOULD GIVE ME HIS SECRETS!* "Noah, how come this writing here looks different from what's in your journal?"

"Ah!" said the hermit with a sly gleam in his eye. "Well, I was just getting to that." He must have sensed something of my misgivings for he added, more seriously: "No, I'm not fooling you, Richard. You're not a nosy-parker like that other fellow I told you about . . . I just got tired of writing all those circles and squiggles.

He motioned as he flipped through the pages of his journal. "Everything's run together with no sign of where one word ends and another begins. I never write doubled letters either; I use that 'two-armed,' mark on a letter if I want it doubled. And repeated patterns—yes, it's true there are some; I can't avoid 'em entirely. But I do the best I can. Every day I write down where I am and what I'm doing—well, I've been here at Cold River City for a good while now, but I'm not sure I've repeated a pattern in the past two months . . ." He leafed through the journal, pointing at different lines of code and reading them, apparently effortlessly, out loud: "Cold River, Town Hall, Beauty Parlor, Mrs. Rondeau's Kitchenette . . . here's 'Beauty Parlor' written backwards, with my backwards-marker from the old HEAVY STOCK code. 'Hall of Records' . . . here I've got 'Town Hall' and 'Cold River' written every-other-letter style, so it looks like CTOOLWDNRHIAVLELR. That's not an easy word to unravel, is it, Richard? Then comes 'Pyramid of Giza,' . . . here's 'Mrs. Rondeau's Kitchenette' written upside down. That's the neat thing about compass points; if you turn them upside down they look just like some other code letter. There's the mark that means 'read this line upside down,' " he added, pointing to a sketch of a friendly-looking little figure with its arms over its head (or standing on its head if you looked at it the other way.) "Here it says 'Big Dam, C.R.' with some square symbols mixed in—I forgot to mention, a square or any symbol with a square in it doesn't mean a thing, just ignore it. I put 'em in here and there just for decoration, to mix up the patterns a little more. And here it says '<GROCE DAM, REVERE FRET>' —these little brackets signify I'm writing something in French, you see—though even another Frenchman might have a tough time recognizing my spelling for 'Big Dam, Cold River.' I never went to a French school, you know, and I've been told my spelling of French is mighty original. I looked some words up in a French dictionary once and it appeared to me they were putting in twice as many letters as they needed— so I like my style of spelling better, anyway. Besides," he laughed, "it makes it that much less likely anybody will ever figure it out."

"You can say that again!" I agreed. "You sure have a lot of ways of writing down that you've been sitting right there in that old rocking chair . . . And if you write backwards and upside down and inside out like that all the time, your code would look like nonsense even if somebody knew which letters were which compass-points. But what about that letter-counting trick? Couldn't someone figure out which symbol was an E, and maybe guess other letters from that?"

"Well," drawled Noah, "as a matter of fact . . . no, that wouldn't work a bit. You see, the letter E in my code is just a horizontal line, and so is W. You can't tell 'em apart. So I connect one end of the line to another symbol so that the free end points east for E or west for W. Or, if I can't do that—connecting isn't always possible—I bring back the circle idea, so a line pointing east or west out of a circle stands for E or W . . . And what that amounts to is that I've got two different symbols for E: the flat line by itself, and the line pointing east out of a circle. If you don't know they're the same symbol you'll count them separately, and so there won't be a clear winner for the most-often-used letter. It might be T, or A, or N, or any number of letters. And if you do guess E for the horizontal line, and you don't know the connection rule about it pointing east or west, you'll start trying to read an E where there ought to be a W and get even worse confused—not to mention there's a bit of a problem even figuring out what the basic symbols are that you're supposed to count, because I run a lot of them together to save time. T and O next to one another can share the circle marker, for instance, and '-ing' just looks like one symbol. And of course the word 'and' *is* just one symbol, just the same as the one for Y but upside down."

I was pretty well flabbergasted at this point. "If you can't tell E and W apart without adding a circle, how do you distinguish N and S? Or"—I looked back at the code key— "A and C, or B and D?"

"You write the symbols for A, D, and N in the upper half of the line, when you're writing a line of code," answered Noah. "S, B and C look just the same, but they're in the lower half of the line because they're really pointing the opposite direction."

"So people would be likely to confuse those letters, too, if they didn't notice the change in position," I said. "And I'm still having some trouble telling your letters and numbers apart, in the old circle code. Can you really read and write in such a conglomeration of hieroglyphics?"

"Sure," said Noah, "with a little practice, it's just like print, you know."

"Make that a *lot* of practice," I said, "and I might possibly believe you. I'm pretty well persuaded that even Edgar Allan Poe might have lost a lot of sleep trying to read your chicken-tracks. I think if I want to keep my head from aching I'd best stick to learning how to read deer tracks, myself, and leave your hieroglyphics to you."

Noah didn't seem too disappointed. "Well," he remarked philosophically, "I suppose the study of deer-tracks is likely to do you a sight more good, in a practical way, than learning my code will ever do. But today," he added, "I find I've been thinking not so much about deer as about another critter, whose tracks are even tougher to read than my journals."

I followed the direction of his speculative gaze, wondering what sort of devilishly clever animal Noah might have in mind. Leaning up against the wall of the Town Hall was a fishing pole. "A trout!" I guessed shrewdly, and stood up with a laugh. "Come on, Professor, put away your squiggles and compass points and let's make some tracks ourselves, over to Seward Pond."

"Don't guess we'll need a compass to get *there*," Noah grinned. He put away his journal and collected his gear, and soon we were walking the old familiar trail to Seward Pond.

We returned several enjoyable hours later with a respectable mess of trout, and after a savory fresh-fish dinner Noah pulled out from under his bunk bed a somewhat dusty bottle and proceeded to mix up a couple of drinks—a little maple syrup, some lemon juice, a dollop of honey, and finally a carefully measured capful from the bottle. As he was pouring I noticed a strip of tape running down the side of the bottle. "Why, that's your trophy bottle, Noah!" I said. "Our catch of fish today wasn't anywhere near a record; what's the occasion?" Noah marked the new level in the bottle carefully and wrote something next to it on the adhesive strip, then handed it to me. "Read it for yourself," he said with a quizzical look.

I squinted at the tiny writing and found to my dismay that it was all written in code. "All right—don't rush me now," I said, steeling myself for the mental effort. A line pointing west with a circle on it—that was an R, I remembered . . . same line with a crossbar was . . . let's see, clockwise from the top after E is F, G, H . . . I. Was that next one an A or a C? R —I—C— . . . H . . . "Looks like 'Richard Smith . . . learns . . . code . . . September 17, 1943.' "

Noah had made a special occasion out of it, something worthy of recording on his prized Trophy bottle, which mostly catalogued such historic events as a successful hunt for a bear or a big buck which provided him with a good share of his winter food supply. And on looking back, I figured it was something of an event. For Noah to tell me all the tricks of his hieroglyphic writing—something that he had not divulged to anyone before (at least not in such a comprehensive explanation) and perhaps never would again—was something more than an hour's casual conversation; it was a sign from Noah of particular friendship, trust and confi-

dence, based no doubt on the similarity of our methods of living and out-
looks on life, and solidified by our long hours together fishing or hunting
or simply sitting around the stove on a cold winter's evening, listening to
each other philosophizing on politics and natural history and the world in
general. Even if I never read another line of code (and I kind of hoped I
wouldn't, it took a head like Noah's to figure out that code, and what he
wrote in it was his business) the occasion was still one I'd remember all
my life.

I picked up the drink that Noah set before me and raised it high.
"Here's to you and your hieroglyphics, Noah, and all the good times
you've ciphered into your journals—and all the fishing and forests and
philosophy at Cold River in the years to come, too, that you haven't written down yet!"

Noah looked at me over his drink, his bright eyes twinkling. "A most
comprehensive toast, Richard," he complimented. "Here's to you, too!"

We clunked tin cans amusingly together and drank down the Hermit's
ambrosial brew, as sharp and sweet as September sunshine mixed with a
healthy glow of good companionship. Life just doesn't come any better
than that.

"Hats off to Mrs. Beebe and her strawberry preserves."

Elric J. Dailey, professional trapper and rival of Noah Rondeau.

Courtesy of Richard Wood

Courtesy of Richard Wood

Richard Wood, 1922.

E.J. Dailey, 1922.

Richard Wood and E.J. Dailey, Duck Hole
Headquarters Camp.

Along the Cold River Trail.

Visitors were Noah's source of news.

Mayor Rondeau warming up 46er Roy Snyder.

Noah tending his flower kettle.

Richard Smith, 1941.

Cold River's beauty was not something Noah could cloak in code.

*Richard had a restless,
pioneer-like spirit.*

Richard "Red" Smith.

Courtesy of Fred Studer

Cold River.

Noah pointing out his code's finer technicalities to Richard Smith.

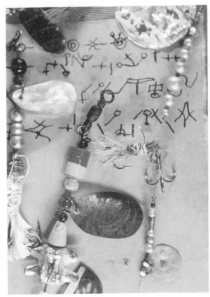

Rondeau's homemade lures.

Courtesy of Richard Smith

Noah John Rondeau, Adirondack Hermit.

Camp Seward. L to R: C.V. Latimer, Jr., M.D., Noah, C.V. Latimer, Sr., M.D.

Duck Hole.

PART III

AFOOT IN COLD RIVER COUNTRY

Courtesy of Richard Wood

COLD, Cold River

Melting **snow**
tumbled in rivulets
as it washed
Seward's slopes each Spring.

Huge logs and boulders
formed **Big Dam.**
It impounded the snowmelt
creating a flow
in the vallie basin.

The river water accelerated,
resembling broad, **silk** cloth
slipping over a deteriorating sluiceway.
The smooth motion was hypnotic.

Continuous cascades leaped
into the **plunge pool** below.
It splashed, bubbled and then was beaten
against fractured rocks of granite
until tiny, churning **whirlpools**
whipped a batter of foam.

Microscopic particles of hydrogen and oxygen
rose skyward catching the sun's rays
and refracted light of a prism.

Early open water provided **few** trout.
The water and air—generally too cold—
made fishing slow.

Hungry trout
would feed on young, **red wigglers**
plucked from warm, decomposing manure.

Happy was a **hermit**
when in a pool of water
an insect hatch was spied
luring fish.

With skillful placement
a hand tied fly joined the hatch.
Hopefully an actively feeding trout
would be fooled and
strike the hook of an ARTFULLY tied fly.

Such were Noah's **Springtimes** so long ago.

The Cold River Mouse

While on a backpacking trip, the summer of 1937, to climb Couch-sachraga Peak, this fellow and his party had discovered Noah's cabins at Big Dam. He decided a great challenge would be to drop by and see the hermit in the winter. So this adventurous outdoor person attempted to cross-country ski to the Cold River Valley corridor, deep in the wilderness, to reach Noah's self-proclaimed city.

Noah, who was a pretty good judge of human nature, had already perceived this fellow was of good character. So when he arrived at the hermit's doorstep in early February, he was invited to stay over. Noah directed him to store his equipment in the Hall of Records cabin and then come into the Town Hall for something warm to drink. Noah and I finished brushing out his snow paths and then went inside to ready a cup of coffee for Noah's weary and cold guest.

As the man was rustling round in the tiny cabin, he dropped his pocket watch and then shuffled it with his foot. Searching the floor with his hands, he brushed against a frozen ball of leaves the diameter of a medium-sized crockery bowl.

Picking up the wadded ball, thinking it was quite an oddity, he entered Noah's cabin rather excitedly. With his hands outstretched he exclaimed, "Look what I have found, Mr. Rondeau!"

Noah immediately knew what it was, but made every effort to act thoroughly surprised. First he turned it over in his hands. Then he began to slowly peel away the leaves as they crumbled in the heat. He had his hermit look of "rather unusual" all over his face. The ball was clearly nesting material. As Noah worked his way toward the core, he acted as if he might be revealing the contents of a mummified Egyptian object.

"See," he observed, "a little forest critter has made a home for himself. What a comfortable place to freeze to death."

By now the guest was grimacing as he watched Noah clear away his scrapbook articles from his hinged table and place down the frozen body.

"Mother Nature can play strange tricks at times," Noah muttered. "You can never be entirely sure of what you see."

Planning to have some fun, since our isolation had been broken by the gentleman's visit, he suggested both the mouse and the skier should sit and warm up. As the moisture began to drip from the melting ice on his mustache, the guest sipped his cup of coffee. Soon all his extremities were warm. The raw feeling in his face was replaced with a warm tingling sensation.

About the same time Noah noted a subtle flicker of movement in the mouse, but he wanted his guest to discover it for himself. Pretending to be doing something on the table near the mouse, his hand movements gained the attention he was seeking.

In an excited voice the guest shouted, "Look! It's alive!" The once passive body was showing unmistakable signs of returning vigor.

Noah acted nonchalant and only noted that it did seem to be stirring about.

"Its eyes are opening," he reported in giddy, almost infantile, gibberish.

"As it should," was all that Noah replied although his guest was entirely engaged by this astonishing display of cryogenics straight from the pages of a science fiction thriller. "Yes sir. You keep your eyes fixed right on him," Noah instructed, "and you'll witness that little rascal making a frail but brave attempt to crawl around. You see. There he goes. He sure is a fine example of a sturdy Cold River mouse."

That night the temperature dipped well below zero degrees. Noah's guest was impressed at how comfortable he felt sheltered against the sharp bite of the blowing wind that raged outdoors. During the next two days that mouse was frozen and restored to vitality twice. Unfortunately, it mistakenly met its death when its curried over the pan of one of the spring loaded mouse traps I had brought Noah during the summer. One thing you can be sure of though, that skier left with a mouse tale to tell his friends.

Cold River Country

The cold January moon rose silently above the distant Santanoni Mountain range. The glowing orb seemed to remain suspended on the horizon, until suddenly it leaped into the sky above Panther Peak. Through a single-paned window rimmed with ice, I watched it climb upward across the star-sprinkled blackness. My eyes wandered eastward, marveling at the small spruce and balsam trees standing like silvery statues in capes of ermine-white snow. In the glow of the moonlight, sparkling frost crystals danced across snow-laden branches, transforming the nighttime scene into a winter fairyland of dazzling splendor. I thought back over the activities that had occupied my first full day in my new trapping grounds. The nighttime, I decided, was surely as extraordinary as the day.

I had arrived at my Duck Hole cabin earlier than I'd first anticipated. It was to be the first time I would spend the entire season on the trapline at a new headquarters. February in the woods is the best there is. It's a lively time; the furbearers seem to be running around night and day during the mating season. Even the most cunning quite naturally lower their guard and ramble the woods haphazardly, leaving signs of their presence.

I wanted to be ready for the trapping season and knew I would need a thorough knowledge of the green timber surrounding the Duck Hole-Cold River country, hence my early arrival. Noah, my only neighbor seven miles downstream, had shared his knowledge of the watershed with me, for my stomping grounds were once part of the three long traplines he tended in the late 1920's and 1930's.

Trapping was another building block that helped to strengthen my budding relationship with Noah. He told me that as a small boy he too found trapping the most thrilling and fascinating thing he'd ever heard of; every track of an animal was a story.

The previous fall we had gone into the woods and learned to read the tracks of the wild forest creatures. Signs are most plentiful in early fall when the tote roads and pathways are dry and dusty and as such the signs of animals traveling at night are evident. The old experienced trapper volunteered to hike to Duck Hole to visit my cabin and accompany the amateur on a survey. In this way I would be able to make a fair estimate of the number and kinds of furbearers found in the vicinity.

The challenge of a successful hunter and trapper is to be able to read the tracks and signs of animals. And Noah, the expert trapper that he was, knew immediately on seeing a set of tracks just what animal had passed by.

We also investigated the muddy strips along streams as well as the entrances, scratch signs, feed beds, and sand bars which coon, muskrat, otter and mink frequented. We noted droppings on logs and large stones and studied the contents to learn their diets. Noah was as kind-hearted a woodsman as you could find—willing to satisfy my hunger to learn

"Richard, a few animals can make lots of tracks," he would point out as we studied signs of mink along a waterway. Noah said someone not well up on tracking is liable to be misled and think there are more furbearers around than there really are. It was sound advice.

With deftness and great skill the master trapper made me aware of my mistakes. To his mind, trapping as well as hunting were not just a way of life or a necessity, they were also an art.

The weather was ideal for snowshoeing. There had been no snow for several days, but the continuous intense cold had kept the flakes as fresh and distinct as if they had just fallen from the sky. There was a foot or so of light powder atop a solid, deep base that amply supported my pack-basket-burdened weight, as well as the heavy toboggan I pulled along behind me. My rawhide webs swished through the dry powder, sending the tiny, light crystals sparkling into the air like particles of fine dust. I filtered another breath through the woolen scarf tied around my face, savoring the sharpness of the thirty-below-zero air, and looked forward to the adventure ahead.

My little cabin was soon lost among the trees behind me. For my first morning of wandering in that wild region, my notions were simple.

Though I knew that the harsh winter environment was uncompromising and might claim my life if a serious mishap occurred, I felt no uneasiness, but rather relished the challenge that Nature placed before me.

I enjoyed watching my movements, mirrored by my elongated shadow, projected on the sparkling snow by the first sun of morning. With each exhalation, puffs of warmed air from my lungs made ever-changing patterns before fading into the mountain air. Water vapor clung and froze to my red whiskers, my eyebrows, and to the frayed fibers of my scarf until I took on the appearance of a graying, grizzled Arctic explorer. I was in my element; this was what I had always wanted to do.

As a young boy, similar feelings were aroused when tracking our family cow that had wandered into a nearby swamp. The farm animal, while not big game, was a prelude to studying the signs of wild animals around the farm. It was fun pretending I was in the wilds, far back and away from home; I also found the playtime to be sort of a safety value. I released pent-up youthful anger—usually directed toward my father—as I began to develop my self-respect. I felt rugged, healthy, and proud of my ability to learn so much about the habits of the wild animals that lived in the hedgerows, meadows, nearby forests and rivers. I was happy and free and on my own.

Most people faced with conditions like this, I thought to myself, wouldn't want to do anything more than huddle at home by the fire and hope for a change in the weather. But I had no such longings. And why shouldn't I be enjoying this? I was up to the challenge. After graduating from high school, I was determined I would make no compromises with life, and I felt I had less to fear from Nature on that score than from the unmerciful forces governing the job market in the days following the end of the Great Depression. The previous winter I had lived alone in a ramshackle cabin-of-sorts on a ridge above the second stillwater on the Chubb River. I earned my bread and butter primarily by trapping and did well enough. The life suited me. Why not make a go of it for real?

I was pleased with my mental outlook and at how pleasant my first day turned out to be. I was embarking on one of the earliest industries the Adirondacks had witnessed. The wilderness has diminished considerably since mountain men first trapped the North Woods. Thankfully, trapping had remained a viable outdoor occupation.

My pace quickened after turning back onto my snowshoe path that would lead back to camp. I was following Noah's advice of last fall, learning the habits of the wild animals I sought as well as a mother knows her child. The trapper was arriving home.

As I silently watched the wondrous evening display through the cold surface of a single-paned window near my bunk, I puffed on the surface and absently scratched doodle patterns in the frost that accumulated. I liked to think that Nature was testing my limits in the extreme cold snap that had gripped the Adirondacks.

Nowhere on earth could there be a scene more beautiful. Restless in spirit, I decided I wanted to experience the entire day for all it was worth and, packing a light basket with only essential equipment, choosing my under and outerwear carefully, I lashed on my snowshoes and penguin-walked out the cabin door into the night. The air, crystal clear, sharp and intensely cold, immediately bit at my skin, but within minutes I was generating ample body heat to keep me comfortable. Indeed, I soon needed to halt momentarily to rearrange my clothing, venting body moisture was absolutely essential. At all costs I could not allow my clothes to get damp or sweaty, for in the event of a mishap that would invite a quick death by freezing.

Swinging in long strides, I headed toward the snow- and ice-clad Duck Hole. Just a few years ago the Civilian Conservation Corps had rebuilt the aging log crib dam at the outlet first constructed by the Santa Clara Lumber Company before the turn of the century. But I still preferred to think of it the way early trappers found it: a sort of hellhole basin full of tangled logs, drifts and bog holes and through the middle, winding a fork of the Cold River and several tributary streams that were regular beaver highways.

The rim of Duck Hole was stripped of all the beauty that I remembered from last autumn. The occasional glacial erratics were almost covered by snowdrifts. Marsh grass, ferns, brambles, and cattails were sealed in an envelope of windswept hardpack snow. Long ago any seeds not harvested by foraging animals had been whipped from their pods by the bitter wind.

But I was greeted by a spectacular view of the Northern Lights, a marvelous ever-changing display of colorful bright blues, glistening soft greens and the deepest of purples put on, it seemed, expressly for my benefit and enjoyment. So bitterly cold was the frosty night that forest trees were snapping and crackling in wild cadence, furnishing irresistible background music for the wild dance in the sky. Some magic spell on these lonely woods must have prevented the leaping, twisting, swaying lights from growing dim or fading away as long as I stood, filled with awe and wonder, watching this gigantic display. How long I stood there watching the hypnotic scene I'll never know. So grand was the performance that, had it not been for the intense penetrating coldness of the night, I felt I could have watched it forever.

The Duck Hole was one of the first destinations that my friend Noah Rondeau reached on his frequent long treks from Lake Placid. In some ways Noah was like other adventurous settlement trappers who used their leisure time to prospect the countryside. The acquired knowledge he gained by learning the numerous lakes, ponds, streams, and marshes helped him locate the haunts of muskrat, mink, weasel, martin, fisher, otter, and fox as well as good places to make sets for these animals.

As a result of his growing discontentment with a conventional lifestyle he lengthened his adventures into the wilder country. There he found the furbearers in greater quantities.

Duck Hole was a remote area. After passing Moose Pond in the bosom of the mountains Noah entered virgin timber. He mentioned that in the early 1900's, New York State's surveying blazes, then over thirty years old, were still fairly reliable along Moose Pond outlet until one reached the "lumbered country." From that point Noah had to rely on reading the topography and compass until reaching the "Hole."

I never asked but it could have been here at the Hole that Noah first entertained the notion to leave his barber trade, lay down a wilderness trap line and live independent of the more accepted patterns of life.

Masked Bandit at Cold River

Trudging along a softening snowmobile trail leading to my employers camp on Lake Placid, I noticed a set of animal tracks paralleling my direction of travel. The mild temperature and sunny skies had melted just enough snow encircling the tracks to make them unrecognizable and thus a curiosity. I've always prided myself as having an unshakable knowledge at deciphering signs left by most woodland animals, so I was challenged to unravel the question of just which mammal had passed by. It was most likely nocturnal and used to humans, I surmised. Probably a 'coon that had received a wake up call from Mother Nature.

In the spring of 1942 beaver trapping season, I returned to Cold River. Noah and I had prearranged during our previous fall hunting trip where he would leave the key so that I could use his Hall of Records cabin. He knew ahead of time that he'd be staying with his friend, Roy Hathaway at his Pine Point camp near Saranac Lake.

I traveled much lighter the following year packing only seventy-five pounds in my packbasket. Arriving at Big Dam I paused to rest and take in the great stillness that surrounded his "City." Snow drifts formed hard banks against the tiny cabins and wigwams and the low rooflines supported a snow cornice that hung beyond the drip edge. With no one to greet me with a teasing comment, I silently thanked Noah for the use of his cabin and began in earnest to dig out an opening around the door. The Hall of Records was his "guest cabin," and the best one of the two I felt. It was a few feet larger than the Town Hall and was even high enough for a person—who was less than five feet ten inches tall—to stand up in. Even if it was only in the peak section of the roof.

Inside there were two bunks both six feet long and three feet wide. A sideboard was positioned on hinges on the back wall between them. When it was let down from the wall that it was attached to, a hinged leg dropped to support the board which converted into a table, the edge of the bunks as benches. Although it was slightly less than two feet wide when lowered, it was a useful surface to work on. A boxstove that was carted in pieces from Shattuck Clearing in pieces was set up in the space by the door. The opposite side was left to pile wood. Every inch of the interior was used and even though not very spacious, it was in every respect snug.

Before I went to bed that night, which was early after such a long trek, I carefully unpacked my riches. At that time grocery stores were offering pressed ham rolls which were both boneless and compact. When sliced and fried the canned ham was delicious; it also produced an abundance of grease that was excellent for frying eggs. Noah always saved the fat as a flavoring for his Slam Bang Stew. These pork rolls of joy eliminated the need to use Crisco or side bacon for frying, as it was more versatile in the back woods. The little gems were called Daisy Hams; the label showed several colorful pigs drawn in a ballet pose. The product label occasionally provoked Noah to make an amusing comment about the animals dancing on their tiptoes around the label. Simple entertainment to be sure, but we never lacked for humor.

Applying what I had learned from the previous beaver trapping season, I decided to carry one four pound Daisy Ham and save the extra weight associated with the usual shortening. After removing my prized canned ham from my packbasket I opened the can, slicing off a tiny portion for cooking grease and flavoring that evening. The remainder I placed in an empty garbage can Noah kept in the wigwam he called the Pyramid of Giza. I carefully wired the top securely to the two handles and then suspended the can from a chain that hung from the inside the wigwam. I remembered some of Noah's comments about raccoons that boldly robbed him of some prime food. I was not about to retire without first making sure my ham was both fool and 'coon proof, if either were around. Unfortunately there was one of each that night. Somehow with the stealth of a cat burglar a raccoon jumped up on the can and worked the wired cover loose making off with my prized Daisy Ham.

The next morning I awakened hungry as a bear fresh out of hibernation and ready for a breakfast of ham and eggs to make my morning repast one to remember. Following the snow path I had brushed out to the wigwam I entered the interior and discovered to my great dismay the untimely disappearance of my prize foodstuff. All that remained as evidence that a Daisy Ham had ever existed was the calling card Mr. Coon left inside the can. I was furious as you may well imagine. Unlike the unfortunate Lake Placid camp owner who accepted his loss begrudgingly, I immediately planned my revenge. I set a series of number four traps in strategic locations and laid in wait for the masked bandit to return as I knew he would. Two nights later he returned to the scene of his crime still with a well greased mustache. Try as he did to look innocent, all signs pointed to his guilt.

After dispatching the raccoon, I reprimanded him about tampering with MY provisions in my sternest voice. Once I had vented myself I condemned him to be skinned to the bone. In the course of two weeks following this incident I used 'coon grease to fry all my pan vittles in and I ate his carcass with relish. Later in the spring following ice out, I returned to fish Cold River with Noah. After telling him about the local raid he asked how the coon tasted. With complete honesty of remembrance I reported the meat was just like Daisy Ham.

I ate many coons before and after that incident, but I can't recall any ever tasting as good. Perhaps because I was so engrossed in my conviction that he should be punished that I actually believed I was eating ham.

Frostbite Remedy

Those were the days, I thought, as I followed the course of the brilliant moon's long, steady upward climb to the heavens. Feeling a slight chill from my inactivity in the open meadow, I decided to melt a small pail of snow for some tea. Less cautious than I should have been, I momentarily removed my mittens to better twist off the threaded cap of the fuel can. It would have shown greater foresight if I had made sure that the reservoir on my makeshift stove was filled to capacity before leaving the cabin, for I accidentally spilled some kerosene onto one of my bare hands. I quickly tried to wipe away the fuel, but in the process I allowed my skin to be exposed for too long to the raw temperature. Like alcohol, petroleum-based products evaporate quickly, causing skin to lose heat. Naturally I was concerned about frostbite, so I immediately hot-footed it back to the cabin.

In spite of tingling fingers upon arrival, I was curious about the temperature, fumbling to strike several matches before one lit to illuminate the mercury in the Coca-Cola thermometer tacked to a sapling outside the shanty window. It registered an alarming forty degrees below zero!

I had read several articles by so-called experts on the subject of frostbite, but I didn't really have much information at the moment except that one should not rub frostbitten flesh or rewarm it rapidly. In the absence of a wilderness doctor to make a cabin call, I poked around in my general bag of knowledge for the most likely remedy. I didn't believe that true frostbite had developed, but it was impossible to tell, by looking, whether any tissue had frozen. I mumbled something like, "The situation is not desperate—" just to calm my mind while I searched for a solution. Then it came to me—snow! Noah had taught me to bury canned goods in the snow to keep them from freezing. It was a good trick. He'd also said the method would work in reverse. From experience he'd learned that sweetened condensed milk had a tendency to curdle if thawed too quickly, but if it was slowly thawed under snow it didn't separate.

If the method worked for milk, I rationalized, it couldn't hurt me. If I caught cold, would I get myself pasteurized? I think not. Putting aside any lingering tendency to stay in the warm cabin, I dragged my sleeping bag out into the snow, crawled in, wrapped my hand in a dry towel and pressed my arm shoulder deep into the snow.

In a short time a greater flow of circulation lessened the burning and tingling sensation. With the renewed feeling came the realization I had only gotten the chilblains and had not really been in any great danger, but I kept my hand buried until my fingers just felt cold. Then I pulled my hand from the snow, entered the cabin, wrapped my fingers in a moist towel and continued to warm them slowly by the boxstove until the towel was dry. Unwrapping the folds, I inspected each finger carefully. They seemed fine, with normal feeling and function. I had a quart of bear oil for cooking and used it freely on the chapped skin for the next few days. I suspected that the dead skin would soon peel away and outside of a bit of lingering redness my hand fared well. In fact, if anything, my skin, with the liberal application of bear grease, seemed softer and healthier than usual. What the frostbite experts needed was a friend as knowledge-able as Noah!

My mishap did not deter me from taking future moonlight excursions. But not wanting to get caught short in the field again, I added a pair of homemade fur-lined buckskin mittens to my survival gear, feeling that their warmth would serve well to encapsulate and reheat cold hands.

I found a special joy in traveling through the night forest and never tired of gazing at the myriad of stars glittering like jewels in the heavens above. Ordinary shadows seemed to come alive in the moon's soft glow. Frost crystals that fell in the crisp air reflected the brilliant moonlight, giving the appearance—at least to a dreamer like myself—of a cascading waterfall of multicolored diamonds.

Fishing Cold River in June

For years I heard tales of the fabulous fishing opportunities at the "Black Hole" in Cold River. Old timers were equally quick to point out the wild land of this river was also mother nature's supreme insect factory. I was about to learn what they had long known.

Noah had assured me the middle of June was the ideal time to fish since the trout seemed to bite at many different varieties of wet and dry flies. He failed to mention fish bites were not all that I would be getting.

I had just returned to my cabin at Duck Hole after some part-time job interviews. I had also gotten a haircut which exposed the tender skin on the back of my neck. June had lessened the black flies' ferocity around town, but they hadn't calmed down in the forest.

The enthusiasm of youth had a stranglehold on me and I didn't think of anything but getting back to the woods. Before leaving I gave my fishing tackle a general overhauling, packed both flies and a generous supply of earthworms, tucked some supplies for Noah in with my equipment and headed out. Amid the constant drone of insects, I made camp in good time.

Early the next morning I hoofed down the Northville-Lake Placid Trail stopping at Mountain Pond. Noah had told me a story about an early sportsmen's outing there the last time I was in camp. The account made me curious and, since I had some time to spare, I decided to investigate.

Mountain Pond was rumored to have large fish at the turn of the century. The men had arrived and established their tent site in the small clearing where once there was an old shanty. The pond's shores were low, its bottom was muddy and it appeared to be very shallow. But after finding an old raft and an even older dugout moored by a stake in the long grass, they became encouraged even though the pond didn't appear to look "trouty."

They chinked the boat with rags and spent the best part of a day casting at every likely spot. The only rewards they got for their efforts were frogs and leeches. Giving up, they planned to fish more profitable waters the next day, and made themselves comfortable around camp the remainder of the day. Someone had told them about an old cast iron boxstove sunk into surrounding stones which could be used as a makeshift cooler. Thinking it a handy place to safely store their eggs, bacon and sausage, they wrapped the food items and placed them inside one of the burner holes. By all principles the set-up was burglar proof from any animal, but only if the cover was replaced and held down with a stone. To be sure, they were amateur woodsmen. Not only did the raccoons have a midnight snack at their expense, but during the evening meal one of the men accidentally tripped causing the cook to became distracted and absently grab hold of the hot wire handle on a cooking pot he was taking off the fire.

Circling to the outlet of Mountain Pond, I found evidence that at one time the outlet had been damned with stones but it had long been washed-out. The water in the pond was shallow and I assumed the best thing about this sheet of water was its scenic appeal.

Noah used to fish for brook trout in Mountain Pond. However, by the early 1940's he didn't fish far from his cabins, he had no reason to. Close by were Cedar and Seward ponds. And Big Dam was still more or less intact, with an immense pool below the spillway of the dam carved in the old days by water action and logs tumbling through. For three miles above the dam, Cold River flow extended where the fishing was quite wonderful.

Noah kept a log raft tethered to the upriver side of the dam and also had a canvas collapsible canoe that a friend left in his care. Noah thought a lot of that person and kept very good care of the boat, dismantling and storing it in large steel garbage cans after using it—so porcupines and mice wouldn't chew the covering. With the canoe he could paddle upriver to within a short distance of the "Black Hole." He said if he had business downriver he might fish the few good holes or the Big Eddy, another cold water pool where big brookies would head. But all in all the rapids and shallowness forced a person to travel two or three miles before picking up a legal limit of ten trout! Fishing above the dam was much better.

Noah had breakfast for me when I arrived. Following the meal, he looked over my fly collection lifting up the black knat and predicting I'd be most successful with it because the trout had been feeding on a new hatch of black flies. Then we were off paddling upstream after the trout of my dreams on our sure-fired fishing trip.

I marveled at the huge stones that stood well above my head. Noah pointed out that the tops of some of them had been blasted away to reduce the chance of logs jamming. I tried to imagine the volume of water that was once impounded in the stillwater and behind the dam on lower Moose Creek. Noah showed me several eye bolts embedded in the boulders explaining they were used to attach cables that once spanned the river, noting that one coil of cable survived from the lumbering days and had grown into a tree along the bank. He was knowledgeable about the logging operations because he had worked at the Big Dam logging camp the last year it operated. He promised to point out an old peavey that he had noticed bobbing in the shallow water near the dam when we returned.

Reaching a point where the rocks blocked any further advancement by craft, we secured the canoe. My education continued when I also learned how hungry the black flies still were as we picked our way along the narrow shoreline with high ledges above us.

How entertaining I must have looked last year when I stuffed cotton in my ears and stitched a net of cheesecloth to the brim of my Stetson when fishing Duck Hole. To avoid the savage beasts, I had made a paste of thick pancake batter, dabbing it all along the stitching in a vain attempt to seal every conceivable opening. I have to admit it worked quite well. But with the double layer of clothing and my face completely enclosed with the netting—it being tucked into my shirt collar held tight with the collar button—I gasped for a breath of fresh air. In addition the cuffs at both my wrists and ankles were tied. My body was drenched in perspiration and I felt as if I were in an oven. But what a creel of trout I had brought back to the frying pan!

This year I tried a different kind of armor, Noah's special bug repellent. Like any of the day, it was effective to a point. That is why Noah always kept a fire going, even on the hottest days. The continual smoke swirling around the cabins and wigwams kept the stingers at bay even though it could often be so pungent as to cause eyes to tear.

I was anxious to begin fishing, but I was equally interested in Noah recalling his days of working for the Santa Clara Logging Company. He explained during the winter that sleighs deposited logs onto the frozen surface of the flow. Eventually acres were covered and, as early spring approached, the gate on Moose Creek was opened releasing millions of gallons of water into Cold River. The rising water added to the water already impounded behind Big Dam. The logs on the flow were entrapped between booms and then positioned by river drivers to be herded through the sluiceway where they cascaded over the dam and were swept downstream.

Men were in bateaus and river drivers walked on logs. The operation required a constant pace, keeping the logs in a continuous line and feeding them over the dam. Even though the sluiceway was twenty feet wide, logs could turn broadside and jam up. That would cause lost water, time and, on occasion, heated tempers. As the water level dropped behind the dam, the gates were closed until the reservoirs were again filled and the process would start all over. Delays were costly and the high water of spring run-off didn't last forever. With such a concentration of logs to be driven, mistakes could not be tolerated, so the best drivers were used for the work, those with the greatest skill and courage. They kept the logs in motion for weeks at a time until all of them were on their way to mills down the Raquette River.

Reaching the place where the cascading waters plunged into a deep hole completely surrounded by high ledges, I knew we surely had reached the famed Black Hole before Noah identified it. We climbed carefully to a small alcove in the face of a ledge from where we could cast into the deep, black water below. I was amazed at the depth of the water. My line seemed to just keep going down. Exaggerated as my dreams might have been, they were nothing compared to what was about to happen. My first catch was fourteen inches of fighting might. But if that was not enough to thrill me, I landed four more soon after. They were so large I could hardly stuff them in my creel without bending the tails. This beautiful pool of water was several hundred feet in length. Noah said he had sounded a good many sections with a lead sinker and found the depth was fairly uniform, but it did have some even deeper holes. Over the years I returned to fish it many times. Sometimes I walked away with my limit and other times I caught very few large trout. But that could be expected as the otter population grew. The otters could reach the "hole" much easier and knew a good thing when they found it.

Returning later that day, Noah held the canoe steady near the area above the dam where he had noticed the old peavey. The handle looked like the end of a rounded stick stuck almost upright in the water. Noah guessed that the spring ice and the lower reservoir level, caused by the yearly deterioration of the log dam, might have had something to do with it ending up in that position. I couldn't dislodge it, so I jumped into the four feet of water and worked the iron end loose. From there it was a simple thing to work my way over to the strip of gravel along the river's edge. The handle was eight feet long, but had slimmed down due to decay. It still felt solid enough to be serviceable. I left it at the hermitage as a conversation piece.

After dinner we reclined in front of a magnificent fire and absorbed the heat while we chatted, as woodsmen chat, about woodcraft. Noah spoke, devotedly, on celestial topics. He spoke of the sheer magnitude of the stars in the heavens that framed our night scene. Where I was enthralled with being in the wilderness, he took me in spirit into the deep, splendid abyss of space. I used to look to the night sky only as a twinkling night scene. But he told me to stretch my imagination and try journeying from the visible field of stars and planets in the Milky Way to beyond, into the deep gulf where "the multitude of stars look like star dust in its fineness." This direction in thinking also opened the door to his many philosophies about a Creator, but the peaceful lethargy sent me to bed. I had tomorrow to look forward to.

"Richard, how would you like to help me carry a load of staples I have cached near High Banks?" asked Noah. Does a dog have fleas! I was ready, willing and anxious to do anything. The plan was to fish downriver. It was going to be a hot day and any fish would surely spoil, but Noah had a remedy for the prevention of spoilage. He showed me his designated place where a large iron kettle was submerged in a cold spring. I never inquired but have always assumed Noah and Dr. Latimer, Sr. set it since it was only a few miles from the doctor's cabin. Once he lifted the lid I had no doubt it would preserve our trout in a cloak of coldness. He sampled a pound of butter he said Oscar had left there for him last fall, and it tasted as sweet as when it had first been placed there.

We fished the holes as far as Millers Falls, then climbed a gradual slope to the narrow footpath that overlooks the river and headed into the woods to a well-concealed storage area. The supplies I had agreed to help tote upriver to the hermitage were cached in metal garbage cans. Noah told me that the cans were confiscated from the former Civilian Conservation Corps camp that was once located at the Cold River lean-to clearing beyond Mountain Pond. Oscar Burguiere, a regular in the Latimer party, had promised Noah that in the future he would help Noah transport larger fifty-five gallon drums downriver to replace these smaller containers.

We carefully loaded our packboards and returned to the spring, picking up our catch, the brick of butter, and the eggs Dr. Latimer had placed in the iron kettle.

Rough and narrow is the only way to describe the trail between Millers Falls and Ouluska Pass Brook. Yet, in spite of the uneven footing, I thought the scenery along this part of the trail to be a superior run of rugged beauty. Along the forest pathway, one can enjoy the pleasant vistas of a boulder-strewn watercourse, framed by huge cedars that droop over the riverbank. The view became even more incredible when the trail curved with a river bend that opened my eye to views of Couchsachraga, Emmons and Seward Mountains.

Where the public trail draws at once from the river to cross bridgeless Ouluska Pass Brook, the water was only a dozen inches deep. Noah came to the brook and, with little hesitation, he launched himself to the flat rock midstream, did a little jug to catch his balance and, with a fluid leap, landed on the opposite bank. If old Noah could do that with a loaded packboard, I would do it twice, or so I thought. When I landed on the rock I wasn't quick enough with the jig and I ended up sitting in the stream with not only a dampened butt, but also a moist slap to my self esteem. When Noah saw I was okay, we had a big laugh and he promised when we got back to camp he would get out the fiddle and teach me "some jig steps I wouldn't soon forget."

Noah was, even at sixty-one years old, very nimble.

We reached the hermitage well before dark. As the first shades of twilight set in, we sat contentedly with full stomachs, having dined on golden brown speckled trout, eggs, and sourdough pancakes spread with butter—a meal fit for a king.

I have never allowed time to be my enemy; that philosophy has allowed me to do the things I have most wanted to do. As I reflect on my years in spent in the woods, I am thankful I chose the course I did. The memory of fishing Cold River in June, so long ago, has always remained as one of my supreme times.

Before I ended my week with Noah, we hiked to his private trout waters he called Seward Pond. His pond was isolated and unnamed on the topographical map, but a neighboring body of water is officially listed with the same name. Perhaps it was a clever way of disguising its whereabouts. The last section of our walkabout was over a decayed corduroy log road where a small rivulet traced a path underneath the rotted timbers on its way down to meet Ouluska Pass Brook. Upon reaching the pond I always stood for a moment and took in Seward Mountain, high above. Beavers had cleared an area around the pond where deer fed on the tender shoots of plants. I felt this was a particularly wild, majestic setting. He boarded the one man raft that was anchored near his log wigwam and I helped push him off. He hollered, "Our raft launching was a great success." I watched him for a minute as he poled to the middle of the pond. He had rigged his ten-foot telescoping fishing pole to catch some big ones. It was manufactured, woodsmen-style, by incorporating a broken tip section from another pole to make up the additional length. His landing net was composed of an onion sack, laced onto a crotched stick. As Noah readied to fish from the raft, I worked my way to the high beaver dam. Soon I had a nice trout leaping and splashing toward me. In the meantime Noah had made a beautiful cast toward a large boulder protruding out of the water and very shortly was reeling in a trout.

My earlier experience bore out the common knowledge that early trout fishing was slow, but I was certainly rewarded this week. By trying to fool the trout by matching flies with what the fish were naturally feeding on, we got a good number of them. I had caught eight speckled trout averaging around twelve inches each. Noah landed four. Two were nineteen and two were twenty-two inches.

We cleaned our catches and had a fish fry of mine along the edge of Seward Pond. Noah wrapped the remainder of the trout in wet burlap, with an instruction to keep them wet all along the trail. I was to keep the large trout to take home. It was an extra ordinary gift.

Later that day I bid my friend good bye. In later years I fished Seward Pond many times often accompanied by Noah, yet never did I ever catch a trout to match the ones he had caught.

Angel On My Shoulder

Tramping alone in the forest, a careful person develops a certain inner alertness to danger. I liken it to the extra sense of self protection those who operate dangerous machinery develop, only the awareness is made even more acute in the wilderness because, from my experience, there has always been a shortage of doctors on call. A safe woodsman is instinctually aware of how to use a saw, ax, knife or fire. He also learns to recognize, before stepping in with both feet, what situations could result in broken bones or deep cuts. Any number of hidden pitfalls exist which might result in a debilitating calamity.

I have had a few close calls along those lines. If I hadn't recognized them and been prepared to protect myself, I would have come out much worse than I did. I do believe everyone has a guardian angel watching over them, but unless you heed their warnings you can get into serious consequences.

My old friend, "Mayor Rondeau" learned exactly that during the 1920's. He was using the old lumber camp along Ouluska Pass Brook as a base and hunting the Seward range when he fell, hurting his leg. He was in pain. It wasn't intense, yet it prevented him from being able to move easily. A careful inspection told him he didn't have a compound fracture; there was no bone bulging or protruding through the skin. He did, however, assume there was a minor break. After splinting it the best he could, he set up an emergency shelter in the vicinity and laid low for over two weeks until it had mended enough for him to hike back to the camp. After that he was forever careful and never had another serious incident.

Early in my tenure he counseled me about how important it was to have a good safety record. It boiled down to knowing what to do and what not to do. He compared it to meeting a bear with no means of protection other than a hunting knife. At that point you have to use your wits. "It's always best to keep in mind if such an occasion arises," he'd instruct, "that you might only have one chance. Your decision must be right. It comes down to you eating the bear or the bear eats you."

There were plenty of dangerous situations just waiting for me in the wilds; I'll tell you about my two biggest blunders. Not only did they happen in the same area of woods, they wised me up considerably! As Noah told me afterwards, "Nothing educates you faster than fear."

Foolishly I was heading into Cold River City on rotting snow. After several hours of strenuous trail work out from my Snowroller camp, I arrived at a fairly large stream I called Boulder Brook, approximately two miles north of the Cold River lean-to's. The brook flowed south, draining the Sawtooths. Not only was the tributary fast-flowing, it was clogged with chunks of shell ice. Long before I reached the stream I could hear the distinctive roar of water. I wondered if I would even be able to find a way of crossing. I studied the scene carefully—ice cold water was leaping and dashing against the boulder. It was dangerous, I knew I would not be able to cross that boiling turbulence. I traced its course upstream to where it was narrower and soon spotted a spruce tree that had fallen completely across the stream. Three-fourths of the branches had been snapped off to short stubs, but there still seemed to be enough longer limbs for handholds near the more treacherous middle section of the swollen water. I was certain I could pick my way over it; heck it was bigger than a tightrope.

When you're young it's very easy to over estimate your abilities to the point of being foolhardy, and I was about to embark along that path. I needed the use of both of my hands so, leaning my Marlin against a tree, I hoisted my pack, loosened the shoulder straps in case I needed to throw it off and nimbly worked my way out. I felt a bit top heavy shouldering the seventy-five pound packbasket, but I confidently told myself I could do it. I warned myself the log's surface would be slippery and coated with a glaze of ice that might not be detected until I stepped on it.

All went well until I reached midstream. With the added weight of the pack, the tree began to settle closer to the water's surface. Chunks of ice were coming downstream just barely passing under the midsection. I had to stop often to steady my nerves and hold my balance. I would have preferred the branches closer together. Twice, I almost hyperextended, trying for a firm grasp before moving my leg another step. Reaching the opposite side, I felt relieved when I lowered my pack and sat down. The worst was over but I still needed to return for my rifle. When I was safely back with my second load, I promised myself I would not attempt such a hairy feat again.

How quickly one forgets. Or rather how foolish can Red get. Not far from that tree in early May of the same year I failed to listen to my guardian angel and performed my most senseless bit of bravado. The northland wind was gently blowing. Robins were singing a half-hearted "cheer-up" song, and the early wildflowers seemed to be struggling much harder to break through last year's leaf mold. I was content just to see the newly formed leaves casting a hint of green all around me in the warm sunshine of early spring. Beech trees had not reached mouse-ear size yet, but that old-timer guide to good fishing didn't keep me from looking forward to fishing with Noah. I was in high cotton and feeling mighty frisky.

Once again I had reached Boulder Brook. The spring freshets had kept the water up; the brook had out-classed its name. I should have rechristened it "Raging Torment." Much to my dismay, one end of my bridge had been washed into the stream bed. I should have heeded Noah's little trick—all I needed was to fall a tree across the water. It would usually last several years and be a reliable bridge. Good idea. The only problem was I didn't have the means to drop one this day. I had actually expected my previous tightrope to be in place and, with the ice gone, I felt it would serve well.

As I moved upstream looking for a favorable crossing, I spotted a tall balsam leaning heavily toward the opposite bank. I noticed the water was undercutting the bank. I reasoned the root system had been loosened and the distance across was not that great. I grabbed a lower branch and began climbing up. I calculated my body and pack weight would send the top lower and lower gently placing me on the opposite bank. I'd call it Boulder Brook Elevator. Upon almost reaching the top, I realized my reckoning didn't work. The tree bent heavily, but it didn't arc far enough. There I sat like an eagle in its nest, waiting for a free ride to the ground. But time was something I had plenty of so I figured I'd wait a while. Maybe try bouncing as the water continued to undercut the slender tree.

I'll never forget the squirrel that alarmed me as it abruptly ran across my legs, up my arm, across my shoulder and, in passing my head, slapped me across the face with his tail on his grand leap to the other side. Maybe he was acting as my guardian. He did scold me as he passed by.

I trusted my instinct though. Sit tight. This process would take time. Not long after I encouraged the tree by climbing just a mite higher, some of the roots snapped and, with a deep groan, it gently settled to the ground.

My smug confidence returned shortly after my heart resumed beating. My youth congratulated me as the spring returned to my legs, but I learned a lesson that day. I would be much better off to recognize foolhardy stunts and instead tread more cautiously in the future—if I wished to see one. From then on I heeded my guardian angel the first time.

Afoot in the Forest

The headwaters of the Cold River was a wild spot in the Adirondacks when Noah first followed the "government trail" in the fall of 1902. Living in Lake Placid, he began to seek the roadless woods as an escape from civilized centers. The region he explored must have felt like a vacation, well beyond the mark of man, where he could shoot and see game.

Reaching Duck Hole, a pond about a quarter of a mile wide, he found the traveling rough around the perimeter because of the maze of downed trees. Laying like jackstraws, the acres of up-turned, wind-fallen trees crisscrossed in every direction. Walking over and on them presented a challenge, but the horizontal trunks also afforded an open area from which to stop and scan the panoramic hills and mountains. High country scenery surrounded this bowl of water nestled in the mountains.

The stream that flowed into the "Hole" connected it with the Preston Ponds—the main source of the Cold River. All along that creek were signs of muskrats, minks, and weasels. After several probes, Noah decided the potential existed to trap successfully.

Noah didn't begin to live permanently in the Cold River country until 1929, but he did trap in a wide district between the Duck Hole to the Raquette River for almost twenty-six years prior to moving into Big Dam. During this time he came on to the logging operations of the Santa Clara Lumber Company. A series of about eight camps were scattered throughout the region. Noah became well-known to many of the loggers who offered handouts of food from the camp kitchens.

Also, during the final years of the logging operations, he came in contact with two experienced trappers who for ten years made the Cold

River-Duck Hole country their base of hunting and trapping. While Noah didn't cotton to sharing the wilderness with Elric Jack (E.J.) Dailey and Richard (Dick) Wood, they all respected and tolerated each others territory.

An old tote road circled the Duck Hole basin along the northern rim. It led to a woods road several miles below the outlet that had well-defined buckboard tracks—a lumberman's road that joined the Cold River trail at right angles north of Mountain Pond.

Noah said a path off the aging tote road led to an abandoned camp near the outlet of Duck Hole. It was in that vicinity, while reconnoitering a trapline, that Noah came in contact with Dailey and Wood. Dailey, at twenty-six years old, was already a seasoned woodsman and professional trapper with some national reputation.

While trapping the Cold River line, Dailey took on Dick Wood, a professional writer and photographer of outdoor sporting stories, for a partner. They made the abandoned Santa Clara Lumber Company's cabin at Duck Hole their headquarters from which they hunted and trapped, off and on, for almost ten years. When new game laws were enacted which made the trapping of marten and fisher illegal, they decided to quit camp permanently. Among the possessions they had gathered at this habitation were three hundred steel traps of various sizes. Not having any use for them, and unwilling to sled the additional weight out of the woods, they voted to dump the entire lot into the muck along the shore of the Duck Hole. That treasure of antique traps rests there to this day. (I could only wonder as I stood on the bank, if I might be near the location of that deposit.)

Down river, by several miles, was the Big Dam camp—another in a series of Santa Clara logging shanties. Noah worked in that camp the last winter it was in operation. The year following its closing, he chose to make the camp his temporary trapping headquarters. After several very successful years harvesting furbearers, he was given permission to set up permanent residence there.

Dailey was also familiar with that camp, having occasionally stayed with the logging crew for meals and shelter. Noah, not one to be openly critical of anyone—except the game wardens, begrudgingly conceded Dailey was a fellow trapper, but reserved judgment about his ability —pointing out Elric Jack just wasn't the woodsman the print media depicted him to be.

From all Noah told me, I think they respected each other from a afar, their rivalry centering over turf. Dailey would probably agree with my conclusion. The highest compliment he ever paid my friend was a descriptive passage about Noah, the famed "hermit of Cold Creek" who he said scraped like a madman on a broken fiddle, and once killed a bear with a homemade longbow, and sometimes fired any weapon that was handy at folks who approached the place.

A rift might have begun over trapping territory, but a battle occurred after this "famous" trapper came into the Big Dam camp seeking shelter one winter. "EJ," as Noah always called him, had been pulling a toboggan load of supplies down the Cold River trail from his headquarters camp. Finding the going exhausting on account of the warming snow conditions, he removed a large burlap bag of traps, stashed them besides the trail and caught a ride into camp with a teamster. Following breakfast the next morning, he planned to pull his lightened sled back up the trail where he would dig out his traps and proceed to his trapline.

The plan was flawed though; there had been a heavy snowfall that evening. The new snow changed the terrain enough that he couldn't locate his stash. EJ returned to Big Dam to ask if Noah would help, which he did with grace. Noah just found folly in the situation. Here was the knowledgeable manufacturer of animal scents, a so-called professional trapper, author of backwoods adventure stories, and he couldn't even find his traps.

As I stood looking across the frozen surface of Duck Hole thinking of all these early events, I tried to imagine the jocular argument Dailey and Wood had at the headquarters camp. It was an incident they both wrote about later.

It all started the year Wood contracted Dailey to guide him to a superior deer hunting ground in the Adirondacks. Dailey chose the Duck Hole country. By the end of the season the men decided to throw in together and trap the region. That partnership lasted off and on for ten years.

Meeting at the train station in Lake Placid, they began packing their gear on the toboggan. Wood, an avid reader, tried to squeeze into the precious space four heavy volumes by Balzac, the French writer. Dailey, restless and edgy, snapped at Wood, "That crap won't save a life nor catch fur." Wood insisted he was not going without the books and won the argument.

A midwinter warm up and accompanying rotting snow about midway through the season, forced the men off their trap lines and back to camp. During the passage of a week cooped up in and around the cramped cabin, the close quarters began to cause their nerves to fray. Throughout the daylight hours chores generally kept them occupied. Dailey even tried trapping a fisher that hung around the cabin, but it eluded all his attempts. He was more successful at making heavy doughnuts that resembled dough balls of fried fat.

As the monotonous days passed they came to know each other too well, until it seemed each had all the faults peculiar to the human race.

Dailey's frustration level rose during the long nights. Finally one evening he could not take the closed-in feeling, close quarters and lack of physical activity any longer. As Wood contentedly read, Dailey stared into the yellow light winking feebly from a candle in a tin can. The glittering flame gave him a wild idea. Taking out his six shooter he shouted: "*Lights Out!*" as he fired at the candle, extinguishing it.

Wood, who was used to Dailey's peculiar antics, was more annoyed than shaken. Having just been disturbed upon reaching the climax of a story, he unholstered his revolver and emptied every chamber into the log wall over his partner's head. "There, half of that ought to stop your damn candle business," he quipped. "The rest ought to encourage you to stop making any more of those damned doughnuts fried in bear grease."

Running outside to escape the smoke from all the gunpowder, they laughed deliriously. It was just the release they both needed.

Hungry in the Woods

I arrived from Duck Hole following a thirty-six hour run with little nourishment. I misjudged how late spring came deep in the wilderness. Beech leaves were approaching the size of mouse ears, a folk observation that indicated trout would begin to bite, but they were reluctant to attack my bait. I had run short of staples, thinking I would be eating buttered bread and fish for a few days.

Thankfully, a hearty supper prepared by Noah healed the rancorous humor of my amended menu of yesterday. Supplied with a pouch of choice tobacco, we smoked our pipes as we reclined before the campfire. To a great extent my happiness in the woods was dependent upon food and warmth from that strange element which we term *fire*.

Lost and hungry are such basic terms with unpredictable outcomes. Such were my thoughts as I sat before the blazing campfire of dry pine logs that radiated a pleasant warmth about Noah Rondeau's camp.

The hermit had just related another incident to me that involved E.J. Dailey. Usually Noah didn't offer me advice about woodcraft survival tricks of the trade in the form of direct lessons. Instead I learned the valuable information from object lessons. E.J.'s was one of them.

During a rare meeting at Big Dam between the two wilderness trappers, Dailey admitted to Rondeau he had been caught off guard a number of times. (I have never heard Noah say that about any circumstance he had ever faced, but he indicated no shame in having it happen. No person is immune from miscalculating. Besides, the most important part is to keep your head and make the correct decisions. That is what E.J. had done, but with a twist.)

It was January and E.J. was tending his trapline in the rugged Sawtooth Range. When he came across the meandering tracks of a pine martin, he decided to deviate from his routine and soon became sidetracked and lost. Engrossed in the animal's movements, he failed to notice an approaching storm. He had no overnight supplies nor time to backtrack, so he surveyed the terrain for a natural shelter. There was little time to locate the typical refuges such as a shelving rock, a windfall, or a large rotted cavity of a tree trunk or hollow log. A rock sheltered den would have been buried in snow.

He headed to a huge spruce with snow-laden boughs that sagged, bound to the ground by layers of snow. The limbs were so closely intertwined that it took some time to enter the interior sanctuary. Once inside he sensed an odd feeling; it seemed warmer than it should have been without a fire. Without matches and birch bark, the most highly inflammable article in the woods even when wet, he had no hope of having a fire. Groping around in the dark, he found the space was virtually free of snow and had an abundant supply of dry leaves. They would provide an adequate insulated bed covering since no blanket was at hand.

As he began to scoop the leaves together, one hand touched a massive furred animal. There was no mistaking, it was definitely a bear. E.J. didn't undergo any weighty resolutions. He was totally unaware of who was more scared, the bear or himself. But the bear won his faculties of locomotion first, and at full tilt headed out into the snowstorm leaving E.J. in ownership of a bed already warmed!

That was a good story. E.J. was quite a man-about-the-woods. Taking my attention from Noah, I gazed over at the oil lantern illuminating the entrance to the wigwam I would sleep in tonight. The lantern was lit by kerosene I carried to Big Dam to help replenish Noah's diminished reserve. Offering him supplies was my way of returning favors. Noah certainly had an entertaining way of instructing. There was no mistaking the hermit as an intellectual. He illustrated that whenever we "blew blue smoke," his description for our lengthy conversations. One fact about him was the manner in which he found humor in all sorts of circumstances other people might only view seriously. That fact was again made evident to me when he related E.J.'s experience. The underlying message being that if I was going to live on my own in the woods, I had to be prepared and be resourceful.

I knew Noah didn't particularly enjoy staying out in the woods at night. Worse yet, he admitted, was to be in the woods and hungry. But Noah was prepared. He cached matches, flour, sugar, and salt in the field as well as other dry ingredients in tightly corked bottles and mason jars —the old style with the heavy, one piece screw top. Assuming he might be forced to eat the flesh of some unappetizing denizen of the wild, (flesh only a very hungry person would consume) he had the ingredients to make it fairly palatable stashed in spots all over the Seward range.

I had not experienced hunger many times in my short woods career, but the gnawing I had encountered earlier in the week that sent me scooting down the trail to Noah's, ended on a humorous note. That evening, as we talked in cheerfulness, I acknowledged I had not planned carefully enough and I was forever in his debt for helping me out.

I recounted how I had netted some chubs from Duck Hole pond after I realized how low my food was without the anticipated trout. With no salt or seasoning I simply boiled them in water, but no matter how long the pot of small fish simmered, the color of the water hardly changed. The towering flames of the dry pine logs outlined the face of my genial friend as he nodded his head as if to say he knew.

About the time I was wondering if I could drink my crude soup, a duck had landed near the dam not a great distance from where I was boiling the liquid in an iron kettle over an open pit fire. It swam near some bulrushes and faced away from me making it impossible to identify the species. With a well-placed shot I took his head off, defeathered the bird and dropped it in the pot not realizing it was the merganser or fish duck. As the contents began to ferment I detected an odor.

Leaving his seat by the fire, Noah disappeared into the Town Hall and emerged holding a baking powder can. Thumbing through his "cookbook" he pulled a "file" and handed it to me. His so-called recipes were written on the backs of canned goods labels.

Noah said that he had tried eating or tasting just about everything. Carpenter ants were not one of his favorites. He thought bears liked them because they had a slight lemon flavor. His recipe can did not contain your typical "Best Dishes of Grandmother." Instead they contained tongue-in-cheek directions for an odd assortment of foods. Scratched across the back of a Morning Glory Evaporated Milk label he handed me was a unique recipe:

THE BEST TASTING ROCK EVER

First, take a large pot and bring a gallon and a half of water to a boil.
While it's reaching the boiling point, find a rock about half the size of
a merganser. Add the rock and the duck to the pot.
After a half hour's boil, a black scum will rise to the top of the water.
Remove the scum with a wooden spoon. Do NOT for any reason use a
metal utensil. It will disintegrate.
When the scum ceases to rise, the duck should have turned black.
Don't be ALARMED. This only indicates it is cooked and time to test
the contents.
Stick a fork in the rock. If you can do this, throw the duck away and eat
the rock.

The following year, I began experimenting with dehydrated ingredients. They were lightweight and were packed with nourishment. On one of my many trips to the hermitage I brought a large package that guaranteed it would serve two people. Noah promised he would try it out at a later date. A few months later I noted he had penned Quack's Favorite Vegetable Soup on a sheet of paper. It was tacked on a pole inside the wigwam where he knew I would see it. Noah had crossed out serving for two and written eight or more hungry mountain climbers. The formula was simple. Add the contents of Richard's dehydrated vegetable mix to a quart of boiling water, if more company arrives drop in more beans and a pail of water. It was his way of being funny.

The flickering and darting sparks were like friendly sprites circling and gyrating in easy play about the camp that evening. Within the enchanted circle of the fire, all was warmth, cheer, and health; beyond was the mist of night that shrouded the river. It sent a dampness to one's bones, adding to the feeling of the forest wilds. But that night friends slept soundly on full bellies.

Exotic Backwoods Cookery

It was October when I came from my camp at Duck Hole making my way downriver in a long circuitous route before reaching Noah's. Following a successful bear hunt earlier that week, he had invited me to share, as he put it, "a very special meal." As I took my last footsteps from the forest into the clearing of the mayor, I looked forward to food, lots of it, for I was hungry enough to eat the whole bear. Before reaching the hermitage's clearing, I had gotten whiffs of an odor drifting on the wind that I couldn't quite associate with anything. The smell was so different, it was sort of an education in itself. It had an underlying recognition of four-week-old socks boiling, and burning hair. I also detected, as I walked up the hill trail, that the brush had a dry, withered look. Could the air have been that caustic? No, not possible. I chalked it up to the frost and unseasonable heat of the day.

After entering the camp yard and greeting Noah, my eyes traveled to a large kettle with rapidly boiling water. A pair of deer horns protruded from the liquid. As Noah stirred the contents, I noted he was actually rotating an entire deer head. I didn't have an inkling of what he might be preparing. I did deem it as looking inedible and wondered to myself if it might not be for human consumption.

Earlier that week I helped Noah dispatch a bear near Seward Pond. It certainly widened my education about hunting and trapping bears. Noah liked to say, "With a trap a man can show a bruin just how to hunt bear and also show him, in no uncertain terms, who is boss!" This particular bear, Noah said, was smarter than some. He actually picked up the drag chain, wrapped it around its wrist and neck, and proceeded into a swamp. Noah and I followed, but once in the swamp the tracks were harder to follow. But the bear, being "so proud of his new bracelet and necklace," kept it rattling until Noah killed it with his trusty .35 Remington. As Noah tested the bear to see if it was dead or just bluffing, he complimented the animal for being a cooperative bear with a "show off vanity."

This hunt was an example of the trust I knew he had in me for, as many of his kills were, this one was not 100% legal. That didn't bother me in the slightest. I knew Noah used every bit of an animal he killed. A bear's hide, for instance, would make a warm comforter. The rendered fat was converted into bear oil (the finest cooking oil ever devised). He ate all the meat. Some of the bones were used for pipe bowls and stems, and the bladder was dried and tanned for use as a pouch to hold tobacco, a sewing kit or what have you. One thing that was very certain, Noah knew how to survive living off the land where a lesser person might have starved.

I quickly dispensed of any notion of the head being part of the dinner I had been invited to eat. It had to be flavoring for his bear bait because, setting beside his iron cooking kettle was the kettle he made bear chowder in. With that observation I smugly prided myself at how quickly I was learning to decipher and classify the many goings on around the hermit's camp. Early in our relationship I learned that Noah didn't appreciate fielding question after question from inquisitive minds. He appreciated silence at times and someone who didn't bombard him with "foolish nonsense."

He motioned for me to sit down at the table; I had timed my arrival well. Placed on the dining table was a chipped white enamel plate holding a half dozen slices of some mystery meat I had never seen before. It resembled a sliced hard boiled egg, but with a clay gray color. It had the same odor as the scent I picked up as I came into camp. While the identity eluded me, I was positive it had been cooked in the stew pot he was stirring. "Richard, you're just in time to sample the appetizers. It's a favorite repast of Oriental men; I only prepare it once in a blue moon. Help yourself, but squeeze your nostrils together before you chew it." Noah paused a moment as I quickly slipped several pieces into my mouth. As I say, I was as hungry as any bear ever was, so I didn't question what it was until he added, "By the way. That delicacy has been used by the Chinese for centuries as a stimulant." Hearing that, I put the brakes on hard. It immediately came to me what part of the bear he had cooked. In short, he had boiled the two male sex organs. "Testees, " he called them. I suppose he believed life was to be lived and that by then I had grown into manhood in a rather innocent way. This must have been a rite of passage, his way of initiating me, for I was in the prime of life and certainly didn't require a stimulant; nor did he, a confirmed bachelor, have any need of it.

Normally I am game at trying most anything, but the small amount I had already masticated was all I was willing to chew. The contents in my mouth ended up being spit out in the woods with Noah calling after me to just pick off a sap blister from a balsam tree and chew it. "You'll be none the worse for the experience."

I was now wary of what the next course might be. I prided myself at being sociable and willing to try things, but when he cut open the head revealing a bubbling mass of gray matter—deer's brain, I couldn't imagine eating any of it. I never cared for the boiled hog's head my parents cooked, so I was positive I wouldn't like his "wisdom nugget soup."

I knew there wasn't a mean bone to be found in my friend's body; he truly hadn't intended to rank me out. I knew Noah used everything he could from his kills, but I just didn't realize how unwasteful he actually was. I had enough and admitted it. I was not to worry. He understood. He had other food planned. Taking a spoon he ladled several thick scoops of the soup into another container. It was to be used as stock for a new batch of everlasting stew, which in itself had a reputation. I'd learned that from Oscar Burguiere. Everlasting stew was just that. Noah kept a kettle simmering day and night. It was there for anyone to take whenever they were hungry. He was a great believer in lentils, barley, bean, rice—bulk ingredients—but also added to the pot condiments and chunks of venison, bear, rabbit, hedgehog, beaver, muskrat, squirrel, partridge "or any other meat that might wander his way," Oscar once emphasized.

It all had to do with survival and I could well appreciate that at times, like along about the middle of February when the broth became kind of thin. Rationing was then in order. But all in all old Noah ate as well as a lot of people, maybe even better because the meat market at Cold River was generously stocked.

Removing the head from the pot, he added the remainder of the contents to his bait kettle, and I offered to help him carve the deer jowl into chunks. With that boring task accomplished, he proclaimed that since "we have the opening courses out of the way, sit down at the table and get ready to enjoy the rest of the meal."

With great relish we dined on sourdough pancakes and choice cuts of bear steak all washed down with great mugs of Beech Nut coffee. As we ate Noah mentioned that, as promised, it was a one-of-a-kind dinner. I certainly agreed it was unforgettable.

Noah's Lickety-Split Ride on Clarence Whiteman's Buck

Deer hunting in the Adirondacks has been a tradition for many hunting parties over the years. The experiences a hunter shares with his companions in camp and on a hunt remain forever part of their lives and can be fondly recalled years later.

The Clarence Whiteman party was one group of hunters who, with the regularity of a well-tuned grandfather clock, bivouacked a short walking distance from Noah's Cold River City. "Our seasonal visits with Noah made it extra special for us," Clarence reflected. "It's hard to explain why we derived so much pleasure from so much work. The hermitage was a long ways back in the woods, but it was worth it. I suppose you would have to have been a participant to really understand what it was like," he admitted.

One unusual event that has never escaped Clarence's memory is that of old Noah himself riding atop of a huge buck pulled by Clarence and members of his hunting party in 1949. And, should Clarence's memory ever cloud, he need only turn on his 8mm home movies to help revive the event that still brings out a hearty laugh from anyone who views the film.

Picture, if you will, Noah sitting astride a large buck. Clad in tattered hunting garb and with his long gray and black flecked beard, he resembles Santa Claus on the hunt. In one hand he holds a rope, the reins, while in the other he's grasping a switch, waving it over his head to encourage his team of four hunters from the Whiteman hunting party to pull him. Dressed in red checked hunting pants, the men have tied crotched branches to resemble antlers to their heads. They are pretending to be Santa Rondeau's team as they dig in and began to pull their load. Noah is hollering to them by name: On Clarance. On Johnny. On Tom and Joe. To the top of Cold River, now on with you go," as he cracks the whip. The team digs into the snow and for a few minutes propels both old bucks over the snow until one of the stead's looses his balance and stumbles, tripping the others. They all laugh as they lay prostrate on the ground. Once again Noah commands them to pick up the slack and off again they go sledding in the direction of the hermitage. A gleeful scene indeed.

Someone viewing the movie might think the participants actions showed a lack of consideration toward the animal. But that would be far from the truth. "It was just a typical prank by grown men who enjoyed each others company. A photo opportunity that only lasted a few minutes," Clarance offered. "It was not intended to be disrespectful or malicious to the deer."

Richard said he recalled Noah mentioned this incident had the makings for the easiest drag back to camp he had ever made. "Unfortunately my reindeers ran out of gas immediately after the film ran out!"

Homespun Humor

A gush of steam puffed into the air as boiling water first spit from the spout. Droplets then rolled onto the hot burner of my boxstove, hissing as they danced on the hot surface. A rolling boil in a large, chipped enamel coffee pot rocked the out-of-round bottom annoyingly on the flat, cast iron burner, interrupting my daydreaming. Once adjusted I tried to resume my pleasant flashbacks, but was too alert.

It was the winter of 1940, I was in the heart of the Adirondacks, as far back as it was possible to get in the woods. I was engaged in laying down a trapline that followed an old tote trail up the valley toward the old Bradley Pond lumber camp. The quiet of the timberland was broken only once when the roar of a small snow-slide on a steep section of the mountain reverberated with a dull resounding echo from mountain to mountain. Stopping atop a low ridge below Panther Peak to take in nature's gymnastics, I decided to eat an early noon lunch consisting of cold, rolled pancakes that I'd buttered with jelly that morning.

I traced my meandering snowshoe path from a vantage point down into the valley. My position gave me a commanding view of the Cold River far below. The wind struck my face and I realized it had a different feel and was coming out of a different direction. Sensing an impending storm, I turned back toward Duck Hole before the weather conditions deteriorated.

My decision turned out to be well-founded.

I had begun to understand the wilderness. I could shoulder a heavy pack and carry it many miles. I enjoyed building a crude lean-to against a tree or rock and spending the night sleeping on a balsam-bough-bed, cradled on four feet of snow when necessary. When traveling across ice, I'd first chip test holes aided by my short handled axe. I liked to watch the ice chips sailing into the air. I even relished the physical tiredness I experienced once returned to my cabin and welcomed the sound of the springs squeaking as I sat on the edge of the metal framed bed to change my socks.

Fascinated by the amount of game that was still to be had at Cold River, I began to do a lot of trapping after I'd graduated from high school. Trapping gave me a chance to do what I most wanted without someone looking over my shoulder. It even provided a big boost to my being a mountain man. Of course Noah had been the magnet that furnished the power. His solitary existence back there kept me fired up until I was older and able to spend some time at his hermitage.

The Duck Hole was still more of a wild state. I rarely ever saw a hiker. And during the hunting and trapping season, the only shots I ever heard were those that friends fired. I was fortunate, as a young man, to be rugged and willing to take the opportunity to roam. It seemed so impossible, but I knew someday those days would be gone forever.

Such were my thoughts as I hunkered down during what turned out to be a particularly long winter storm, complete with dramatic and massive whiteouts. I remember I was cabin bound for a week. When the temperature on my outside thermometer dropped well below the zero, I didn't cuss one bit, nor did I wonder why I had allowed myself to get stranded so far from kith and kin. There would always be something to occupy my time or so I thought. I matured following that storm and never once did I question why Noah preferred wintering at Pine Point Camp near Bartlett Carry rather than remaining at his Cold River City. On the heels of that storm I came to understand the need to exercise alternatives. By the time I had decided to follow in his footsteps, he was becoming less agile and less interested and able to face the challenges of nature. While I, decades younger, thrived on the challenge. As I look back I realize it was the persistence of youth. The seemingly impossible things were challenges to be attempted whether sensible or not. I often gave very little thought as to how things might turn out.

Toward the end of that week, after running out of reading material, I considered that I just might reach the point of madness. To keep from getting cabin fever I unlaced the webbing of my snowshoes, resoaked the rawhide filling, restrung the shoes, turning the worn part of the lacing over and in the process learned several new knots and how they were laced to get the proper sized holes. Sometimes I got so interested in the intricate weaving pattern I stayed up past midnight working on them. When finished they were sag proof and, with a glistening coat of varnish, looked like new.

Following this particularly long storm I decided to wander down the Cold River trail and check out the cabins of the absentee Noah, since I was the only resident caretaker in the area.

Not long into that winter day I found the frozen remains of a deer. Its life shortened due to starvation. Later in the day while roaming the thick cedar swamp around Cedar Pond, I chanced upon a deer yard with about twenty deer bunched together trying their best to survive the long Adirondack winter which had deposited four feet of snow. They were apparently so weak from hunger, they showed little fear of me. Coming across the dead deer that morning convinced me a helping hand was now needed. Mother Nature provides, yet sometimes not in over abundance. For over an hour I cut and broke fresh cedar boughs and stamped out several paths leading out of the yarding area. After they became accustomed to my movements, they seemed as trusting as farm animals. I'm sure they welcomed my efforts. Certainly this humane gesture wouldn't be so meddlesome as to upset Nature's plans very drastically. Later that year I learned members of the Tupper Lake Rod and Gun Club, under the supervision of Game Protector Earl Vosburgh, Noah's arch enemy in the Conservation Department, set out almost 800 pounds of "deer cakes" for the relief of deer snowbound and hard-pressed by hunger in the Tupper Lake area.

On my return trek a couple of days later, I checked on my handiwork. Apparently Mother Nature had approved. The herd appeared friskier and were using my snowshoe trail, now frozen hard enough to support their weight. This time I brought an axe and cut several larger cedars. The only visible alteration was the condition of the deer I helped. It at least made me feel better. During the winter of 1939 I had learned what hunger felt like. To a small degree, I am sure my minor efforts eased their suffering. When I returned to fish Cold River later that spring, I liked to believe I saw all twenty alive, well and rejuvenated from their weakened condition. In fact I never once heard one of them sneeze or cough which just goes to show that Cold River was a healthy place for man or beast. Maybe the little effort it took to provide some feed even helped insure a more bountiful harvest of fawns.

Before leaving the "diggings" I tacked a Christmas card, complete with a handwritten epistle, next to Noah's bunk. It read:

Dear Noah,
        I'm writing this card to tell you
    The economy slump has taken away
    The things I really needed—
            my pack, my reindeer, my sleigh!
    So I'm making my rounds on a donkey on snowshoes.
    He's old, crippled and slow.
    So if I miss you at Xmas;
    You will be sure to know.
    There's nothing I can do about it, you see,
    I'm out on my ASS in the snow.
                                        Santa Claus

When next I visited my friend I mentioned what I had done for the deer. Sounding knowing yet sensitive to my feelings he philosophically addressed the issue. "Richard, I'm glad you have compassion for the deer. Your assistance slightly reduced some suffering. Still, though, as seemingly cruel as it might seem starvation is Nature's way of weeding out the weaker animals and therefore producing a stronger herd. Of course if you had a razor sharp double bitted axe in each hand, you couldn't possibly feed all the deer in the Adirondack forests. So it seems reasonable, though cruel, that Nature's way is best. Yet, if you take pleasure in feeding those you find, don't stop. Cold River deer are living under more trying weather conditions than those of other regions and a little extra help is never a bad thing. Who knows, helping Nature may make the Cold River herd the best in the state."

As I listened to his conclusions I understood exactly. I was proud he had taken me "under his wing" and cared to share his knowledge. His teachings over the years produced many first time happenings that I would never have experienced had it not been for my old, unforgettable friend—an extra ordinary man whose honesty was always foremost in his way of life.

Once he'd masterly taken care of my lesson-of-the-day, Noah queried, "I hear ole St. Nick fell on hard times last season." During the pause I studied his facial expression trying to guess what might come next.

"Uh huh," I answered, "I believe that's so," playing right along. "By the time he arrived at Cold River it was well past Christmas. I'd suspect his team pranced too hard all over the Town Hall roof. I had to gather up most of the beaver, deer and bear bones that rattled off the siding when I checked things out in mid-January."

"Santa was a mite hungry too," he continued. "Ate up all the cookies, drank too much scotch, and slept in my bunk. He must have been busier than the proverbial cat on a tin roof. Yet for all the fussing, I didn't think Christmas was any duller than last year." I simply smiled and nodded. "I'll be ready for him next year, might even roast a raccoon marinated in my special sauce. A special Christmas dinner certainly would be a fit gesture, since Claus left me a personally autographed, handwritten note. On second thought, I shouldn't be impressed even though that card came straight from St. Dominique. He took liberties in my absence. Next year he'll have to obtain the proper permits. I just can't have people landing on my rooftop without first receiving the proper authority from the mayor."

Thus began a jocular Christmas ritual we continued for many years. Noah's homespun humor always filled me with delight.

Far Back and Beyond

Since that summer in 1934, I had often thought of Noah especially when challenged by less than favorable weather. Although I was unable to spend as much time as I wanted to at Big Dam during my high school years following my initial visit, we did correspond through the mail. His handwritten letters were beautiful in penmanship—decorative, flowing letters. Unique to Noah's style of writing was his capitalizing anything connected to the natural world: Sun, River, Thunder, Bear. I couldn't wait to read his opening remarks. His flowing penmanship made me feel his presence even from afar; he was a wonderful letter writer. Our year-end correspondence evolved from newsy Christmas and New Year's greetings to humorous and cynical remarks. How I would give my shiniest hounds-tooth to have them now to reread. Noah felt our ever changing "List To Saint Nicholas" was especially "a scream." He at least had the foresight to preserve some of his sentiments in his journals.

Noah's Letters to Santa

Santa:

If you have something worthwhile in your Pack; To night you may come in through my Town Hall Stove Pipe. And please understand, —I've had so much of somethings, that, I don't want anymore. Please don't bring:—Radio Advertisements, Old Tricks (as new deals), Gods (Old or New), Frame-up arrests (by the dishonest American Conservation Commission of N.Y. State.) And no more Rooseveltisms; (Democrat Ass Bray.)   And—POSITIVELY no more snow. Further; I have so many natural Trees, that, your half tone Pictures of little Trees make no appeal; neither; Tin Whistles, nor Japanned Teddy Bears even if made with American Metal. Therefore,—if You come in under the circumstances; Be darn careful, that, you don't wake me up.

Noah John Rondeau

My Letter to Old Saint Nick

Nick,—attention: I've heard about you; and frankly, I have not much use for "Saints" But if you have something good; Leave it at my Town Hall to night, at Cold River near the Big Dam Between Santanoni and Seward Mountain Range. And if you're a Saint like Peter; with crowns at Pearly Gate No matter how they glitter, after I'm dead I'm not interested. And if you come down my Stove Pipe Look out for the traffic. Santa Claus may come tonight with a Pack of Monstrosities. About noise making: be careful, Nick. When I'm sleeping I don't want noisy Saints.

Noah John Rondeau

December 25, 1943   Saturday Cloudy and moderate temperature
Christmas Day at Cold River   At Town Hall

My little Christmas Tree looks nifty, standing in snow bank near Wigwam in front of Town Hall. For 3 hours a little Deer feed in sight of camp. I hear a woodpecker knock his Pipe on a dry limb in the forest.

Memoranda: Christmas Day. "Notice to Old Man Claus"

You white whiskered,—Red Nose—Old Fool! Inspite of my warning to the contrary, you brought more snow; and that's all You did bring. You snooped in the Wigwams and Town Hall; like a hateful American Game Protector; You made all the noise you could with your big feet and just about woke me up. All you have,—is diversity of colors on tissue paper and thrash to fool kids. And because I don't want your trinket,—You sore, you try to wake me up and you bring "More Snow." If I had you here today: I'd take you by a Roll of Neck Fat, and the seat of your Old Red-Britches,—and I'd brush your New Snow out of my snow Trails with your darn Old Whiskers. And remember, if I ever catch you in my Cold River City, I'll give you a kick in the ass—that will make you bite the Stem off your little Pipe.

N.J. Rondeau

Memoranda: Christmas Day 1943 "Notice to Sanctimonious Nick"

Nick Dominie,

You have nothing but cheap cloth Dolls with Butts full of Saw Dust; and a "Saint" name, to get in snoop, wake up nice people (even the Mayor) and when your thrash is not wanted you bring a snow storm, then make the wind blow. Be it known to your fraudulent Sanctities; that Peter and Paul, Antwine and Saint Jaco,—I discarded long a go. And you (Nick) if I ever catch you at Cold River—I'll give you a K.I.C.K kick in the Saintly back-side that will make you shed the fuzzy tassel off your little Red Nose.

N.J.R.

December 28, 1943
Tuesday

The Thaw caught cold (Froze) last night. Today: calm and Sun Shine. Cold atmosphere. Crust is new now and on top of two to three feet of packed snow. I chop ice away from Hall of Record Door. Three air planes go eastward over Vallie. I chop Slam Bang off the frozen Buck.

December 31, 1943
Friday
Cloudy and moderate temperature At Cold River City

I read and I write. The chickadee Birds call many times per day and get their ration. I fiddle 1943 out and 1944 in. I pity the poor Hermit that can't fiddle;—I can't see how he can change year.

Remains of Big Dam on Cold River.

Noah Rondeau at camp in the 1930's.

One of the many crews that cut, hauled and drove logs to their final destination.

Sluice dam similar to the Big Dam on Cold River.

Noah preparing to fish.

Memories of fishing with Noah lasted a lifetime.

The frozen Cold River was often the best trail. Winter 1924.

Noah's how-to-hunt concoctions were legendary.

The hermit's aim was deadly accurate.

Noah stirring a kettle of "Everlasting Stew."

Phil and Richard's cabin, concealed at base of Bear Trap Mountain.

Richard's time-blackened iron cookware.

Construction of Richard Smith's log cabin along the Chubb River was very basic.

Richard Smith's Duck Hole cabin.

Phil McCalvin relaxes with Noah.

Noah's cabin in the Cold River country, the scene of decades of "hard times."

Duck Hole, a frozen wasteland, 1922.

Seward Range from Cold Fiver Flow, 1924.

PART IV

RICHARD'S REMEMBRANCES

Courtesy of Richard Smith

Nature's Art: Frost, Snow, and Ice

The raging winter blizzard of the past few days had begun to breed a touch of cabin fever within me. I first recognized it when I realized I was washing breakfast dishes a second time, just to have something to do. The snow had stopped coming down; the sky was turning blue; the sun, which I hadn't seen for days, was glinting from the draped spruces. It was time to break the fever before it got any worse. My one room cabin's walls had been crowding me, and I had to get out if only for a tramp in the new snow.

I had been thinking about some beaver ponds on Boulder Brook that an old friend told me he once trapped in his younger days, and although it was well below zero, I decided to look them over.

As I set out across the fluffy white snow with my snowshoes singing a happy song, it was like traveling into a world of virgin newness. The ermine whiteness of the newly fallen snow seemed unreal in its fresh beauty. The several inches of snow made the whole forest seem devoid of life—wild and lonely. Not the best remedy for cabin fever. With a few curious chickadees for company, I was soon back in my element, enjoying the new snow which was now sparkling, as if a giant hand had sprinkled it with glittering diamonds.

Crossing the outlet of Moose Pond a short ways from where Boulder joined it, I spotted the old tote road. Long ago, logs were drawn to a field on the outlets bank to be driven to the big holding dam down river in the spring. I made good time on the road. But as it grew steeper, the rushing waters had broken loose from the icy bonds and were now sending a fine spray of mist that was instantly freezing on small spruces and infant hardwoods along the bank. Reluctant to leave the fine walking on the surprisingly clear road, I kept on, enthralled by sculptured formations of ice along the river's bank. As much as I was enjoying all this shimmering wonder, I soon realized I was rapidly becoming a part of this lacy finery and decided to move away from its freezing fingers. With the guttural roar of the cascading waters as a guide, I climbed with more difficulty than on the road, but could still enjoy the muffled song of the winter brook.

After climbing steadily for some time, the sounds of the brook mellowed and, once more returning to the brook's course, I found I had entered a long valley, the mouth of which had once been partially closed by a huge beaver dam. Now the dam was a mass of ancient, nearly unrecognizable beaver cuttings. Part of the dam still clung to a granite ledge several feet high, indicating at one time it had flooded the valley.

The nameless mountains I had seen from the outlet soon appeared more ridgelike. Where once a great expanse of water had been created by these fur-clad engineers of Nature, now stood an almost impossible jungle of saplings and spruce, cedar, and balsam trees. Surely the beaver had vacated this beautiful little valley when they had run out of food. From the size of area involved, several generations of beaver must have been here at one time. At the far end of the valley a small dam of new construction was in progress. Perhaps a new colony was in the making and would eventually reclaim the valley, as there was plenty of new growth.

These new settlers appeared more intelligent than the original planners. Rather than build a large dam to flood the whole valley, they planned on doing it in steps—moving the dam as the food supply dwindled at the old dam. Perhaps their ancestors had done the same thing and the old dam at the entrance was the effort of many. I was a bit disappointed I hadn't seen the large beaver pond that was once there.

Rather than go back the way I came, I went through a notch into another narrow valley. At its end was a sharp little peak covered with cedar trees. As I moved toward it, at times it disappeared, than came into view again, as if it were watching me. I named this cedar-clad little outcrop for my own amusement "Peek-a-boo Peak." Upon looking back, it had again disappeared in the protecting folds of the guardian mountains and ridges that surrounded it. It seemed no time at all before I came once more to Moose Pond Outlet. By using small passes, and winding pristine valleys and ravines, I had found an easy way to the hidden beaver dams on Boulder Brook, but it seemed I was years too late.

It was, however, a pleasant outing. I had witnessed first hand the magical beauty of Nature's handiwork of frost, snow and ice. As the cold Adirondack night slowly closed around me, I came in sight of my snug little cabin, no longer a breeding place of cabin fever, but a haven of warmth and comfort in the freezing atmosphere of the winter wilderness.

Mosquito Madness

The first shadows of twilight were falling across the pond. I was seated on an old beaver house, admiring the string of trout I had caught. Across the pond, a black bear cub was busily scooping ants from a rotted log that had been split open by its mother. In a nearby backwater covered with lily pads, two deer were extracting roots and succulent grasses. All was serenely quiet; only the gentle lapping of water kicked up by a mild breeze broke the silence.

As I sat, wrapped in thought and wonder, an ominous drone of startling magnitude began to emanate from a deep, dark swamp across the pond's tranquil waters. At first I thought it might be a diving aircraft, but the rapidly approaching black object quickly became recognizable as a cloud of giant mosquitoes.

As fast as was humanly possible, I hit the pond's edge on a dead run, for I knew I had to hide quickly before the sharp eyes spotted me. I immediately realized, however, that I was too late; the mosquitoes had seen me.

My only chance, however slim, was to hurry as if my life depended on it to the abandoned maple sugar works a half mile away. I arrived at the site hardly a jump ahead of the blood-thirsty hoard of insects. I was able, with no small effort, to pry a large iron boiling kettle from its overturned position in the dead leaves and to crawl under.

Safe at last, I thought, proud of my record-breaking run and quick thinking. My only concern now was how long they would keep me imprisoned beneath the kettle before giving up and flying away.

My safe refuge was not to be! Seconds later I felt a sharp jab on my neck and saw a mosquito stinger poke through the kettle. Don't worry, I told myself; perhaps it's just a rusty pinhole, but suddenly several more appeared. I pulled my hand axe from its sheath and frantically squashed the stingers against the inner surface of the kettle. My arm began to ache in the frenzy of my work. But just when I felt secure, the kettle began to stir and rise. Suddenly it was airborne!

All I had time to do was dive under another kettle. Again and again I repeated the strength-sapping procedure until at last there were no more kettles to be found.

My only chance now was to make one last desperate run through the pitch black forest. Finally I reached the trail, but just when I thought I was safe, I was snatched into the air by an insect at each shoulder!

In my half insane state, I thought I could hear my two captors bickering over my disposal. Their dialogue went something like this: "Do you think we should eat him here?" The replying voice said, "Are you crazy? We had better take him deeper into the swamp before the big ones come along and take him away from us."

Daylight was now filtering through the forest, accompanied by a weird sound from the pond, not unlike the bugle call reveille. I was abruptly dropped to the ground and again I heard the bickering voice saying, "I told you we should have eaten him when we had the chance."

I know this occurrence must have begun as a dream, which got twisted around and turned into a nightmare! Funny thing, though, when I went to the sugar works the next morning, all the kettles had mysteriously disappeared. Only their imprints remained deep in the leaves. I am convinced, however, that my experience was only a nightmare, in spite of the size of the mosquitoes at Moose Pond. I'll let you decide.

P.S. As I sit alternating writing this and sharpening my old Case sheath knife, I am amazed how little it has changed over its valued lifetime. The bone handle has turned a golden yellow, and the blade, although worn considerably by years of honing, still remains razor sharp and shining. It seems indestructible, as if time has had no effect on its usefulness. Long ago I lost count of the deer and bear it has carved. The man who crafted it surely did a marvelous job.

One autumn when I was young, Noah and I went downriver to Camp Seward that was soon to be occupied by Doctor Latimer and several of his friends on a hunting and fishing trip. We went down in advance to clean and cut firewood. We had neglected to bring an axe, and the axe belonging to the camp was nowhere to be found. Luckily, there was enough firewood already cut. But a huge balsam had blown down upon the roof of the camp in a windstorm. With my knife, Noah was able to cut the tree into sections small enough to remove from the roof. With each blow, I expected the blade to break, but the knife came through it all without so much as a bruise. Never again did I doubt its capabilities.

Roaming & Trapping

One time I packed a few hundred pounds of traps and food supplies into the Duck Hole and had a worthwhile excursion harvesting beaver and otter. My snug little log cabin was situated there with traplines running like the spokes of a wheel. Every pond had a beaver colony, and my main cabin was the hub. At times, I even got as far as Noah's hermitage, where we compared notes and news, the proper sets to use, and the best way to prepare the furs for market. Believe me, we had a time with many "slambangslum" stews of beaver tails and steaks of bear and venison.

During most of my trapping years, so-called conservation laws set a limit of six beavers, and game protectors attached a foolproof stapled tag to keep the limit legal for each trapper. This was done to keep the beaver population active and in balance. It worked fairly well, too, in keeping the market prices higher. I placed sets away from the beaver houses where I trapped only the larger blanket beavers. To conserve the beaver ponds from year to year, I caught only one or two beaver at each pond. At one time, I set only one trap at each pond so I wouldn't end up with more pelts than the law allowed. Usually when my take reached four skins, I would cut most of the sets to only a couple. Because Cold River for many years contained so many dams in both rivers and ponds, I hardly dared to set over six traps. It's a scary business to set out a dozen traps and have six beaver in the first seven sets. Having more beaver then was allowed by law was a constant source of worry.

Most of the years I trapped beaver, the price was a dollar an inch. A blanket measure was seventy inches length and width. One huge fellow, after stretching and drying, measured an even 86 inches. That year, with my take of muskrat hides I made over $1,000, which wasn't bad in those days when coffee was thirty cents a pound.

When trapping I roamed far and wide and often stayed overnight in thirty degrees below zero weather in rough balsam lean-tos with never a thought of hypothermia. Building a fire against a ledge or boulder to reflect the heat of a good hardwood fire, I was snug and warm. I also traveled many miles in the moonlight, cross country to Tupper Lake, hiding my snowshoe trail on windswept ridges and lakes. All the years I did this, never did a game protector come to my log cabin. Without a doubt, those were the happiest years of my life.

Fishing has become so poor that it's almost a lost cause due to acid rain (deer hunting, too, has not been the greatest in the past few years), although there are a few lakes (the deeper ones) with great trout fishing (lake, rainbow, splake). I also have a secret beaver pond nestled in a deep mountain valley in the Sentinal Range that has good-size speckled trout ranging from eight to fourteen inches, native trout that are almost extinct in the Adirondacks. The environmentalists say there are none left. I agree with them, but I enjoy eating them every summer and keep my peace.

In 1944, they also say that the mountain lion has been extinct in the Adirondacks for a hundred years. While trapping between Moose Pond and Duck Hole one February, I found, in a huge swamp, a blood trail of a deer and a pursuing animal. The paws were the size of a woman's fist with heart-shaped pads. No nails showed in the tracks. After following the tracks a ways, I found the imprint of a tail mark on each side of the trail. Following along cautiously as possible and as silently as my creaking snowshoe webs would allow, I saw the dead deer, and pausing a few minutes, I finally saw the two big cats on a ledge. The heads were about the same size as a German shepherd's. The tails were almost as long as their bodies, with a characteristic curl at the end. In my mind I was convinced they were "panthers." Not wanting to disturb them, I backed off and went about my business.

Another time, while packing some venison to a camp at Moose Pond, I heard a scream. It was close to midnight and I froze, the hackles on my neck standing straight up. After a moment of frightened immobility, I turned my flashlight down the trail just in time to see four feet of tail disappear into the balsams. I reasoned that they meant me no harm, but were following the scent of the deer meat in my pack. Half a mile ahead, the trail went to some ledges and I decided I wouldn't go any farther. I built a fire and stayed till daylight. When I reached the top of the first ledge, I found where a big cat had lain in wait. I can't say if he would have jumped me there if I had ventured on; I'll never know, but by stopping I was sure he wouldn't.

I gathered from that experience that before they attack, they scream in such a way that it immobilizes the intended victim so they can deliver the fatal blow. I know that their screams do vary in pitch. And I know for a fact, if my life had depended on it, I would never have been able to get my rifle to my shoulder. Another thought I had at the time was that they had caught my scent and they had remembered that I had not harmed them the year before in that swamp. One thing for certain, I saw their sign on muddy pond shores among the driftwood on occasion. The Conservation

Department would have liked to have known about the "panthers" that they called cougars, but I never contacted them. If I had, they would have been in there in force to trap, tag, remove, or study. I kept their secret, and it was nice to know they were there, and I like to think they still are.

Roaming the winter wilds as I did, I saw lynx, bobcat, wolverine, all at a long distance from me on the big flow above the Hermitage. Rondeau remarked at each mentioning, "Yes, they are all here, but let it be our secret."

I once lived to hunt and roam that beautiful country. I went in year after year in the 1940's because the old Hermit was a fine friend and a powerful magnet who pulled me that way at every opportunity.

Bear . . . BEAR . . . BEARS!!!

Depending on your vantage point there might be something sinister in the word bear. I can attest that seeing their tracks in the snow can unbalance a slight-hearted person, causing their heart rate to rise as well as the short hairs on the back of their neck.

Some people also react irrationally during a rare bear-man contact. Consider Oscar Burguiere's experiences. While deer hunting near Shattuck Clearing, he looked back to discover a bear was smelling his tracks with great interest. Later on he said he thought about shooting the animal, but he didn't think it was the best option. Instead he decided to put as many miles as possible between himself and Mr. Bear. If the bear wanted to smell tracks, he would gladly oblige and make a lot of them quickly! Of course the animal wasn't causing any harm. Oscar simply became alarmed and overreacted. For his part Oscar said, "It seemed a fine way of ending my brief encounter." But the local Cold River crew knew differently. Even though our friend was armed with a big powered rifle his reputation for accuracy was legendary, Oscar probably would have missed.

Roaming the wilds, I have had a few meetings with black bears and from those encounters bears earned my respect. In a split second a bear can change from a gentleman in a fur coat to a savage, roaring demon of destruction. To be fair the vast majority are skitterish, preferring to turn and run, but I have seen a few possessed with a very short fuse and a dynamite temper.

I remember the day when I was at Noah's, sitting in the summer heat around his smudge fire, just relaxing and passing the time of day, when our big talk fest was interrupted by shouts and screams. Following the incident Noah said he would have to record it in his journal, but all he chose to write was something like: Two fishermen come and go.

Hearing excited screeches coming from the downriver side of Big Dam, I jumped up from my seat in alarm. Noah showed none. Shortly, several very scared fishermen breathlessly crested the hill and entered the clearing blurting they had just met a bear on the trail. Noah tried calming them saying, "With all the noise you're making the bear is probably as scared as you were and run off by now." It helped some but they remained edgy while they were in camp. During the course of their conversation, one fellow asked Noah what he would do if attacked by a bear if armed with only a fishing pole. Noah replied in all seriousness, "I'd slap his nose as many times as he allowed me to with the tip of the pole."

"Would that stop his attack, Mr. Rondeau?"

"No it wouldn't," he responded matter of factly, "About all it'd accomplish would be to make him so mad he would finish me off quickly so I wouldn't suffer."

To calm their lingering fears, I volunteered to accompany them back to their tent site. On the way we retrieved the scattering of creels, fishing poles, and some clothing they had discarded during their flight. I pointed out to them where the bear had crossed the trail and made its exit. Out of curiosity I tracked it for about a half mile before returning to the hermitage. Reporting my find to Noah I told him he had been right. The bear probably was as scared as the men and ran helter-skelter up the mountain. With a twinkle in his eye he replied, "I'm glad you followed the bear to verify he was as scared as our friends. I don't think they believed me. If I see them again, I will be sure to give them your report."

As the years passed I grew more knowledgeable and skilled. I helped Noah trap bears as well as shoot them with my trusty .30-.30 Marlin —usually with only one shot.

Noah and Bears

Noah's friends never understood why he trapped and hunted bears. The time it took to skin one out, tack it up, prepare it for sale, and carry it out was not worth the effort. The hide had little value. It wasn't for the meat. Noah preferred venison and never lacked for it.

The springs on the steel-toothed traps were so strong that it required two clamps to set the pan—one on each spring because no one man's weight could depress both at the same time. Stepping into one of Noah's bear traps could be fatal. If a man stepped into one, his leg would be broken and, without clamps, he could never open the jaws.

Noah maintained he had no mercy if someone footed it into one of his bear traps. "No one has any business stepping into one," he would snap. Fortunately no tragedy ever did occur.

Several of Noah's traps still remain in caches in the Seward Range and under a large boulder near the Cold River lean-to's.

Fifteen Frog (Trout) Pond

Not far from the hermitage was Fifteen Frog Pond. Noah's recollection was, for the most part, the trout had evacuated the waters, but on rare occasions a few could still be caught there. He fished them more or less for something to do. He told me about one time when he made his city available to sportsmen in the early days when he guided occasionally. Two anglers complained that the trout were not as plentiful due to the low water and hot weather. Noah understood they were disappointed, but said it couldn't be helped. The next day of their stay he suggested they try a little beaver pond up the trail. They followed through and within a few hours caught fifteen fairly good trout. This made them happy and Noah declared he was just going to have to christen that body of water Fifteen Trout Pond in their honor. A couple of days later they returned to try their luck again. But this time instead of catching trout, all they saw were frogs everywhere they looked! Since they never caught another fish Noah told them he would have to revise the name and ever since it has been referred to as Fifteen Frog Pond.

I didn't have any better luck. Noah knew I wanted to catch a mess of trout before I had to pack out to Lake Placid on business. So, in the true spirit of a seasoned guide, he promised me a good time fishing the Black Hole and Seward Pond when I came back in June. With a promise like that my feet were sure to fly over the trail on my return.

The Big Cast

April 1942 turned out to be one of those rare spring months, the kind one only dreams about. Snow had fallen early last fall and winter seemed to go on forever as one snowstorm followed on the heels of the last. Several times I was driven indoors long enough to develop cabin fever or what someone might call boredom between four log walls. But life in the backcountry around Duck Hole was new to me, so everything was an experience.

The streams were still high from meltwater and rain, but I had too much energy that morning. I had enjoyed my coffee outside under the trees. The morning had all the earmarks of a blue-ribbon day: a light, sweet-smelling breeze, bright sunlight; blue skies with puffy clouds. By the time I finished my coffee, the temperature had risen and the soft touch of wind had disappeared. Chickadees fluttered around my suet feeder—I was getting restless. I felt like catching some Cold River trout.

Dreamy pictures of a fry pan full of speckled trout filled my mind, giving me high hopes and big ideas in spite of the chunks of flowing ice in the water and the patches of snow in the woods. I didn't want anything to burst my bubble as I hiked down the river trail to Noah's camp. We had talked of many fishing get-togethers in June, a hungry season for trout, and I just itched to be at his hermitage once again.

I didn't have any bait and my high hopes diminished considerably when I couldn't find enough worms to launch my grand assault. I dug in Noah's garden plot for an hour and only produced three shivering earthworms, which, if all of them concentrated their efforts, would hardly create a wiggle, as Noah commented, "that would interest a day old tadpole."

As we sat in the warming sunshine, a pair of robins settled on our excavation and pulled out a granddaddy nightcrawler. With that success

I began digging again, but soon relinquished the search to the birds. It was humbling.

To get any fishing plans into action, Noah suggested we tear apart rotten stumps "bear-like." His operating plans produced six white grubs, three beetles, a potato bug and several large carpenter ants. They were all quite slow to move, but by placing them in a quart jar and laying it in the sun, they came out of their dormant stage and began crawling about —having been disturbed by two inconsiderate trout-hungry anglers.

With our precious bait bottle we descended the "golden stairs" to the river below. We planned to bait our hooks in a sequence of one ant, one beetle, and a strip of bacon rind, topped with a fat grub. A very appealing combination, we thought, for hungry trout. Of course we had to limit the ice cold exposure to a short cast or our bait would stiffen and lessen their appeal. Our plan even included trying to rewarm them in our glass incubator.

But plans do not always go the way one expects them to. As Noah gingerly worked his way out on a large piece of imprisoned ice frozen in spirea below the sluiceway of Big Dam, I had my eye on a bit of promising water between the base logs of the dam where the water churned in a framework of old log cribs that held the dam in place. This pool was surrounded with huge blasted pieces of granite. Over the course of years the smaller stones had been washed away leaving a gravel bottom about ten feet square.

Noah warned me the water was too high, but I wanted to defy logic. It wasn't long before my once wiggling bait was as stiff as a board. I tried to get some life into one of them by slightly jigging it up and down, but any trout that might have spotted it probably laughed and just lay there fanning the polished gravel. Moving downstream toward Noah, I noticed four trout he had tossed up on a patch of snow. Just as I was about to call out to him I noticed the floe of ice he was fishing from had cracked and had begun moving toward the faster current. Quickly I stepped into the edge of the water and cast my line over a span of twelve feet to him.

The next occurrence seems more like fiction, but I assure you it really did take place. Noah grabbed the line, wound it about his wrist, and I slowly reeled. Little by little the ice chunk started to move back toward shore. Within a few minutes Noah was able to grip the end of my rod and jump from the ice to shore. Once on dry land he complimented me on the fine hermit I had caught.

Noah also complimented the fish for having "wintered so well," but added we would fish off the river tomorrow. That afternoon as we dined on his catch, we talked, and he mockingly summed up life with one of his favorite saying. "Yes sir, Richard. These are hard times. Hard times indeed." Indeed, it did turn out to be a day to remember.

Bears I Have Known

The Boss King

One day as I was hiking along the Ward Brook fire control road north of Mountain Pond, I came upon a bear track that was wider and longer than my size nine hunting boot. A king of bears I decided. But I was not alarmed—I was carrying my invincible Marlin. As I had chalked up an impressive record of deer and bear kills, I considered myself a good marksman. Certainly I wouldn't be intimidated by an outlandishly large bear.

Approaching a telephone pole carrying wires for the emergency phone at the rangers cabin at Duck Hole, I noticed the cross tie that carried the wire was broken where it connected to the pole. At the base of the pole were prints of a very large bear, the same size I had spotted earlier. I reasoned singing wire was not to his liking and he decided to show them who was boss in these woods. Each succeeding pole showed damage in one way or another from this aggressive bear's teeth and jaws, or his paws. Rounding a bend, I noticed a six-inch spruce tree broken near its stump. Further evidence. It was a display of frightening power. Then suddenly, and without any warning, a bear bounded onto the road and came to an abrupt halt facing me. He was close enough for a hug or a handshake. There was one thing for certain, my forward motion had come to a stop and retreating was out of the question. He stood glaring at me with a great show of teeth in his massive head and sent forth roars of anger. Fortunately, I remained steady as a rock, which was easy since I had become partially petrified. His huge paws clawed the ground. Stomping my feet in retaliation only produced a puff of dust. His roars made my hair stand out as if in a gale. I returned with my own bluster, but it seemed no louder than the first time a puppy barks.

After we had both put forth our best efforts in shoulder hunching, foot stomping, roaring and arm waving, to my great relief he finally decided such an insignificant challenger was hardly worth his efforts. With one final roar which I didn't try answering, he turned and lumbered up the road proudly proclaiming victory.

When I calmed down and my heart started beating once again, I decided victory should also be mine. After all he was the one who had backed down and left. Although maybe I'd call it a draw. I finally decided if we met again I would try just taking my hat off in the King's presence. It seemed a more sensible way to settle who was really the boss.

Sweet Bear Dreams

Early in my days at Duck Hole I was exploring the ledges around Beartrap Mountain when I came upon a small opening, a cave of sorts. I was sure it was occupied by a bear because I noted some frost feathers on the rocks as I poked my head into the entrance. Indeed it was rented for the season. He was a fair sized bear, far into the process of hibernation and only made a feeble effort to raise his head. As he gave a half-hearted growl, half-hearted snore, I quietly left him with a courteous "goodnight."

Step Once, Look Twice

From my black bear experiences over the years the word unpredictable seems the best word to describe them. They never do the same thing twice and keep you guessing at what they will do next.

While hunting one year along the high ridges between Moose Pond and the Duck Hole, I came upon bear tracks in two inches of fresh snow. It was perfect for still-hunting, so I spent several hours using every trick I knew. But not once did I get more than one short look at my target. At one point in my silent stalk, I came out on a knoll where I could look over a small opening along side a brook. A short distance beyond the main water, I knew there was a bog where bears often wallowed. I sat down, adjusted my rear sight, and waited two hundred yards away. Soon after taking watch I was encouraged to see a black nose rise above the bushes, checking the wind. I figured sooner or later the bear would leave his private tub once he'd had his fill of frogs.

My chance to shoot it, however, would never come. Eventually the impatience of youth won out, and I began to cautiously approach the bog.

Carefully parting the bushes surrounding the hole, I noticed evidence of much dredging but no bear. Instead, as lady luck would have it, tracks were heading toward the very log I had been sitting on. He'd probably smell my scent and wonder what darn idiot would be so interested in his bathing facilities. There was no question about it, I had been out-foxed by a smart or just plain lucky bear.

Bear Stumped

On a fine summer day I backpacked down the Northville-Placid Trail to Moose Pond for a weekend outing. It was a wonderful day and, having deposited my gear at the lean-to above the pond, I walked down to the outlet to do a bit of fishing. By late afternoon I had caught enough speckled trout for an evening's fish fry. Returning to the shelter with nothing more than visions of browning trout, boiling coffee, and pungent cedar woodsmoke, I spied two bear cubs clawing ants from a rotted log. I stepped behind an old pine tree that had been sheared in half long ago and watched the animals. I told myself the older member of the family had to be close by. As time ticked away I began to wonder where mother was. It was unusual not to have spotted her.

Then I detected a telltale odor of fish. I determined it was reaching my nose on air currents that drifted from the nearby beaver pond. Then I had a creepy intuition—a feeling that something was behind me. My fingernails sank into the stump I was holding on to. Venturing a glance I slowly turned to see Mrs. Bear, in all her glory, looking at me from six feet away. Now I knew where the smell of fish was coming from! I fully expected her claws would rip into me at any moment, but instead, after giving me a short "woof," she was gone in a vault toward her cubs. The only explanation for this fortunate outcome was that I had not caused her any alarm or that she didn't feel threatened by my clawing over her territorial markings on the stump. It was lucky for me the stump was there simply to hold me up. Whatever her reasons, I was happy she politely left me alone.

My Closest 'Shave'

One day in midsummer I was heading toward my cabin by a bushwhack near an old beaver meadow. Out of simple curiosity I diverted my direction to look into what was making a tearing sound. Dropping my pack, but taking my rifle, I noticed the slight depression of an aged tote road leading to the brushy clearing. I elected to followed it. In my haste to cover the distance quickly I lost my footing as I leapt over a fallen tree, landing my body close to a bear cub who was about half a step from dreamtime until I chanced into its life. He erupted from his bed with a wail that caused the old she-bear to come-a-running with flashing teeth and cold, courageous eyes. There was a neon sign blinking in her brain flashing over and over, "Save your baby at any cost."

Trying to halt a charging bear intending to destroy anything in its path is a lot like a person standing on the tracks in front of a runaway train with an upraised hand. A dozen thoughts went through my mind. The only good one was to drop momma in her tracks. My shooting ability was certainly not lacking. That alone gave me an abundance of confidence, but I didn't want to kill her and leave her baby an orphan.

As the mother headed toward me with froth dripping from her chin, her cub veered into the forest. With a split second calculation I swung my Marlin to the running cub and sent a bullet through the top of its ear that set up a wailing you would not believe. Instantly the mother stopped in mid-stride and turned toward the new menace that she thought was attacking her offspring. This took place just short of twelve paces from where I stood poised to squeeze off a fatal shot if need be.

I don't mind admitting that after it was all over I felt my steel-like nerves had become a bit shaky. In my mind I could have stopped her charge. I did wonder if her adrenaline would have given her the ability —even though dead on her feet—to reach me.

I was happy, though, it worked out as well as it did. Outside of one slightly bloodied ear, the bears left in fine shape, and I learned never to be overly anxious when investigating unusual noises. In fact, you might say I treated all future instances with caution and intelligence worthy of Solomon. Amen to that!

Overall, the black bears in Cold River country must have accepted me for they never molested my cabin. For a short time in my life we lived amicably—side by side you might say. I having great respect for the fascinating creatures, the Adirondacks largest mammals.

I Shot My Last Bea . . .

The approach of fall weather is like a shot in the arm after the hot summer we have had. The cool, pleasant breezes make me want to shoulder my favorite rifle and head into the Cold River wilds as I did years ago. Although thirty years have passed since I last explored the area, I often think of those times when youth and freedom were as much a part of me as needles on the pine. Alas, time has passed!

Last weekend I went on a random scoot into the North Notch country, where once the ponds teemed with trout, but I only managed to get enough for a small fry by the brookside. It seems chemical wastes from man's factories have drifted into the pristine mountains and are slowly killing all the fish in the lakes and ponds. The destructive tread of progress once more!

Some years ago, while I was trapping in Cold River, I was caught in a sudden snow squall and luckily came upon a cave on a ledge. The snow was coming down so heavily at the time, I lost all sense of direction. I decided I would spend the remainder of the day or night in the shelter of the cave. It was late fall, and not having a watch, I didn't know what time of day it was because the snow had caused total darkness.

I managed to scrape up enough dry wood in the cave to get a fire going. As luck would have it, just outside the cave's entrance was a supply of dead wood. I busied myself for a better part of an hour collecting enough wood for the night. As the fire got brighter, I was amazed to find that some of the rotted wood I had found within the cave had ancient axe marks. After a satisfying lunch, I lit a birch bark torch to further explore the recesses of the cave.

Upon careful examination, what appeared to be a brown stick leaning against the cave wall was actually the remains of a rifle barrel, encrusted with rust and eaten away almost to the back sight. With more torches, I sat down to examine the find. The only part worth salvaging was the brass blade of the front sight. It was then that I saw, in the flickering light, some writing scratched on the cave wall. I was excited about this, and I began carefully to remove the lichens and moss so that I might read the message, written there, beyond a doubt, by the owner of the old muzzle-loader.

After what seemed like a few fleeting minutes, I finally made out the words: "I killed my last bea..." That's all I could read.

A thousand things went through my mind. What happened to the ancient writer of those words? Had he surprised a bear in the cave and wrestled him? Perhaps he killed the bear with a knife or hatchet? Did he die as a result of the fight? Had he died of old age? A mystery unanswered.

After the storm, I went out and eventually made my way to my camp at the Duck Hole, near Cold River. That night it snowed again, destroying any chance of backtracking to explore more of the cave. I did search several times, but the country there is wild, and so many places look alike that to find the cave again would be as accidental as the first discovery. I asked Noah and the other old-timers if they knew of anyone what had been missing, but they had no idea who may have been in the cave.

The exact year of that encounter with the bear is anyone's guess. I decided the rifle had stood against the wall of the cave for one hundred to one hundred-fifty years to rust away that much. The stock lasted perhaps twenty-five, and the metal was eaten away in another seventy-five.

If I were able to find the place again, I'm sure I could find the brass hardware from the rifle that must still be buried somewhere in the forest chaff. The mosses and the leaves of countless years made about a foot of carpet. But the mystery still remains and the answer may never be known.

Lost . . . Lost . . . Lost

Today is Groundhog Day. After a warm night and thaw, a wet, heavy snow is pouring down. Mr. Groundhog will be unable to see his shadow. Thus, as the saying goes, there will be a shortening of the long winter. Still, I know there will be another six weeks plus. Oh well, it is the price to pay for living here among the mountains, where the air is pure and the wild beauty of the mountains, lakes and forests prevails.

In March, spring gave little indication that it was ever to begin, as the temperature remained twenty degrees below zero during the long nights. The snow was four feet deep. At the time, I had a trapline on Moose Creek running several miles. One morning when I started my rounds, it was eighteen degrees below zero, but the sun was out and I felt warm out of the wind. As I went along, I picked up three beaver, each weighing between thirty-five and fifty pounds, and reset my traps. As I neared the head of the stream, my load grew heavier.

At my last trap, I decided to go to an old abandoned cabin. Although the roof had fallen in years before, part of it was still intact. The cabin was roomy enough to skin my catch, thus lightening my load, for I had about six miles to go before I was back to my cabin. Before I had two of them skinned, it began to snow hard and though it was only midday, I noticed that I was in semi-darkness.

I hung two carcasses in the spruce to be picked up on my next trip, and started for camp with the two skinned pelts and one unskinned beaver. I had 75 pounds less in my basket, but by now the trees were covered with snow, and not having a compass, I wasn't sure if I was heading in the right direction. Everything in the woods looked alike.

Crossing a steep ridge, I got my bearings in a notch between the mountains. This place I called Painted Notch. It was unmistakable, because on the highest point was a large spring that flowed in both directions. I even went a bit out of my way to make sure it was the familiar spot, as there are many look-alikes.

It seemed to me that it would be an easy four-mile walk to my cabin. Not so! After several hours, I became completely bewildered. The storm developed into a raging blizzard, blocking out all landmarks. I may as well have been in Siberia.

At times I contemplated stopping at a likely shelter, building a lean-to and a fire, and spending the night. But it was getting colder all the while, and I didn't relish staying out overnight without a blanket. I did, however, have the remaining beaver that I could eat.

I knew I was on the right side of the range, and if I stayed on fairly level ground, I would eventually get to the Duck Hole—if I didn't stray from my direction. After a time, though, I decided that I must be going in circles. What to do!

I know those big mountains have a lot of echo chambers, so I yelled once. By counting the time for the echo to come back to me, I found I was still on course. Thirty seconds from the ridge on my right, sixty seconds from the ridge on my left, and nearly two minutes from the ridge in the direction I was heading, which I figured had to be Santanoni Peak. After checking at regular intervals, I found that the longer echo reduced in seconds at each sounding.

Once, the echo time on my left became almost equal to the echo from Santanoni. I wondered what had caused this to happen. I concluded that echo had come back from Street Mountain or Nye through a notch running to the east.

Another mile farther on, the echo on both left and right became identical, and the Santanoni echo came back in less than a minute. I knew now that the valley I was following was close to Roaring Brook on my left. I knew I had reached the beaver dam, because I could not hear the water. I was only a short way from my cabin.

Turning sharply to my left, I reached the beaver flow and finally came to the dam. A short walk over a ridge led to my cabin.

Had I stopped overnight, I am sure I would have survived, but at least I didn't have to spend a night in the cold.

The next day when I made my rounds, I discovered that up until I started to use the echoes, I had been going every which way except the right one. After I had the echoes zeroed in, my trail became almost a beeline down to my cabin.

Many years later, I read that Verplanck Colvin, the early state surveyor, had used that same method on one of his trips on Mt. Marcy when he became lost in a white-out. It is a proven theory.

My First Deer Hunt with Noah

Hunting season was over for me. The Duck Hole cabin, where I spent the majority of my venery pursuits, was winterized, bear proofed and closed. The only remaining thing I planned on doing before hoofing out of the woods was to swing down to see how my old friend, the hermit of Cold River Flow, was faring; it would be several months before I would return to his neck-of-the-woods in late February, in advance of the beaver trapping season.

Following our customary 'hooty hoot' greetings we invented for fun, I settled my heavy pack for a chat. I noted only one buck hanging in the meat wigwam so my ears especially stood up and took notice when he began talking about the possibility of having a rather lean diet this winter. "Even bean soup, you see Richard, spruced up with rice, barley and grits would soon become tiresome without a bit of meat to thicken it."

I knew he was driving at something, but this wasn't the time to ask questions. "Yes sir," Noah continued, "it sure pays to get a deer. With a partridge alone you can have yourself a fine meal; but a big buck, well now, there's enough for a formal state dinner—good enough for any mayor—and then enough leftovers for standard-fare meals that would last quite some time."

Following his preachment he asked if I'd care to stay a few days to help him "teach a buck a lesson" that had been giving him the slip all season. I was electrified. Asking me was like offering a wolf a T-bone steak.

Yesterday C.V. (Dr. Latimer, Sr.) and his friends had put on a final drive in Holy Lost Marsh in hopes of assisting Noah in bagging this elusive buck. But even with their combined energies, the enterprise proved unsuccessful. Apparently it didn't, however, put a damper on the delicious ham dinner the doctor put on at Camp Seward that night, complete with C.V.'s famous Cold River cocktails Noah always enjoyed sipping on.

During the evening campfire, I regaled the feat Phil McCalvin and I put ourselves through earlier in the season. In turn he filled me in on the latest adventures of Oscar Burguiere and his future plan to tote in two brand new cast iron boxstoves for the Town Hall and Hall of Records. Oscar wanted Noah to have these gifts before his anticipated move to "Lost Wages," Nevada in the next few years.

Before retiring that evening, Noah outlined the drive we would make tomorrow on the southern slope of Emmons Mountain. What was perfectly clear to me was that this skillful woodsman did not take lightly being given the slip as often as this buck had done. One final, properly executed drive might change the outcome of the story.

I had listened intently as Noah gave precise instructions, cataloging every detail, positive I could find the exact spot he described from which to begin the drive. In the morning, though, Noah wanted to review the plan before we continued any farther. It amazed me how much I had missed in the first telling. Although I had rehearsed the points in my mind as he spoke, I was thankful he wanted to go over the guide points; everything became more identifiable. Surely, the second telling is the mark of a true guide and Noah was one of the best. Noah's precise instructions helped my confidence in this vastness of forest. Shortly afterwards we reached what he called Seward Pond.

Crossing Ouluska Pass Brook, I surveyed the forest. I never tired of walking through that section of woodland. During the waning days of September, Noah and I had tramped over this exact route to reach Seward

Pond, a small unnamed bowl of water separated from Ouluska Pass Brook by a high ridge. I've long contended, as others have, that this private trout pond of Noah's was, in fact, the location of the fabled Lost Pond in the Seward Range so often reported and written about for over a hundred years. Noah said he, "had heard of such tales" but couldn't "verify them." However he was interested in reading the old magazine accounts I brought telling about Lost Pond.

During the perfect days of autumn, Mother Nature seemed to put extra effort into her annual display of forest colors. The mural she painted from her multi-colored easel made our fall walk to the pond seem more like an endless parade through ever-changing beauty. I felt so strongly about my association with this region of the Adirondacks, that it was often the sole thought that would bolster my morale during my army years when I served in Europe.

As I look back on those days before the Army, life was less demanding. I saw the Cold River wilderness as nothing less than a land of magic. The hues seemed so much brighter on the slopes of Seward than anywhere else in the valley. Noah's sensitivity toward the environment did not fall on deaf ears either. His interest in nature was contagious. From him I learned to take the time and gaze upon those beautiful scenes. "The crimson red of maples," I recall him saying he liked to imagine, "were modestly blushing as if embarrassed to even think they could forestall Old Man Winter."

Now, two months later as I stood in the same forest, naked of its beauty, the once many colored leaves, lay crisp and browning, products of several frosts. Now the leaves were more like a protective blanket draped over the roots of the trees from which they came, helping to insulate their feet from the cold winter that would soon be on them.

Arriving at the high slopes after an hour of steady climbing, I surveyed this stretch of forest for the landmark tree I was to start the drive from. For one fleeting second I thought I might be taxing my woodsmanship to its limitations. I didn't want to make a mistake and disappoint Noah. But then, right before me, I found the immense burl hugging the giant trunk of a stately old maple exactly where I was told it would be. I breathed easier. The trust my old woodsman friend had placed upon my abilities had just been bolstered.

I've often thought one of the main reasons people get mixed up and disoriented in the woods is that they underestimate distances. That, in turn, causes confusion and doubt, possibly leading to being lost. I've learned it is wise to add an extra half mile or additional minutes to the best of instructions.

Continuing beyond the burl by the sloping ledges, I reached an area of infant cedars and balsams growing amid a mature wood screen. This seemed hardly more than a pleasant morning's walk. A backward glance was immediately distracted by a glimpse of Seward Pond glistening like a silver ribbon, now and then shrouded in shadows cast by Panther Mountain brooding in shaggy elegance, as if it knew winter was not far away.

But back to the task at hand. Just beyond the ledges and clump of cedars and balsam, a tiny vly came into my vision. This was the exact spot where Noah cautioned the buck liked to bed down. The tiny green swamp, the moss as quiet as a thick carpet, allowed my progress over it to be noiseless—or so I thought. Stealthily I neared its center, silent as a shadow creeping across the ground. Then, all at once, I heard a crash ahead of me and caught a flash of a deer's white tail and a glint of sunlight reflecting off antlers, as the buck instantly bolted and quickly outdistanced himself from me.

Reaching the deer's bed I located his point of exit and continued on his track. Less than five minutes passed before I heard the dull authoritative roar of Noah's .35 Remington semiautomatic rifle in the distance. Then a moment of silence followed by a one shot salute, which Noah said he would perform. That signal told me the drive had been successful.

Following the route the buck took on his wild race down the range's lofty crags, I saw Noah rise from his task of cleaning the deer. A smile of success covered his happy face. He was definitely pleased with his ten-point buck that weighed, perhaps, 180 pounds. He was equally pleased I had followed his instructions exactly. He even went as far as to say he'd consider hiring my services again! That comment pleased me coming from such an accomplished woodsman and hunter.

Dragging the deer downhill was easy enough for both of us. We reached the Northville-Lake Placid Trail shortly after midday; from that point it was only a short drag up river before we reached a secret spot, near camp, where we hung the deer temporarily out of sight.

After a rest followed by some necessary chores, we "had to celebrate by preparing a meal fit for any mayor, or king," Noah gleefully announced. Following the main course of deer liver, bear steaks and "trimmings," we were reluctant to end such a perfect day with sleep, although we were both tired. Interspersed between the many stories and confabs, we enjoyed some quiet moments where we simply stared into the fire. I reflected silently during those times about all the experiences Noah had willingly given over the last six years. My original perspective might have contained a wee bit of hero-worship, but as I matured I came to view our friendship as that of teacher-student. Following my greatest achievement so far, of being invited to hunt with Noah, I realized that not only was I benefiting, but I was also a positive force for Noah. The old saying that teaching transforms not only the student, but also the teacher, was true. Certainly Noah's ego was bolstered.

After a short prelude of blowing blue smoke to the four winds from my standard pipe while Noah puffed on his enormous goose-egg Merchaum pipe, Noah announced that it was time for a very special occasion. Rummaging in a crevice near his bunk, he hauled out a large bottle of aged scotch left by friends years ago. I had seen other bottles of spirits left by friends or mountain climbers, many of whom were not teetotalers, but this bottle was different. He called it his Special Occasion bottle that was truly aged in the woods.

I knew the bottle held significance because Noah had a long strip of yellowed adhesive tape glued to opposite sides that extended from the base to the neck. Level lines and coded markings were penned indicating it had some history. I felt I was about to be inducted into a special inner circle.

In the wee hours of morning we finally retired, lulled to sleep by the flowing water of Cold River plunging over the spillway of Big Dam. Its magical powers blending into a symphony of musical softness, as we drifted into sound and restful sleep, deep in the wilderness.

The Trapper's Ghost

During my travels of this wilderness domain on trapline and trail, I often came upon ancient blaze marks on giant trees. As a woodsman, I scorned their maker, who had to blaze a trail to find his way about. The blaze marks often followed along brooks, and I surmised they were made by some long ago trapper with very little knowledge of woodcraft. As the years went by, however, I forgave him. I realized he was traveling in the days when this country was all virgin timber, before there were trails of any kind, and before the lumberman's axe had disturbed the solitude of this vast wilderness.

At every opportunity, I tried to locate his cabin, or its remains. For several years, I found evidence of those tell-tale blaze marks. Some were overgrown by age, but the visible marks were always at the same height on the tree and the same size, as if made by the same axe.

One day, I decided to explore to the northeast, along Roaring Brook. With some luck I might pick up the blazes. It was one of those rare fall days when the sun sends shafts of colored light through the autumn foliage, today it cast miniature rainbows on every ripple along the stream I had elected to follow. After several miles, the brook had greatly reduced its size from twenty odd feet to "jump across" size. Soon I came to a point where it forked, with crystal clear water running over polished stones that lined its bed.

I was undecided which of the brooks to follow, when I spotted a blaze on a gnarled old cedar. On closer examination, I found a clear, cold stream of water coming from beneath its roots. As I followed along its course, it often disappeared completely beneath the forest floor and, if not for its gleeful gurgling to keep me on course, I would have lost the stream altogether. On higher ground, it became more distinguishable. I can't begin to describe the excitement I felt as I stepped through a crack in a ledge that opened into a basin a half-acre in circumference, surrounded completely by ledges and cedar trees, several of which were dead and dry. Axe marks revealed that huge slabs of bark had been cut from them years ago, perhaps to construct a shelter. Hastily I went on and soon came to the remains of an age-old cabin. The roof had long since caved in, but the cedar logs were still marvelously sound.

The cabin's floor, made of split cedar, though mossed over and choked with dead leaves, was still sturdy. A half hour's work exposed it completely. In the center, where once stood a table, was a trap door. Upon opening it, I found a rocked-up spring, boiling with eternal vigor through pearl-white sand. I had found the camp of my friend, the Old Trapper!

Any doubt I ever had of his woods ability vanished. He had made the water available even in the coldest weather, when arctic winds sheathed all in ice. I made plans to restore the cabin. After several days, I had new rafters in place. On another trip, I brought in tar paper to replace the cedar bark roof. The stove, made of cast iron, was still usable. With a new stove pipe and a window, camp number two was established.

I found several dozen traps hanging in the hollow butt of a huge white pine. This indicated the time when the Old Trapper had made his camp there—sometime around 1840, I thought. The traps had been dyed in wood bark prior to the catch and were in excellent shape.

I used the cabin for several years, and it seemed I felt the presence of the Old Trapper on many occasions, guiding me on my many trips to the wilds. Once, in a blinding snowstorm, just when I was about to settle for a cold night's camp, but before starting my fire, I sensed the unmistakable smell of cedar smoke. Following it, I made my way to the cabin door, only to find the stove completely out, as I had left it that morning. But when I touched it, it was warm. My imagination? I wonder!

Eventually, I had to give up those precious years of forest life and return to the settlements to make a living. But before I left that little glen, I re-dyed the traps and hung them in the hollow pine.

When I reluctantly left that last time, I looked back at the cabin. It seemed that I saw in the doorway the ghost of the Old Trapper, waving his hand, with a look of approval on his weathered face.

Moon Flower

A long way back along my many trails in the infant days of the 1940's, I was packing a load of canned goods into my Duck Hole camp in preparation for the fall hunt. As the morning drifted into afternoon shadows, I crossed the last ridge above Roaring Brook. The weight in my packbasket seemed to be getting heavier with every step. What seemed feather-light at the start, felt heavy now.

I had a few more miles left to reach my cabin. At a bubbling spring on the crest of Paint Bed Notch, I began a mental game of promising myself a rest when I reached a certain part along the route. My next stop would be a rocky ravine overhung by huge ledges about a half hour distant. I especially looked forward to reaching that spot because it marked my approach to a long sloping valley above my cabin.

I was above the ravine on an approach ridge. As the top of the ridge leveled off, I rested my heavy pack on a log. Below me were a series of ledges that were not as visible from the bottom of the deep ravine. Peering over the top ledge, I saw slabs of jutting granite forming a stairway down to the flat grassy ledge below. Reaching the center ledge I looked up. The upper ledge extended a dozen feet over the flat ledge I was now standing on, making a roof of solid granite. In disbelief, I spied a small three-walled cabin with gray cedar logs butting up against the ledge wall, seemingly as old as the granite surrounding it. From the cabin came the pungent smell of cedar ashes, indicating a fire within. The small door was simple hand-split cedar slabs held together by crossbars fastened with wooden pegs. I rapped as I called hello, but no sound came from the interior. I opened the door slightly and could tell in the semi-darkness someone lived there. Two browse beds were along the side wall. A stone fireplace was built against the granite ledge and was directly in front of the door. A fissure in the rock wall allowed smoke to escape outside. On wooden pegs driven between the logs were various articles of clothing, some made of deerskin. A pair of moccasins in the last stage of manufacture lay on a stool by the fireplace.

Strips of venison were strung on a wire, between the narrow side walls, curing over the fireplace. I could easily reach my cabin in short order, but the aroma of the meat not only smelled good but tempted me to try a strip. I rekindled the fire and hung my tea pail to boil. With the fire built, I drew a loaf of bread from my basket and cut two slices. With the venison, bread and tea I had a regular picnic. After eating, I rearranged the meat strips slightly to fill in the space made by the one I had taken. Then, rummaging through my pack, I found a token for my gratitude to show proper respect for the woods hospitality.

After dousing the fire with a dipper of water, I hoisted my pack and was away, reaching my cabin by suppertime. Throughout the final leg of my tramp I mulled over just who was using the tiny makeshift camp. All indications pointed to the inhabitants being American Indians.

Several days following my stopover at the ledges, I had some visitors. While I was chopping wood a voice called from the forest, "Hello to the cabin." I put down my ax and said, "Come in," as I turned in the direction I thought the call came from. Then, sensing someone was behind me, I turned to find a man. His features clearly indicated he was Indian. Good naturedly he said, "It takes an Indian to sneak up on a white man."

I smiled. On first glance I liked him immediately. We exchanged names. He introduced himself as Running Fox, but I could also call him John. I told him mine and acknowledged I was positive his voice had come from the opposite direction. "Don't feel bad," he replied. "I have to confess I took unfair advantage of you." Upon saying this he gave a sharp whistle. An Indian girl around fifteen years old presented herself. She was dressed in a buckskin shirt, short skirt, and leggings. His daughter, Moon Flower, was an attractive teenager. Surely if flowers grew on the moon, she would have been the fairest of its gardens. She kept her eyes cast down in what I thought might be a shy gesture. For living out in the woods her black hair was neatly combed and braided.

Our forest encounter was friendly and causal. I told John I took the liberty of eating some of his jerked venison. He was pleased I had helped myself. He knew someone had been in the camp. "Had you counted the venison slices?" I asked.

"No," he replied. "You extinguished the fire with water which allows a small fire to smolder. The ashes insulated the few remaining hot coals. It's easy to rekindle a fire that way. All I needed was to do was blow on them until the embers were red hot, then add birch bark.

I shared with him the lesson I had learned when I chanced upon a fire that had spread from an open fireplace at my friend's camp. Noah was forever leaving a fire when he left to fish at Cold River or Seward Pond. Once, when coming into camp, I spotted a dry rotted interior log in the Pyramid of Giza wigwam, burning. The wind probably was the culprit, carrying a hot ember from the stone and sapling fireplace inside the log shelter to the surrounding combustible material. Because the log was standing upright it was like a stovepipe in the breeze. Noah used an old washtub to place over the fireplace for protection, but he was often forgetful about using it.

I figured another half hour and the whole winter supply of wood might have burned. Maybe even his cabins. While there was not much of value outside of his rifles, violin and so forth, he would have been wiped out of all of his worldly possessions, home and all. I purposely placed the charred log in the clearing so Noah would see it when he returned. I thought he would realize how close he had come to losing everything. Did it scare him? No, not a bit! He thanked me for putting the fire out and told how much he would have lost. He even shared a bit of wisdom, saying fire is a fine servant but it can also be a hard master. But he never changed his habit of leaving an open fire unattended. On the other hand I learned a lesson well. Never did I want to take a chance of losing my things nor run the risk of causing a disastrous forest fire.

From our brief meeting, John learned of my interest in hunting and trapping. I had assumed he was here for the hunting season, but I learned that was not the case. John was a school teacher in his village in Canada. He taught French and English as well as his tribe's native language. He had a personal interest learning the stories he heard from elder tribesmen. One of those stories he had heard from his grandfather. The story turned to how he first came to this land.

We made plans to meet at John's camp when I headed home later that week. He would tell me more at that meeting. For two days I mulled over what John's purpose was. Mysteries seldom arose in Duck Hole country and I was curious. I also looked forward to seeing Moon Flower again. She was not too much younger than I, and I thought she was beautiful.

John must have thought enough of my woodsmanship for he asked if I might be able to help him with the lay of the land. His grandfather, once the chief of his tribe, had hunted and trapped this territory as a youngster in the company of several adults. On the hunting party's last trip they had left a ceremonial bell that had something to do with tribal boundaries. When his grandfather grew to adulthood, the story of the bell was one he often told. Now an aging man, his grandfather wanted John to retrieve the bell. When the decision was made to move the tribe from their long-standing home to a new location, finding the bell became a paramount issue because it was to be used in the ceremony of breaking camp.

The ceremonious bell had been placed on a rock ledge above a pond about 1860. John had not located it yet and was feeling some pressure. Time was running out before snow arrived. I offered my assistance which he gladly accepted. I warned him that by now it could have been found by lumbermen, destroyed by natural causes, or moved by the ravages of time. He agreed those possibilities existed but held out hope for its retrieval.

Working with the original description of the pond, I suggested he narrow the search area to west of Moose Pond, concentrating on a pond in the Sawtooths that had returned to more of a bog. Many generations of beavers had changed the characteristics of the surrounding landscape, but according to the legend he had told me, steep ledges were in the vicinity.

In return for my aid, John volunteered Moon Flower's and his assistance in transporting the remainder of my cache up to Moose Pond outlet.

The next day we climbed up high to the source of a tributary that drained into the Moose Pond outlet and skirted the boggy shoreline, looking for a large boulder that was supposed to have a carving that would point to the direction of the bell. Not finding the large stone, we fanned out farther from the shoreline as we circled the old pond. After many hours, John found a large boulder well hidden in a thick growth of black spruce. On the surface was scratched a faint marking. Closer inspection revealed it was the sign made by the men his grandfather had accompanied. It took another two hours of our combined efforts to locate the ledge of rock where the bell was supposed to have been hidden.

Finally, with John's sharp eyes and his memory for details, he located it in a weather-tight crack in the ledge and drew forth a small bundle bound in ancient white birch bark tied with now-brittle spruce roots. The bundle was sealed with melted spruce gum. Handling it carefully, he placed it safely in his packbasket. We were all extremely anxious to open it, but John wanted to wait and unwrap the fragile package back at his camp.

Pausing before he removed the layers, John offered a silent reverence. His grandfather would be so pleased. Each layer of the small package was carefully removed until the bell was revealed inside an inner parcel of old cracked leather. It seemed well preserved and had ancient Indian signs engraved on its surface, many of which John could not decipher. But he easily identified a small sign that his grandfather had made. John was overcome with joy, and he had every reason to be proud of this seemingly impossible accomplishment after almost eighty years. The bell was a part of his tribe's history.

That evening, around a fire, John conducted a solemn ceremony thanking the Spirits. As part of that ritual he gave me an Indian name that in translation meant "man who knows the forest." I felt very honored.

The following day my friends helped me transport my remaining supplies to Duck Hole and stayed the night. I cooked dinner. Moon Flower seemed interested in the small stove top oven I baked sourdough biscuits and potatoes in. The small heat indicator located in the door never failed to steam over on the outside. I gave her the job of wiping the condensation away with a cloth so the rising dial could be watched. The breadstuffs were a perfect complement to our supper for we had packed jars of jams and jellies that day. The sweetness tasted especially good back there in the woods.

The following day before my friends parted, Moon Flower said she had left a gift for me by the spring, but I would not find it until evening. John told me earlier how much his daughter enjoyed hunting small game so, before they left, I presented her with my old .25-.35 Winchester carbine. It was a very light rifle, great for small game, but underpowered for deer and bear. I laced a hawk feather on it and told her with practice she would become an excellent markswoman. Expressing their thanks, John commented the rifle was a fine gift. He knew how much it meant to his daughter.

With packbasket shouldered, Moon Flower addressed me in the familiar way she had previously. It sounded like "asme-na-ista." When I first heard her say it, her father grinned and told me it was a word of respect, and she would tell me what it meant before they departed. Before they began their trip she told me she was saying "fire-beard." I realized then my beard and hair must surely have seemed as red as firelight. I liked the name. As I said my farewells, I told them I would always value our meeting.

We never met again but I often thought of them. Moon Flower had placed a mindful gift of fluorescent wood called "fox fire" near my springhole. In the pitch dark it emitted a greenish glow. For years as I neared the Duck Hole cabin, I would catch a whisper of scent, a combination of cedar oil, balsam and sweet grass roots in the softly rustling breeze. The woodsy smell would remind me of Running Fox and Moon Flower. I even imagined they would come with the twilight shadows and sit by my fire. They were never to be forgotten. And now, years later, I will confess I was a bit smitten over Moon Flower.

My final contact with them was a package I received in the mail. It contained a pair of beaded moccasins, a neatly wrapped and bound birch bark package containing strips of dried venison, and an empty box of .25-35 cartridges. John wrote that his daughter was going to be married to the son of his oldest friend and that they had established new tribal hunting grounds in the far north of Canada. He closed by saying: "May the Spirit of the wilderness always be with you."

In the Woods With Noah

Tramping through the rustling leaves in a forest now bleak and barren of green, I could hardly contain my joy and excitement, for not only was I back in the wilds of the Seward and Santanoni Mountain ranges that I loved so well, but I was about to embark on another deer hunt with my friend Noah Rondeau.

We started early on a dogtrot that lead into the forest behind Noah's city. It was the same route I had taken when I hiked to Seward Pond. Accustomed to noticing incongruent forest features with my experienced eye, I noted faint clues revealing that the twisting pathway we followed was once a tote trail. Long ago, large draft horses skidded jumpers loaded with logs chained together, cut from the surrounding slopes. Lanterns, set on poles along the icy snow road, illuminated the way for the teamsters. Road monkeys kept a fire going and slowed the descent of the metal runners on the steeper downhill runs. All winter they piled logs on the frozen Cold River Flow in preparation for spring thaw, when they would be released to wash downstream to where the Cold River joins the Raquette. Log drivers followed the logs all the way to the mill.

Seedlings were becoming established in sections of the old roadbed that received goodly amounts of sunlight. In the years to follow, I knew they would grow so close they would clog the way, as they already had across the river. Former sections of the maze of abandoned logging roads that radiated from the bygone Bradley Pond logging camp into the wilderness, below the towering peaks of Couchsachraga and Panther, were now too difficult to follow. Noah once relied on these roadways in the early nineteen twenties when he ran out his longest traplines. Too often a wall of needles was impenetrable, making tracing the old pathways fruitless.

As we skirted down a gradually descending slope, I spotted some large boulders in the distance and recognized those landmarks as the location of the hermit's Mammoth Graveyard. This was a term he used to describe the hiding place where a few galvanized garbage cans, scavenged from a disbanded Civilian Conservation Corps camp, were kept. It was a secretive spot known only to Noah's close friends, and the place where he and several hunters stashed valuables. Noah also used the weather-tight cans for safeguarding a number of personal articles whenever he left Cold River City for any length of time.

Arriving at Ouluska Pass Brook, I asked Noah about the trail we had followed. "I've taught you well, Richard," he replied. Crossing the stream, he turned and pointed out the route the trail formally took, north along the east bank. "The fishing Cauldron, you recall, is upstream about a quarter mile, near the old tote trail that winds over to Boulder Brook. Just beyond it, on the right side of the bank, opposite a small drainage from the lower slopes of Mount Emmons, is the site of an old wood choppers camp where my anvil came from."

During my earliest visits, I had noted the large, black iron anvil that stood outside the Town Hall, but never gave it much thought. I had assumed it was just another remnant from the Big Dam logging camp, the site Noah occupied. Much to my surprise, I later learned that if the anvil could talk it could have told quite a story about Oscar Burguiere. Noah befriended Oscar and together they skidded that anvil, over several years, down the mountainside and into camp. "We had a blessed time," was all Noah said laughing. *[Noah noted in his journal that on Sunday, November 27, 1939 the iron anvil finally reached Cold River Hill.]*

Eventually I met Oscar and came to realize why he accepted such a Herculean task. Oscar was a young cook for a group of hunters Noah named the Highbank Gang. In the early 1920s Noah had a running feud with the gang over territorial rights. The vendetta grew to where serious threats were hurled; Noah eventually emerged the victor. During a few armed, surprise visits to their camp downriver, he met Oscar. Oscar was harmless, honest and impressionable, not like the men he worked for. All Oscar ever wanted to do was to be a woodsman, a skill he never learned (according to Noah). Noah liked his sincerity, but never failed to tell countless tales about poor Oscar.

Paths From the Past

It seems fitting that I write a bit about the huge lumbering operation that went on for many years at the turn of the century in Cold River. Much has been written about the millions of board feet of logs that ended up in those mills, but little of the struggles of the hundreds of men that cut, hauled and drove the logs to their final destination.

I spent many years hunting the country around the big dam on Cold River where the Hermit of Cold River lived the greater part of his life. The lumbering had ceased for nearly fifty years, but the corduroy roads, the dams, the bridges and the lumber camps were still in evidence. Noah and I often walked those roads, nearly always a foolproof way of getting deer, as they too used the roads and lumber camp clearings for both travel and food. There were hundreds of miles of these roads, still well preserved—a fitting tribute to the skilled men who had built them.

One bridge, which spanned a deep ravine, was a masterpiece of construction. Built of huge cedar logs, this bridge was over eighty feet long and its center rose to a height of fifty feet. It seemed unbelievable that this huge quantity of cedar could be harvested to build such a structure when one considers the thousands of logs also used for other construction. Endless miles of roads were corduroyed, flood dams and log cabins were built that housed the hundreds of men and teams of horses that were employed in these great projects. But we must remember this was virgin timber country.

The bridge itself was a thing of awe as it was made with only a few simple tools and ingenious fastenings made by the blacksmith's forge. Each log was fitted with mortise and tendon joints. Each end, squared with cross cut saw and ax, fitted precisely into a mortise fashioned with large hand augers and chisels. These joints were so true in construction, so tightly fitted that I wondered why wooden crosspegs and iron spikes were needed.

The center of the bridge was several feet higher than the ends, which checked the momentum of the heavily loaded log sleighs as they came down the approach incline onto the bridge; once over the center crest of the bridge, the momentum of the sled increased sufficiently to climb the incline at the far end. This center rise also kept the horses from prancing as they couldn't see the whole span of the bridge.

Of the hundreds of log crossings on that bridge, only one sleigh had a mishap. The twisted wreck remains at the bottom of the gorge. Noah, who had worked at the Big Dam, recalled that the accident had been caused by a broken triple draw bar, which secures the horses to the sled's tongue. When the bar snapped, the horses ran clear across the bridge with the teamster sliding along the iced road bed in a ski jumping stance. The sled leaped the safety log and crashed to the rocky bottom of the gorge. The teamster continued on to Big Dam, picked up another sled and returned for another load, as if it were all in a day's work. The bridge was then named: "Near Calamity Bridge."

I well remember the first time I crossed that bridge, as I was going up the road to fish Seward Brook with Noah. The bridge was then nearly fifty years old, and though cedar is a hardy, long lasting wood, the corduroy top logs were moss covered and small balsam and spruce had taken root, thus making a moisture trap that had caused some of the cross logs to contract wet rot. As Noah approached the center of the bridge, a log under his foot broke and noisily crashed through the structure amid shattering bark and dust. There seemed to be no hesitation in Noah's stride, only a nimble skip and a fluid jump to the next log. With not as much as a backward glance, he continued to the other side of the span. When I overtook him, I asked if he wasn't "just a little worried" when the log broke beneath his foot. With that old familiar twinkle in his eye he replied, "Not at all. I was worried more about the next one!" It seemed the bridge was well named.

High in the Seward Range the log road became quite steep, and I thought surely loaded sleds couldn't navigate on such an incline. Then we came upon a simple, yet ingenious setup that allowed the sleds to cope with the steep mountainside. A double incline plane was positioned on either side of the road. Here the teamster unhooked the rear sled and continued on with the front until the team could no longer climb. We found a cable with a rusted hook. Two miles later we found a drum winch run by horse power. It all became clear to me. The cable was hooked to the tongue of the sled and all was pulled up by the winch. The logs were then loaded on the front sled bunk, a chain secured the dragging ends and again the winch cable was played out until the sled reached the back sled that had been left at the base of the incline. A log was then chained so as to roll and slide up the incline until the back sled could be slid under, refastened, and as the log rolled down the opposite incline, it positioned the dragging back logs onto the rear sled bunk, which was then chained. The teamster settled down the task of the long downhill ride to Big Dam.

These roads were always kept in tiptop shape. Each new snowfall was packed by a huge water roller, pulled by a span of several teams of horses. I have no idea how much this roller weighed when filled, but it must have been heavy, as it was ten feet wide and as many feet high with a seat for the teamster. On the steeper inclines the roller was hauled up empty, filled with brook water and then rolled down the mountain road. After the snow was packed, a water sleigh would wet it down and it quickly froze to a concrete-hard surface. This was usually done very early in the morning so the day's log hauling could begin at daylight. Some roads were lit by lanterns at the more difficult points. The bridge had several lamp posts that had guided the sleighs across. Perhaps on a moonlight night there was also much activity on the roads. At one lumber camp I found an old sled tongue that supported two hooded lanterns and a reflecting bullseye, a device which sent the lantern rays far ahead.

Harvesting the logs was certainly hard, cold work, but I imagine it must have been a lot of fun too. The lumber camps themselves must have been beehives of activity. The sounds of the blacksmith's anvil making horseshoes, plates, spikes, and sled runners mingled with the talk and laughter of the woods gangs. The ever-present smells of cooking and baking attended the coming and going of hungry loggers.

How different it is today with giant bulldozers gouging out tote roads and chainsaws clean cutting the trees. Modern day lumbering has taken all the romance out of the industry. The demands of the ever-increasing world population, driven at breakneck speed, have resulted in the strip and slash method of lumbering, which in turn has turned our woodlands into denuded wastelands.

I am grateful I was able to walk those old roads with Noah, reminiscing about the old days when the pace of life was slow and easy. Like the lumberjacks of the past, I took the time to sit on a felled log, light up a fresh pipe of fragrant tobacco, talk of days gone by, and dream.

Writing about the road rollers brings to mind the time I found one not far from the trail down from Moose Pond. Amazingly, it was in good condition, but it was covered with a layer of moss which had caused some surface rot. Using levers, rope, block and tackle I spent half a day standing it on end. I cut a door in with a crosscut saw and lugged a cast iron boxstove from an old nearby lumber camp that was locally known as the "Blacksmith Shop." Once I installed the stove and added some refinements I had a fairly decent camp but seldom used it other than for an overnight stop on my way to Duck Hole. I only wish it were not so close to the public trail. It did give me a base from which to learn the surrounding country, and soon I found a shorter route through Paint Bed Notch.

The last time I traveled over that route I could hardly locate my trail. I recall there were plenty of bear signs. The camp, too, had rotted away leaving only the stove to mark the location. At its center, the floor space had spanned eight and a half feet. My interim camp must have been one of the smaller snowrollers. According to Noah, some towered twelve feet above the teams.

Lonesome Jim Meets Sourdough Smith

Emerging from my blankets that cold winter morning was not the easiest thing I had ever done in my life of backwoods travel. I had spent a warm, comfortable night in the brush lean-to I had hastily constructed against a large granite boulder, a short distance off the Northville-Lake

Placid Trail, a few miles in from the Averyville trailhead. I had just finished the last of my wood cutting jobs and was eager to leave the rows of neat cordwood in Lake Placid for my cabin and Noah's hermitage in the wild lands of the Duck Hole-Cold River territory.

I generally confined my early and midwinter wanderings to around the Chubb River, Moose Pond and the Moose Pond Outlet near my snowroller camp at Paint Bed Notch. So it was a special pleasure to travel as far as my cabin at the Duck Hole and down to Rondeau's at Big Dam.

I was soon laying down new snowshoe tracks on a fresh blanket of snow. A whisper of a southern breeze warmed snow laden small spruce and balsam trees along the trail. The trees were springing back in shape as if flexing their arms in morning exercise following their awakening from a long sleep. A new fresh smell came from the surrounding forest bringing a promise of an early spring. But this warming trend was softening the snow and causing some annoying ice clogs to pack between the webbing on my snowshoes and the bottom of my boots.

Typically I allowed myself at least two weeks of leisure prior to March trapping. During midwinter snow is intermittently falling, making snowshoe traveling a difficult matter when pulling a loaded snowboat of supplies. The snow cover in the latter part of February is usually frozen sufficiently to hold the weight of medium size fur-bearers and is ideal for snowshoeing.

I picked up, from old-time trappers, that the best means of learning an animal's habits is to follow its trails in the snow, observing every action and reason for such action by the trail "signs" the animal leaves. A trapper improves his skill in direct proportion to his keen observation. It has been written that there is "romance, adventure, humor, suspense, drama, character traits and all other 'story qualities' in an animal's trail." Small wonder that I felt my observations along the trapline seemed to parallel stories by my favorite author, Edgar Allen Poe.

At this time of the year my method of trapping depended on getting out lines of skillfully camouflaged blind sets, although I didn't completely abandon maintaining a few bait sets. Muskrat, raccoon, skunk, fox, mink, and nearly all other fur bearers start moving about with renewed energy in February. A time when they are instinctively less cautious.

Hibernating raccoons come out during warm spells and run the streams with mink. The fox and white weasel travel all winter. The weasel being the easiest to trap, usually with part of a rabbit carcass. Fox trapping on snow is an art few understand.

Skunks also can be trapped all winter, and a skunk carcass placed just outside a den hole is the best bait in the world to catch a skunk. Muskrats live in hollow logs on the banks, in bank burrows, or in any kind of nest possible on higher ground. Trapping marsh rats present more of a problem, so I avoided them. During bad weather fisher hang around rock bluffs where porcupines live; it is the only animal that feeds on the quill pig regularly.

Noah described to me how the fisher, an animal the size of a house cat, scents a "pig." It first walks out in front of the porcupine. When the "pig" sees danger it curls up into a ball with nothing but quills showing. The fisher, knowing his business, crouches low with every muscle tense. A waiting game ensues. After a considerable time the porcupine, believing he is safe, starts to uncurl. With a lightning quick spring the fisher pierces the "pig's" throat with his needle-like teeth, at the same time ripping the under part of the "pig" which is not covered with quills.

The otter, unlike the fisher, travels both the hills and the far back country. It follows streams and is capable of covering a dozen miles in a single night. He's a playful fellow. Noah has followed, out of curiosity, an otter's tracks as it has climbed the southern slopes of Seward's Mountain when there is snow on the ground, and then has seen it double its short front legs under him and slide back down the slope.

And, everywhere there were signs of beaver. There is scarcely a stream to be seen without a family of those busybodies living in it.

Mink are particularly easy to catch in a blind set, as they dive into every hole or den, run through hollow logs and under bridges. I remember Noah telling me that after the streams freeze over and snow piles up, he would look for mink signs under ice and snow. They frequent log jams, bridges, dams, rock piles, and old muskrat houses. They congregate, sometimes in great numbers, around big dams, or places where the fishing is good. Noah said that E.J. Dailey had boasted he had caught seventeen mink on Cold River at one place in 1919. By coincidence they were taken in one set under the debris of the dilapidated horse barn a short distance from the "Big Dam" camp where Noah eventually set up housekeeping. For thirty years prior to 1919, the country had been lumbered over extensively. Evidently every mink that went up or down that river, even under the ice, would nose around decaying logs of man-made structures.

When scents were effective, their worth was proven. Most scents for spring use contained animal musk, urine or the reproductive organs of the female. I also remember Noah saying that when he began trapping in this country that poisoning was still carried on to some extent. Some trapper's attitudes were: "Catching comes before hanging." Some bold outlaws even boasted of outwitting the game protectors. Little did they realize they were the actual losers every time an infraction of the game laws was committed. The honest trappers and hunters knew, as the wise farmer did, that "some seed must be saved if there is to be a crop the following year."

While my mind was on the great number of fur-bearers that roamed this part of the Adirondacks, I also knew that it wasn't just getting back to my old haunts around the Hole that was motivating me as I blazed a snow-trail along Moose Creek Outlet. Another prime factor in going was my desire to see Noah.

The weather became increasingly mild as the day progressed. Had I worn a coat, I would have overheated pulling the toboggan behind me. I switched to the shadier side of the creek. As I neared Boulder Brook, which drained the southside of the Sawtooth Range, I started to anticipate a well deserved rest. I planned to put up for the night in one of the Cold River lean-to's built at the former site of the CCC spike camp. It wouldn't have been practical to veer off my route and travel extra miles just to stay at my cabin. The snow had deteriorated to a point that my snowshoes were sinking into rotting snow four to six inches deep. My legs were becoming tired lifting wooden snowshoes so high out of the snow; the heavy pack I also carried added to my burden.

Where the brook enters the outlet stream, I came upon a fresh set of bear paw snowshoe prints. Compared to my 12" X 60" webs, the maker of this trail was sinking in at least a foot. Every so often the imprint of a packbasket marked where the traveler had taken it off. The rest stops seemed too frequent. I figured whoever was leaving these signs had to be tired, yet young and green to endure such punishment.

The Cold River lean-to's were not farther than three miles away. I usually left the water course at this point, but decided I would follow the trail a while, possibly sighting who was spoiling my snow.

Long before I reached the lean-to's, I caught the smell of charred wood and a strange odor not completely unlike wood, but thick as fog. My first thoughts were of a burned lean-to, but I also didn't relish the thought that someone else might be trapping in my territory.

As I neared the lean-to, I smelled a sickly smudge and caught the sight of a gray cloud spreading through the needles of the evergreens. As I came into view he caught sight of me and hailed a greeting. I called back a question. "Have you seen an elephant go by?" as his bear paw pug marks had resembled.

"Sorry mister, but the trail you were following was not that of an elephant, but rather one of a jackass!" he responded with a good-natured laugh. "And if you are still not convinced have a closer look at my ears."

I drew from his initial response a curiosity; he seemed as if he would be an amicable sort. After removing my pack and snowshoes, I took a longer look at the feeble, sputtering campfire he had made out of green balsam logs. It was filling my beloved forest with billowing smoke that choked my lungs each time the breeze shifted.

I surmised that he didn't know the first thing about taking care of himself in the woods or how to be a trapper. However, he was likable and the reality of the situation was that I did not feel up to pushing the remaining miles down to Big Dam that day.

I suggested we gather ample firewood while we had the opportunity and ease of daylight. Armed with axes we donned snowshoes and broke a trail to a dry maple and a tall, hollow dry cedar stump. Within a short time we had an overnight supply of burnable wood.

Back at the lean-to a blazing fire soon shed a warming glow about the interior of the horizontal log walls, driving away the cool gloomy shadows of early evening. Taking a coffee break, my new acquaintance told me that he had selected his bear paw snowshoes from an outfitter in Tupper Lake who had informed him that style was the favorite of wilderness trappers. But he had quickly learned that carrying a heavy packbasket required larger shoes to distribute the weight. He told me he was a first time, would-be beaver trapper, which became more obvious when he proudly unwrapped four different skinning knives recommended by each of the authors of four how-to books on trapping. If that wasn't enough, he admitted he'd never even been out with anyone on a trapline.

I tactfully explained that books would not give him much specific information, possibly just enough knowledge to make an experienced trapper laugh. And as for his traps—they were too small to hold a beaver. To him I might have appeared to be kin to Daniel Boone with my fur hat, made with fisher and pine martin, complete with teeth and claws dangling as ornaments.

Probably feeling a mite conspicuous about his shortcomings, he invited me to join him for supper, offering to cook while I gave him some pointers. I agreed, assuming his greatest ability might be in cooking, but it became apparent that he was far more inexperienced and naive than I had originally thought. He pulled a container of rice down from the wooden shelf. He had salvaged it from a temporary lean-to farther up the Ward Brook trail, apparently a surplus amount left behind, he assumed, by last fall's hunters.

He said he had eaten some last night. He held some notion that as a true woodsman he was somehow living off the land. However, he pointed out that the grocer had incorrectly filled the container with a great deal of unprocessed rice, mixed with the normal white kernels. That error didn't cause any great change in flavor, since he hadn't minded how it had tasted. I didn't have the heart to tell him that rice was not naturally black. I did, however, strongly hint that he should keep all food in covered containers. It was all obvious to me that knaw-it-run-a-bouts were responsible for the so-called "discolored" rice. I promptly found an excuse to prepare my own supper. Not wanting to make him feel extremely embarrassed, I remained tight lipped about his rice.

Later that evening I showed him one of my #4 Blake & Lamb beaver traps which was the largest legal trap at that time. After an evening of "shop talk" he wanted to throw his twenty-five dollars worth of books into the fire, but I convinced him to keep them to look at whenever he was in the need of a good laugh. He could call them his "Wilderness Joke Books." Extending to him an offer of help, I explained that I would be traveling downstream on personal business in the morning but that upon my return in a couple of days, he was welcome to accompany me to my cabin. Once there not only would he be more comfortable, but I would also be willing to instruct him in the rudimentary art of trapping.

Anyone who has ever camped in a trailside, state lean-to can readily appreciate the rustic lodgings were not meant for winter comfort, especially when the temperatures would lurk below zero. Warmth would be little problem today with the highly insulated down and synthetic fibers, but at that time wool blankets and makeshift bags were the most readily available as well as affordable.

Before continuing on my trek to Noah's that morning, I gave him several instructions. One was to fashion tails for his snowshoes, filling the open space and lashing them on with extra rawhide I carried. I also carried a small can of spar varnish, brush, and brush cleaner. After drying the rawhide I directed him to apply a coat of varnish all over. Once out on the snow, he would find this refinement would improve the performance of his webs. I also pointed out to him that he should build a windbreak of snow around the front of the lean-to beyond the fireplace, using a combination of spruce boughs and snow, and using his snowshoe as a shovel to scoop and pack the snow. Not only would he be gaining wood-craft knowledge, but he would also find enjoyment from the ever chang-ing musical sounds that would drift through the needles. He should also experiment with a deeper, springier browse bed and place balsam under his pillow. The aroma was enticing and would encourage a sounder sleep.

I never went empty-handed to Noah's hermitage. Once in awhile Noah would specifically ask me to pick up an item. As a rule of thumb, I always brought some kind of food and Victor mousetraps. Neither one of us had very much and weren't in a position to do much for each other than provide companionship. The least I could do for all he gave me in friend-ship was to liven up his daily menu of "Everlasting Stew" which seemed to be his main fare in the dead of winter. Deer and bear meat laced with barley, beans, dehydrated carrots, potatoes and other vegetables seem to offer "a good start on an old man's lunch" as he would say in thanks. Always of course followed by, "Hard Times, Richard. Hard Times in Cold River." Then he'd laugh and give a little jig step.

Returning from Rondeau's, I found my words of encouragement were "cheer-up's" to my new acquaintance. His sense of self was restored upon successfully completing the tasks I had laid out for him.

We were of nearly the same age and got along splendidly. He was quick to smile and laughed easily. As I made sour dough pancakes every morning he began calling me "Sourdough Smith." I named my apt pupil "Lonesome Jim" because I found him out alone. We really had a great time making the rounds over my beaver trapping grounds that season. When showing him the fine art of spreading the powerful jaws of the beaver trap as they were placed across the tails of my snowshoes, he watched with rapt attention. He hardly blinked an eye or missed a verbal instruction.

After watching the process several times, he wanted a try at it. It was tricky at first for him to get the feel of bending over, reaching backward between his legs, grasping the jaws and forcing the trap over and then, once in a flat position, hooking the pan's retaining trigger. The move was tricky and called for exceptional balance, but it was the only way of doing it. Mastery eventually came, but not before he lost his balance and tum-bled headlong into the snow a number of times. He looked so comical, blowing snow with the behavior of a surfacing seal. The antics of his frustrations were funny each time I helped him back to a standing posi-tion. Eventually he became the official trap setter.

Under-the-ice sets with landing platform and drown pole, the use of beaver lure, the skinning and preparing of pelts, all fascinated him. They were all first time things he devoured as I had once done when taught by my old friend Noah.

How quickly the days passed. We caught eight beaver, two less than the legal limit. But if we had had no luck at all, we would have been content just enjoying the out-of-doors. It had been a wonderful wilderness adventure for him. Jim learned much about survival and how to be comfortable in the wilds. He learned quickly why I did all the noisy preparations such as chopping and hammering way beyond ear shot of the ponds. He would never have considered the noise would scare the beaver, keeping them in their lodges for days. He especially appreciated all the shortcuts I volunteered and being shown how to construct drown sets.

We made some money. But more valuable than the dollars was the friendship made by chance in the wilderness. We promised to keep in touch. Later that year he moved away. I didn't hear from him until years later when a letter arrived from far off Alaska. He hadn't forgotten me or his first trapping experience after all. After moving to Alaska he had married and had a "house full of children." Through many years of occasional correspondence he sent photographs and stories of his adventures. He had grown to be an accomplished hunter-trapper. The impression I got, though, was that while possessing a lot of nerve he took too many unnecessary chances.

I never got the particulars, but learned from his wife he let his guard down once too often and was stomped by an enraged moose. Along with the fateful letter announcing his death were included the four "Wilderness Joke Books" and a personal inscription to me. It was saddening to hear he had not heeded my warnings to never trust any wild animal no matter how "tame" it appeared. Maybe he wanted it that way, I don't know.

Hunger: A Valuable Teaching Tool

I spent my first winter in a makeshift cabin above the Upper Chubb River. I ran short on shekels and was forced to eat primarily rabbit all winter. I shot eighty-five of them and ate eighty. I tried them in every conceivable way. I boiled, broiled, fried, stewed, braised and baked the meat even coming up with a tasty enough recipe for rabbit pie. I also substituted muskrat, beaver, porcupine, coon, and fox meat—victuals others might have bypassed, choosing to starve to death instead. I didn't like fox. I tried eating it camouflaged in a thick burnt flour broth, but I just couldn't get the tiniest morsel to stay down.

Noah was amused hearing me tell of my predicament. He matter of factly asked whether I had noticed any peculiar tracks on the runways, made by a man hopping on snowshoes. Clever of him to think I might just have developed a hopping gait by the close of the season.

My first experience of being hungry in the wildlands was not my last. Some lessons were hard won.

Poverty Casserole

While living in the winter wilderness of the Adirondacks, most of my errors in judgment revolved around underestimating my appetite and overestimating the lasting qualities of the supplies I had packed in to camp. One year I packed in a sack of potatoes to offset my bland routine. They were a wonderful addition; I didn't even let the parings go to waste. I mounded them on a large flat rock outside my window and enjoyed watching the birds and mammals feast. The weight of the potatoes, however, prevented me from making a habit of including a lot of them.

During the March beaver trapping season the temperature seldom rose above zero at midday. Regardless of the cold, I ran my trapline every day. I often envied bears, raccoons and other "hiber-natives" asleep in their warm dens. Arriving back to camp I was always hungry. When my basic staples of sugar, tea, coffee. powdered milk, cornmeal, flour and baking powder were alarmingly low, I tried creating emergency dishes. Admittedly my creations were feeble, but by then anything would do.

I generally had plenty of cornmeal on hand because it was the least expensive item. It served as a substitute for flour. The chef in me discovered the yellow meal could take on many forms such as cornbread, pudding and porridge. I even fried slabs of cold cornmeal. But a steady diet of cornmeal in any form quickly looses its appeal.

Following a snowfall that kept me cabin bound, and noticing the E of empty on my cabin shelves, I began to stretch what remained, experimenting with what I came to call Poverty Casserole. It turned out to be my favorite dish!

The casserole consisted of anything considered edible—within reason. In a deep pan lined with jellied cornmeal mush, I added layers of wild meat and whatever scraps I had around: rabbit, beaver, grouse, squirrel. To those layers I added a thin spreading of sourdough pancake batter. I even added the potato parings that I removed from the frozen pile the animals had not eaten. To that I sprinkled raisins and beechnuts. That concoction was baked until golden brown. It turned out to be a backwoods delicacy. I often ate it along the trapline and found my casserole served as an energy booster that was guaranteed to quicken my pace on snowshoes.

Although I liked it, after eating Poverty Casserole repeatedly for many days, my taste buds would get saturated with the flavor even after I sparingly poured maple syrup on it. One year, when the beaver decided to stick close to home during the later half of the trapping season, I found myself with no meat in store. I was tired of the monotony of the same feeds, so I decided a change was in order. Desperate for a taste of meat, I attempted to dredge up a mess of hibernating frogs in a bog near Duck Hole. Certainly the legs would add variety.

Life wasn't easy in the woods. All I had to do to put my circumstances in perspective was to think of my friend Noah. How did he manage to get food when he stayed year round in the wilderness?

Managing your food took planning, I know. Yet, after many years of practice, Noah figured it all out. He earned a hundred dollars trapping with which he used to buy dry staples: beans, lentils, barley, rice, sugar, flour, coffee and the like. If his budget allowed, he would also buy sweeteners like honey, corn syrup, condensed milk and a few other bulk items. The heavier supplies would be carried in by his ranger friend from Long Lake to Big Horn camp located at Shattuck Clearing. From there he only had a seven-mile carry to the hermitage.

On several occasions I had gone with him to pack in loads, and he had mentioned that other friends, especially Oscar Burguiere, often helped him bring his winter supplies upriver when they came to hunt during the fall. Oscar was so enthusiastic that he never flinched carrying heavy packboards of canned goods. Doctor Latimer and the men who hunted with him at Camp Seward, near the High Banks, helped immensely—not only by bringing food, but also by providing money for clothing and other needed equipment.

Combined with his annual deer, rabbits, raccoons, normally a bear and at time porcupines, he got along just fine until the lean months of March and April. All things considered, Noah fared well.

By 1938 Noah didn't always stay at his hermitage throughout the entire winter. But one of the years he did, I remember deciding to pay him a "beggars" visit. I presented him with an offering of beaver meat and hinted that anything he could spare would be much appreciated and the favor returned. I knew that by this time he too would be running low and would be glad to receive the meat. I only hoped he would have something to break the monotony of my Poverty Casserole.

Before I left he placed a rather large package in my pack. The contents were hidden, wrapped in newspaper, and I didn't want to ask as if I were picky. I envisioned bean soup and baked beans on my way back, but when I unwrapped the package at my cabin, my chin dropped to my boot tops, for there in my hands was a five pound package of cornmeal!

In advance of the close of the beaver trapping season, I was soon tramping along the trail toward Averyville and civilization. Once back in the world of conveniences, I sold my pelts and made a beeline to the grocery.

Following a few days of rest I was back at Noah's with a package of repayment for his borrowed food. I figured large bags of flour and beans would hold him until fishing season. Then between the trout, his remaining root crops and the fresh food his fishing friends would be depositing, he'd be in fine order.

Lost Youth Ridges

The fall hunt had been successful for both Noah and me. I had a 9-point buck hanging at the Duck Hole, and Noah had killed a bear a few days prior to my visit. During my visit we worked together on a drive and Noah killed another buck, a large 10-pointer, hanging it in the "Butcher Shop" wigwam. Nineteen forty-three was certainly one of the "good years." In addition to our hunting success, we also enjoyed the pleasures of a very pleasant Indian summer.

By November 21, squaw winter was close at hand. Time for me to return to Duck Hole and prepare to leave for Lake Placid. The day before we had taken a trip to the lower slope of the Seward Range to pack the remaining half of Noah's bear back to Big Dam. Noah had previously skinned the bear, so when he hooked the carcass out of the water of a brook, the sight of the naked bear ridged in thick layers of fat brought out a bit of witticism. Noah addressed the bulk in a half-pitying, half-scolding voice: "Just because I borrowed your fur coat for the winter, I see no reason why you should go and drown yourself!"

We cut the slabs of bear fat away for later rendering; Noah estimated it might produce four gallons of oil. Then steaks, chops and a pile of stewing meat were cut. The meat filled a pack basket. The fat, rolled in the bear skin, was tied on to my pack board. Once shouldered it felt as if it would be a staggering load, but I came down the mountain with little trouble and reached Big Dam first. Depositing my load in a wigwam I backtracked, joining Noah where he had taken a rest foot of Ouluska Brook. I insisted I'd shuttle the packbasket the remaining distance. He consented saying, in return, he would cook my evening meal. I had volunteered to pack the basket of meat also to make three lighter loads, but he quipped that he wanted to have half the fun of carrying it down the mountainside.

The gloomy overcast sky hinted of foreboding weather. The water in the drinking pail had frozen over, imprisoning the dipper. Noah had to give it a good thrashing before it would let go. When we had retired that night Noah said he "smelled" snow in the air. Being only the 22nd of November, it wasn't something to be alarmed over. By the time we had finished eating breakfast, snow was falling. Large wet flakes soon covered the ground. Before I left the hermitage to return to my cabin, six inches of snow covered the ground.   Noah invited me to stay another day and watch the storm's development, but I thought one early storm wouldn't last too long and was anxious to leave.

By the time I had arrived at Mountain Pond, the snow depth had reached my knees and was not slackening. If anything it was coming down heavier. By the time I reached my cabin, I was wallowing through snow waist deep. Walking the last miles had been an effort.

I built a fire and I went to check my buck. No bear had happened upon it, but the front shoulder had vanished—probably into the stomach of a fisher or bobcat. Chickadees had also been working at rounding the shoulder blades. The snow stopped by evening, but by then everything was buried under three feet of a fluffy blanket.

During the evening I fashioned a pair of crude snowshoes using springy cedar branches. I made them oval in shape, with crisscrossed branches for the webbing tied in place with strips of deer hide from my buck. For handles I cut four inches from my boot tops, shortening them from twelve to eight inches. The snowshoes worked well enough but I didn't think they would last the entire trip.

Early the next morning I secured my cabin and the remainder of the venison and started up the trail. Progress was slow even though I carried as little weight as possible. I knew I would need to lay my ears back like a mule in order to keep a good steady pace. During the second uphill drag I slipped, falling into a hole and demolishing a snowshoe. I repaired it as well as possible and tried to stay on the higher ridges avoiding swampy lowlands that were much more snow chucked.

By 1943 I foolishly didn't carry a compass any longer, feeling I knew the country like the back of my hand. But it would have come in handy now as I bushwhacked along aiming to intersect with the state trail to Moose Pond.

Finally in the half light of early evening, a short ways from a brook, I spotted the sagging outline of Frank Fay's tent not far south of Moose Pond. A brutal trip but I had made it! I cleaned the heavy snow from the sagging roof and soon had a warm fire going in the little sheet iron stove. It felt good to shed my sweaty, wet woolen shirt and dry off. I cooked enough venison and pancakes for two men—sort of like rewarding an overworked jackass with an extra measure of oats. As my strength returned I settled back, sipped tea and repaired my webs.

After a restful sleep, followed by a hearty breakfast I ventured out. I thought about the two important lessons this trip had taught me. First: carry a compass regardless of how well I think I know the lay of the land. Second: Make my bearpaw snowshoes an essential piece of equipment whether snow is expected or not.

In those days the Conservation Department kept, at all wilderness lean-to's, a pair of bear paw snowshoes for emergency use, sealed in vermin-proof containers. There had been a pair at the Cold River shelters. Still, if I had used them, I might never have known my capacity to deal with emergency situations in the woods. Outside of a few anxious moments of indecision, I didn't experience too much discomfort a bit of rest wouldn't cure.

The wild land I bushwhacked between Bear Trap Mountain and Paint Bed Notch, I named Lost Youth Ridges honoring this experience as a watershed between my youthful enthusiasm and my greater adult understanding of how to anticipate and plan for situations. The antlers of the nine-point buck hang on my wall to his day as a reminder of this snow-bound trip.

Stubborn Irish Pride

Although I was overjoyed to be back at the hermitage, on a hunt with Noah, I couldn't help but spill out the events of an earlier hunting experience on the opening day of deer season.

It had all started weeks earlier when the color in the woods first peaked, dressing the forest in autumn finery. My friend, Phil McCalvin, and I toted supplies into his Duck Hole cabin. The journey was bitter-sweet for Phil. He was looking forward to joining the Air Force by year's end but he would be leaving his beloved Adirondack Mountains. My tale awaits, but first a short history lesson.

The Civilian Conservation Corps' side camp near Mountain Pond where Phil served for two seasons, was dismantled in the late nineteen thirties. Phil returned to collect the many discarded materials left behind, much of which he had squirreled away for safekeeping. He was determined to establish a green timber camp (built from freshly cut trees) somewhere in the vicinity of the Duck Hole. He raised a small, squat, well-concealed, horizontal-walled log cabin complete with a wooden roof. The roof was an added bonus. He originally planned to have a canvas one, but found most of the rough cut boards left over from the construction of the new dam at Duck Hole still sound. The structure, built on state-owned land, was blatantly illegal, but it was not uncommon in those days. Old timers, once guides working for two dollars a day —heroes of ours—had learned just how difficult it was to adjust to the state's new regulations after World War I. Before then the state generally overlooked tar paper shanties built for temporary shelter for hunting, fishing and trapping. Permits were even issued allowing a permanent edifice to be constructed. Large canvas-wall tents could be erected over wooden platforms. Even rustic improvements to the surrounding property were condoned. All this was legal until the Conservation Commission began to build lean-to's and develop marked trails to other places besides fire observation towers.

Phil knew that, in spite of the new conservation ethic, a woods-smart person could still maintain an outlaw camp if it were placed in a concealed, out-of-the-way area. The location would be whispered by those few who had knowledge of the locality, but the whereabouts would be kept a tightly held secret.

Two private camps were already hidden away between Moose Pond and the "Hole." They had remained undetected for almost a decade. Without feelings of maliciousness, we maintained a "State be dammed" attitude. Many native Adirondackers felt New York State already owned more land than it could possibly police.

Before the state purchased large blocks of woodland for inclusion in the forever wild preserve, native Adirondackers enjoyed a mutual arrangement with the logging industry which encouraged the building of temporary camps on company property—each year a small fee was paid for the privilege. Individuals as well as the landowner benefited since woodsmen were placed in the guardian position of looking out for wildfires and illegal cutting of timber.

I first met Phil during the summer of 1937. He often traveled down river from the CCC camp on his days off to visit Noah, as did a number of other recruits. During one of his weekend jaunts I happened to have also dropped by. He was a few years older, but we hit it off well since we both shared a love for hunting, trapping and remote living.

Phil and I reminisced as we headed down Moose Pond Trail talking about our first converging at the hermit's and of our mutual appreciation of his friendship. Excitement filled our thoughts, for we were anticipating the joy all hunters feel when first reaching camp. Hunting season wouldn't begin for a few more weeks. We were the advance team whose turn it was to perform a number of jobs before a party of friends came in.

A quick inspection of the cabin showed it had remained impenetrable from bears in spite of the claw marks around the heavy wooden door. Throughout our work session we cut and tacked sapling poles for chinking between the openings in the log walls, installed larger interior support columns under the roof's ridge pole, cut additional firewood, relocated the fifty-five gallon storage drums and otherwise tidied up the way a man would. With the majority of the preparations completed, we headed out of the woods vowing to meet at Noah's a week before deer season began.

The color had left the woods by the time we returned. In an honored tradition that I had begun a few years earlier, I delivered Noah his hunting license. I continued to do so until I joined the Army a few years later. After a lengthy confab that caught us up on each others goings-on, we bedded down before heading upstream the next morning to reopen camp.

Reopening camp didn't require much labor. After unlocking the door, we started a fire, removed window boards and set down to organizing the supplies stored in drums. The next day we began to reconnoiter the territory looking for telltale signs of bucks.

On the opening day of deer season—as luck would have it—Phil killed an eight point buck near the Duck Hole. Borrowing a line from our hermit friend we quipped, "That's one buck that won't be laughing as he bounds away." We hung it in a thickly sheltered thicket where a cold roiling spring arising from some rocks would help keep the deer from spoiling, if the temperature rose.

After a couple more days of hunting and no further luck, Phil wanted to take his buck home. I tried my best to convince him to cut the deer up and pack out only the most desirable parts, but he insisted we drag it out to Coreys via the fire road—a distance of sixteen miles.

The Irish are noted for being stubborn—even if half English. But a full-blooded Irishman would not take no for an answer if his life depended on it. Phil was full-blooded!

No amount of convincing arguments would sway him. If we dragged a hundred and fifty pounds of venison that distance over a gravel road, by the time we reached Coreys, I was convinced, we would only be dragging the horns. The remainder of the deer would only make a long trail for a bear to follow, assuming the bear had no other pressing things to do.

Realizing I would never convince Phil of the folly of such an impossible stunt, I consented to be a human mule. I would rather lay my ears back and poll than to have ever been an unwilling participant. We were both young and like brothers in friendship. To solve the problem of distributing the dead weight, I rigged up a travois with poles and a canvas pocket for the carcass of the buck and lashed a drawbar across the upper end for the two Irish jackasses to hitch up and draw the deer on their young shoulders.

For food we packed only five pounds of pancake flour, Phil's homemade fudge, and a package of cocoa I was sure we'd need for extra stamina. Bright and early we started the draw from the cabin. By noon, having only covered four miles, we stopped to eat. Hungry as bears we built a fire to warm a pail of water for cocoa and devoured the flapjacks we had premade on the griddle that morning. No sooner had we started again when the sky opened up and it started raining hard. Carrying nothing for protection beside a few articles of clothing, we pushed on to the site of old Camp Four just short of the Ward Brook lean-to. As we sloshed on, the gravel softened up enough that the pole ends of the travois created an additional drag as they penetrated below the surface of the road.

We were soaked to our skin. By the time we reached our destination for the day, an old tool shed left by the CCC's, we were chilled and exhausted. We built a fire in front of the door in order to dry us out and agreed to alternately tend the fire. I drew first watch while Phil slept for an hour. During the second hour I tried to sleep, but in those days of living in the woods, the least little thing out of the ordinary would snap me wide awake in a split second. In this case my sleep was interrupted with the smell of over heated hair. I woke just in the nick of time to save Phil who had slumped forward, face down, too near the roaring fire which was singeing his hair.

Waking before daylight, we rekindled the fire which was hissing from the extinguishing raindrops. The pancake flour was soaked, and all that was left was cocoa and a few squares of fudge.

Ward Brook lean-to was a little over a mile beyond. Surely we thought we would find food left on the shelves. But all we found was a tin of bouillon cubes which we made into a pot of soup, drinking like the two starved Irishmen we were.

After dragging for another hour, we saw a string of burros coming toward us. They were lead by a group of hunters from Pennsylvania who were packing in gear for a long fall hunt between Seymour Mountain and the Sawtooth Range. Later on the burro tenders passed us going back out. They said we were doing great, but never offered to pack out our deer. They certainly weren't the kind of men I was used to being acquainted with.

A short time later we met a lone hunter on the trail. He looked at the deer we were dragging and asked where it had been killed. Phil regaled the highpoints of the hunt. I saw the hunter grin as I tied my bandanna around the buck's head to cover the eyes. For what we were putting his dead carcass through, the buck deserved not being gawked at.

When we finally reached the turn-off to Ampersand Park, we were as gaunt as a couple of starving coyotes. I told Phil he could shoot me if he liked, but I was going to cut some meat from the deer. At that he crowed,

"No!" He couldn't allow me to spoil the appearance of his trophy. Ignoring his wishes I cut some venison, although he glared with flashing eyes fit to kill. But once I cooked a strip, he calmed down and put a good meal of venison under his belt as well.

At dusk we arrived, at last, at the road to Coreys. Exhausted and damp, we were still a fair distance from a telephone.

As luck would have it, a couple of army men were setting up a tent where the trail came into the road. They had a lantern which wasn't operating, so we volunteered our help setting up their camp and getting the lantern going in exchange for a ride to an occupied camp at Coreys. An older gent came to the door of the first camp with a phone. I recognized his name. He was one of a number of Coreys natives on Noah's less-than-favorite list, but that had nothing to do with us. The man allowed us to use his phone and offered us up some beans, coffee, bread and butter while we waited for Phil's brother to arrive.

The next morning Phil told me, in retrospect, we should have cut up the deer and packed it out, but he wanted to impress his girlfriend. It was a memorable trip for no other reason than to recall common sense had been defeated by stubborn Irish pride.

Gone Like a Puff of Smoke

As a boy, Richard enjoyed listening to the old woodsmen tell stories. He never felt radio stories measured up to his neighbor's tales. This account about a fox and a hound was one of John Schmoll's favorites. John was one of several men Richard enjoyed hanging around as a youngster. John was a man who shared his kindness and wisdom freely with all children. In order to reach the Ausable River, by Lake Placid's dump and airport, Richard had to cross over Schmoll's property. Each time he did, Richard would first stop to say hello. Often Schmoll invited the boy to first join him in some target shooting with his pair of .22 Woodsman's pistols. When Richard grew to adulthood, he always made a point each fall to bring back a couple of venison steaks to John, a small token of his gratitude for all the happy hours he had spent in his company as a youth. Richard credits those old-timers with influencing him. Richard's

greatest wish was that his own writings preserve some of those personal
narratives for a generation who, someday, might discover them—if they
ever tire of video and computer games.

The winter sun, in a final glow of color, seemed to stand still momentarily on the shoulder of the distant mountain. In a final farewell to the daylight hours, falling snowflakes began to flicker in the reflected light against the backdrop of the setting sun as the darker shadows of twilight descended upon the landscape. One by one the stars of evening began to appear, filling the early winter sky. As I stood admiring this atmospheric splendor, my hand felt the cold, wet muzzle of old Blue, John Schmoll's blue-tick foxhound, followed by a greeting from John. A freshly killed fox was slung over one shoulder, and across his arm rested his double-barreled shotgun.

"Come along Red," he coaxed, "I'll buy you a warm drink." I didn't need any further encouraging, for I knew where his invitation would take me. Within a short walk the lights of the general store sent out rays of welcome; it was the local gathering place for men after the day's work. I always enjoyed going there. It gave me a chance to listen and talk some to old timers, while they relaxed around the oak heater and drank hot buttered rum or a glass of spiced cider from the store owner's cider mill.

Leaving the fox just outside the door in the guardianship of Blue, John hung his gun on the coat rack and we joined the crowd. Someone asked John if he ever had a real outstanding fox hound, one just a tad better than all he had ever trained. "Yep I did just that," he admitted in a lowered voice. "I had me one hound that was about the best darn foxer a man could hope fer, but I best tell you about him in soft talk so as Blue out there doesn't hear me. That hound likes to think he is the best there can ever be."

"That dog was a mix, part walker and blue-tick. I picked him out of the litter because of his extra long legs. I figured they'd enable him to get along just fine in deep snow. The funny thing was throughout its puppyhood that squirt's ears kept growing until they were almost as long as his legs. It was with relief when the hound's ears finally stopped growing lest they'd grown so long as to be stepped on by his extra large feet. I named him Smokie for his predominately gray color. By the time he'd grown to full size, I figured he had also become the best fox hound in Essex County. In fact, the third winter I had him he became a sort of local celebrity, for it turned out he's run just about all the foxes for miles around so I decided to take him into Hamilton County, down Long Lake way to see if any foxes had moved in there.

"In the middle of January, with a blanket and enough grub to last a few days, and following an all day's walk, we arrived at a large pond deep in the wilderness. A beaver meadow seemed to stretch for miles. Fox signs were everywhere and Smoke didn't take long to get one moving before darkness settled in. In the twilight I saw the fox and Smoke several times crisscrossing the frozen pond and meadows, but each time it was out of range to shoot with my eight gauge.

"Once full darkness came on I rustled a bit to eat, fully expecting Smoke would smell my cooking, give up the chase and come in. But he didn't. I must have stayed up half the night watching the moon, but never once caught another glimpse of dog nor fox.

"Come next morning, the air being so clear and all, I thought I heard Smoke 's bay way out well beyond the range of my voice. I stayed all that day and all night on watch, but not a further sound did I hear of the fox race. After three days I figured Smoke could have chased the fox clear down to Old Forge. As my grub had run out I reluctantly returned home, half hoping my blue ribbon foxhound would come home by himself.

"The rest of the winter I hunted all over for that canine, made several trips back to the beaver meadows and even offered a cash reward, but Smoke never showed up. Come spring I had to admit I'd lost him for sure.

"That summer, remembering how good the pond looked for fishing, I made me a trip to fish for large trout. As I sat on a beaver house on the edge of the water I heard a dog's bay and then saw a dog run smack across the pond. Boys, there was no mistaking that sound; it was Smoke. Why I'll tell you, to hear that hound running a fox once again was like listening to Gene Autry yodeling! From the combined noise I could tell the race was coming right toward me.

"I had my .22 along, but didn't like shooting fox in the summer. But in this case I would if it would end the race. I waited, then took careful aim as they hit the shore and circled towards me. It would be an easy shot as it was all open except for a few low bushes. I was ready when all of a sudden everything turned to a blur of red followed by a long trailing whooshing sound. I lost track of what happened momentarily then realized Smoke and the fox were a merry-go-rounding around the lodge. Determined to get my dog, I leapt off the house intending to wrestle the fox to the ground, but it run by too fast. So my next instinct was to seize Smoke when he came by. As he rounded toward me I grabbed, but didn't have a thing for my efforts except air and the sound of his voice trailing off in the distance.

"I cussed myself for not trapping that dog, but the more I thought about it the more the incident became a mystery. Then, as I walked home, it finally came to me what had happened."

With that John called for me to leave. He handed me his shotgun, opened the door, shouldered the fox, whistled to Blue to follow, and we headed out when all at once, in seemingly one voice, the crowd of listeners called after us. "John, what happened?"

My neighbor halted, turned and answered, "It's as plain as can be if you think about it, but I'll tell you what happened. Smoke had chased that fox so long and so far all that was left of it was his tail and all that remained of Smoke was his voice."

Early photo of Noah.

"Food's ready!"

Fifteen Trout Pond.

Abandoned Santa Clara Lumber Company along the Cold River.

Duck Hole, 1920's.

Noah and members of the Whiteman hunting party.

Abandoned Bradley Pond Lumber Camp, 1920.

"Red" Smith, 1940's.

Noah and Richard at Cold River camp.

Handsome Hill, Richard's cabin on River Road.

Singing Pines Camp, Rondeau's last home.

Richard Smith consented to my picture-taking, if I promised not to get his "paws" wet.

William J. O'Hern

For a very long time we just sat quietly.

Courtesy of Richard Smith

Red's packboard and Marlin.

William J. O'Hern

PART V

HOME IS THE HUNTER

Home Is The Hunter

The following stories were favorites of Richard's. He told them many times—each telling a nostalgic reminder of his rich past. I like to think they also provided brief intermissions from his pain.

I flipped pancakes on my blackened iron skillet this morning. Several cups of coffee followed. The combination of pancakes, a sprinkle of brown sugar, maple syrup and coffee was also a standard when I was at my snug Duck Hole cabin. Many times I stood at the woodstove in the yellow cast from a kerosene lamp, preparing an early morning breakfast like the one I had just enjoyed. Back then it was just an ordinary day: packing sourdough pancakes, sometimes spreading butter and jelly, then rolling them like cigars, all stored in a small lard pail complete with wire bail—a very versatile container that served many purposes beyond a brew pot for tea.

In those days I traveled over my traplines from daylight until almost twilight. I looked forward to a trail lunch and warm tea along my route. The meal was not only sufficient fare, but the break provided time to focus on how quiet and peaceful the forest felt. I was a lone trail-blazer, a nomadic trapper. My territory was Cold River country from Preston Ponds to the South Gap in Ouluska Pass. The land lumbered many years ago had, by my time, begun to grow back though it did not resemble the old growth forest of its original state. My lines generally ran in wide circles through green timber to ponds and streams and back to camp. I was deep in the Adirondack forest.

How I longed to be a time-hardened "natural born" trapper. For a time I attempted to emulate the lifestyle of my friend Noah. If it were possible to turn back the calendar to those days and nights, I wouldn't change a thing. Everything would be as it was, with the exception that I would have more appreciation. I would know those days would be very special—the happiest times in my life. But, alas, those bygone days will have to remain reflections of the past, to be enjoyed only by bringing up files from my springtide, stored in memory, there to brighten me in the fleeting, twilight days of my life.

As I write, the snow which began to fall again last night is ruthlessly covering the exposed stump in my backyard, blotting out almost all traces of the last tree I had felled. From the kitchen window I estimate fourteen inches of snow has draped the landscape since yesterday. That makes a total of thirty-nine inches. No matter how strong my log rafters are, there is a limit on how much weight the roof will withstand. Mother Nature is certainly sending a roaring old "south-easterner."

Longjohns and a wool sweater are a necessity for me. I've never been cold in my cabin, but the fabric is warming and makes me comfortable here on a hillock overlooking the Au Sable River that I call "Handsome Hill." My health? It's not the best, and I'm growing tired of the many oil changes (my way of saying blood transfusions), but my happiness remains supreme.

I've been thinking of the many old timers I once knew, who were fortunate enough to live into their nineties complete with teeth still white as a hound's tooth and nary a missing hair, as when born. Younger people say they live better today. Bah! Humbug! says I. All technological advancements don't always promote a quality lifestyle.

Everyone must tolerate and make what they can out of a rapidly decaying world. Noah was always good at illustrating particular points of his philosophy with examples such as this. "A drunkard, after getting tanked up, was wobbling down the road with unfounded manly pride, when his rubbery legs began to weaken. He lay down in the gutter along the roadway to sleep it off. Soon after a pig wandered by, spied the man and laid down by his side. Soon some ladies passed, noted the two and were heard voicing their disgust. 'You can detect any person who boozes by the company he chooses.' At that the pig's ears cocked, head turned upward, stood up, shook and slowly walked away."

So what did I do with my life? Only what I could physically do and did not offend my pride. I always strived to do my best, no matter how small a task. None of us ever knows what our destiny will be. It might be preplanned and, unknowingly, it subconsciously dictates our particular path through life. I think the best of life has to be having good friends. They help make one's life contented and happy, and we in return do the same for them. Amen! Pass the gravy!

During one of my visits with Noah, when he was hospitalized in 1967, he conceded, "Old father time keeps picking my pocket, I can't make him stop." It was his way of letting me know that what was to follow was a gift. The gift happened to be his hand-carved ironwood cane. It had an interesting natural curled handhold. When he gave it to me I never thought I would need it, but Noah knew better. I always felt he possessed a great deal of common sense and wisdom—wisdom about everyday life, happiness, real wealth, friends. Things that should matter most in life. Time has once again proven him right for I find myself relying on his cane to move from room to room, especially after returning from recent lengthy hospital stays.

The rain and snow of previous weeks has made the air chilly and damp. The ground cover has frozen, and the sun and winter breezes that followed chased week-old clouds from the sky, clearing minute spots of pastel blue. This pattern will repeat itself at the end of this storm. Winter will end eventually, and regardless of how many false starts, spring will return. It is as it always has been.

While I always looked toward the future, I feel the winter of my life provides a pleasant tempo to reminisce. My physical disability puts me in a position where I can do very little but keep my Case hunting knife sharp and my rifle ready, just in case I get the old urges. This winter storm is bringing back strong memories.

One winter when I was working at the Tahawus mines the deep snowpack was much like this winter. So with a weekend available to me during the last of January, I decided to hike into my Duck Hole camp to shovel off the roof. I invited a friend who also worked at the mine to come along.

At the close of our 4 p.m. Friday shift, we started over the route that traced the Santanoni Brook. By the time we crossed the brook and began a steady climb toward the pass, we knew the night sky would be illuminated by the strong moon glow. Snowshoeing was not difficult, but as we worked ourselves farther up we lost sight of the trail. The snow was deep at that elevation; trail markers were not easily visible, although I had a sense of which way we should continue. We pushed on for a short time until my friend lost his balance and fell. As he regained his position, pulling himself up with the aid of some tree limbs, he uncovered a trail marker. It was the last one we would see. Scuffling against fatigue—we had started out after working all day with very little to eat—we decided to avoid any hazardous predicament and make a camp for the remainder of the night.

Finding a good-sized boulder we dug, using our snowshoes as shovels, a small hole large enough for a fire, the pack bags and ourselves. With ample dry boughs for fuel, we had a fire going in no time. The reflection of the heat off the rock made a cozy nest. The fire warmed us up and was used to melt snow for coffee and to heat a bite to eat. Soon after, we fell asleep. Occasionally during the night I woke to toss more wood onto the fire. It wasn't a roaring blaze, but it did keep us fairly comfortable. Around daybreak the odor of rubber burning woke me up. My friend had moved his feet, clad in rubber-soled Bean boots, too close to the fire. I did him a favor, but he never forgave me for waking him up, "That was the first time my feet had been warm!" he quipped.

Bradley Pond was a short bivouac. I had only been in the area once out of curiosity. It was at the far end of one of three trapline's Noah laid down in the mid nineteen twenties. It was one of several areas of competition with the famed trapper E.J. Dailey, since they both disagreed on the other's claim in the waning days of Dailey's tenure.

I stopped to view the landscape at the head of the ravine, the site of an old lumber camp. First built in the late 1880's, the Bradley Pond Lumber Company buildings were quite old when Noah set mink traps around them. The dilapidated buildings were made to decay faster because the roofs were removed. That was standard operating procedure when buildings no longer held any usefulness. Also customary was the preservation of one small building where the roof was left intact. That building was used primarily for shelter by hunters and others who happened by. By 1925 the log structures that stood in the clearing at the end of an old tote road coming up from the Duck Hole were well over thirty-five years old. Noah's trapline followed that road.

By the 1940's nothing remained. Any useful wood had been removed. Any solid timbers had been cut out and moved to build woodland shanties. I know that Noah and Dailey both confiscated boards from old dry goods boxes to form stretchers and helped themselves to discarded pots, pans, stovepipes and other articles left behind.

We headed down the valley tracing the route Noah took so many times over rotten, slippery corduroy where black muck oozed between spaces in the logs. Now this overgrown and often washed out tote road was a popular pathway for the mountain climbers who approached Panther Peak and Santanoni from the Duck Hole. The path followed the old roadway that generally kept to the north side of the brook which flowed right down to the dam at the foot of Duck Hole.

I was growing anxious the closer we came to the bottom of the valley. My camp was illegal, having been built on state land. In the days it was constructed, game protectors did not search for outlaw camps unless they had evidence the occupants were violating game laws. I used the Duck Hole camp for almost ten years and never met a game protector until the fall of 1947. The warden politely mentioned that if I might know the owner of the unlawful camp, I might want to pass on the message that any valuables stored there should be removed, since it was scheduled to be burned during early spring when snow still covered the ground.

Sooner or later I knew that my time would come. Fifty years earlier, and more, a man could still go out into the woods and build a camp on open land—land not owned by a club or organization. By 1900 the method of choice was to build log camps where once only lean-tos were built. Those rustic camps were hidden in the forest and fitted with an outside latch string allowing anyone to gain access to the interior. It was unusual to find a camp locked. Woodsmen had an open door policy. Anyone was welcome to use another's property. The only condition was the occupant should exercise reasonable care and replace all the dry tinder and firewood used.

This arrangement worked very well. A lost, wet or wayward hunter, fisherman or forest traveler could find shelter and food, spending a night of comfort beside a wood-fired stove. There was little thought of stealing or destruction of camp property.

My camp was not only well hidden, but was situated in a remote location. It was never vandalized, nor did I ever have anything stolen. I was fortunate. Eventually it became a common practice by most camp owners to lock the cabin door and board shut the windows, often barring them on the inside. This was not a precaution for bears. It was a dramatic departure from past practice, and was meant to keep people out. I left the camp open in the time honored Adirondack fashion and to my knowledge it was never used by anyone I wasn't aware of. Yet it was there if someone needed to escape a miserable night in the woods. After all, I could have been that injured, hungry or half frozen man in need of shelter.

On the other hand I wasn't naive. I knew that the days had long passed when woodsmen could build a camp wherever they pleased, as well as leave it open. It wasn't natural for the old Adirondack woodsmen to steal, but the character of the woods had been changing. My friend Noah found that to be true and had for a long time padlocked his door and stashed his most valuable items in Mammoth Graveyard.

Since the early 1900's individual land owners and clubs began to buy large amounts of forest land, setting limits on who could use the property. Owners of large preserves often ordered the burning of all illegal shelters on their property and in the surrounding state land. This infuriated the natives. Sooner or later the private preservers would suffer. I know respectable natives supported the arrest and conviction of camp robbers, but they also couldn't help but feel a twinge of revenge when a particularly unpopular landowner lost personal property or game was plundered from his land. Naturally this type of situation could not go on forever. Both parties were at fault. Natives were aware of the written law and in time came to respect it. Times were changing; natives just couldn't go into the forest and build camps wherever they pleased nor should they consider the land they once freely hunted and fished on, but did not own, an inalienable right. Land and camp owners, on the other side, also needed to be more amicable and build better relationships with the local residents. Only then would they begin to earn the good will of their Adirondack neighbors.

I always experienced anticipation a short distance from my little cabin whatever the season. Dropping into the Duck Hole basin was the point I looked forward to the most As we crossed the outlet, I pointed out the low lying rise behind the camp known locally as Beartrap Mountain. Never tiring of my wilderness paradise, I felt the same kind of excitement that anyone would when they were about to be reunited with something their heart was immensely fond of. Rounding the pond, we headed toward an evergreen-deciduous forest that ringed the base of Beartrap. My senses were kicking in. The balsam smelled sweeter, the snow purer and whiter, the wind blowing through the conifers sang to me, as the hills and faraway ridges urged me on. Fifteen minutes, now five, and then finally I could discern the roofline projecting slightly above a low lying hillock. I softly uttered to myself, "Home is the hunter," something I began years ago. It was a way of expressing that inner feeling of contentment, home and heart. Noah had a similar ritual each time he returned from his extended holiday vacations on the outside. I truly knew this spot in the wilderness had been set aside for me. My beloved Adirondacks.

Upon seeing the mounds of snow that encapsulated the cabin, I knew the trip had been a good decision; the snow-dome roof looked more like an Islamic mosque than a mountain cabin.

I thought it best, as we began the process of clearing an opening around the door, to point out the half-hidden rabbit droppings that lay just under the fresh layer of snow. The snowshoe hares had been busy during the winter, concentrating their activities near two sides of the building. They used their big hairy hind feet to get around in the deep snow in search of a nibble, as we had relied on snowshoes to get into camp. Once a new runway was broken out leading to a food supply, they would travel it until the grocery store was empty. Very often some runways would be used most of the winter. Well used ones, high speed pathways, were like our interstate highways—direct and fast.

Sixty-five years ago, when I was just a lad, January was the first month we would begin to experience deep freezing night temperatures. In order to keep warm, rabbits hopped around seemingly in constant motion. Winter was sure rough on rabbits. Old timers used to tell me then that the best way to catch rabbits on such nights was to go out into the swamps with a party of friends and build a grand bonfire. After a spell of drinking and story swapping, the snow would begin to turn to liquid. Come midnight they'd all head back to the settlement, allowing the fires they stoked one last time to continue burning and melting the snow throughout the night. When human noise and activity in the swamp stopped completely, the rabbits would come out of hiding and gather around the fire. I was never sure if the rabbits were in a storytelling or drinking mood like the men, but the theory was that as they stood enjoying the heat from the fire, the melted water cooled. As it did, the rabbits were caught off guard and their feet froze fast in the ice that formed as the water lost its heat. The next morning the fellows went back to the site of last night's gathering and simply clubbed the animals over the head. They claimed on real cold nights, they could fill a couple of bran sacks. But I always sort of wondered if they were telling the truth!

All newcomers to my wilderness cabin were given the job of camp snow scooper and it was not to be taken lightly. On more than one occasion the resident scooper had dashed outside in the cold snow, in the pitch dark, clad in only longjohns and rubber bottom boots. The trick was to dash outside, scoop and pack enough snow into a large metal kettle held in one hand and a white baked enamel oversized lumberman coffee pot in the other, then hightail it back into the cabin before you began to chill down too much. Naturally with the action moving at high speed, there were apt to be slip-up's. Those shortcomings would only be noticed the next morning when, in full light, a solid mass of soggy rabbit droppings would occasionally be seen layering the bottom of the containers. That discovery was always good for several laughs, and served as fodder for tales which aged gracefully as they were retold over the years. Evening tea was generally enjoyed with a bit of spirits, thus the reason why I referred to my brew as Wild Rabbit and Whiskey Tea.

Once an entranceway was cleared to the door, I started a fire in the stove to begin the process of thawing out the frost. While the heat slowly began to circulate and soak into solid objects, we started scooping snow off the roof with short-handled coal shovels, the only official tools I had available. At the rate we were working, the lower and heavier layers of harder packed snow would require more time to shovel than I wanted to spend on the job. Looking around for an alternative, I eyed my long two-man crosscut saw hanging against the wall. It was the perfect alternative to shoveling. The long teeth easily cut the packed snow into blocks we could manage, and by maneuvering them on to the long blade, we skidded them down the slippery steel-inclined plane. By the time we'd finished, the snow on the ground was nearly as high as the drip edge. I knew the dense snowpack would provide an extra barrier against the wind and act as additional insulation. It was too bad I wasn't able to stay longer, but at least I didn't have to be concerned that the roof might collapse.

With the interior dried out nicely, warm and snug, even cozy in appearance, an afternoon nap was in order following a small late lunch. As we ate I fielded questions about my cabin and my hermit friend down river. My companion was taken by the entire trip. It had been his first venture into the mountains and he was interested in hearing about my adventures.

He picked up a fungus growth I had setting on the table and told me how much he liked it. On the smooth surface I had scratched a crude drawing of my camp and penned my sentiments:

> To live your life in your own way
> To reach the goals you set for yourself
> To be what YOU want to be
> To do the best you can with what you have.
> That is success.

I was proud of my accomplishments as small as they might appear to someone else. I was surrounded with the satisfaction of my toil.

Most of the camp's equipment was second hand. The abandoned Civilian Conservation Corps side camp had provided a treasure chest full of useful items. From the tent platforms came many boards for making fleshing and stretching forms for the heavier hides I trapped. I also trudged miles back and forth carrying enough boards to allow me to lay a floor, build a table and benches, and fashion two bunkbeds. Nails were plentiful for the gathering, along with sheets of galvanized tin that required little pounding out to restore them to a useful shape. I even lugged back to camp a heavy galvanized tank that I converted into a cooking stove. By placing it horizontally on a raised platform and cutting the top off, I converted this useless tank into a useful stove with a thirty inch cooking surface. I placed a hinged door in one end, fashioned a smokestack, and added a flat iron cooking surface. When completed, I could place a fry pan, coffee pot and pancake griddle side by side with no crowding. I fiddled around with a damper and draft control until I was able to kept a space about the size of a coffee pot's base red hot. This produced perked coffee in very short order.

Later that evening, while we ate supper, the conversation leaned heavily toward outdoor life, the woods and mountains. We were young adult men and felt as if we had the world by the tail, with a downward pull. Jokingly we made a up a poem comparing true wilderness life to what we might experience nowadays.

> Two hundred years ago
> When wilderness was truly here
> With powder in their guns
> The men went out to hunt the deer.
>
> But following another plan and in another age, for—
> True wilderness has disappeared
> With powder on her face
> The dears go out to get the men.

We thought we were terribly funny, but it echoed a reality I often thought about. I was attempting to live like my friend Noah. I was happiest when I was trapping, hunting, fishing or just being in the woods. Spending time with Noah sort of helped set my way of life, but it was too late to make it completely work. I realized I was treading on the fringe of a departing era of time.

"Perhaps you'd like to return another time," I mentioned to my friend. "I'd introduce you to some real ice fishing—Noah Rondeau style." His eyes popped wide only to turn into a confused look.

"But the ponds and river are frozen so thick and the streams frozen solid?" he replied.

"Ah hah. So you know how to recognize the best winter fishing conditions already," I bantered. "One of the beauties of the Cold River country is that the temperatures do drop well below zero, thirty, sometimes forty below. But fishing can be just as good under those conditions as if it were mid summer. My hermit friend taught me that. Both Noah and I have caught some of the largest trout during the dead of winter when streams have been frozen clear to the gravelly stream bed."

I'm sure that sounded like so much woodsmen boast, a tall tale perhaps. So I pointed out how useful the cross cut saw had been to use earlier in the day. He agreed it indeed saved much time.

Winter fishing was just as easy. Did he remember the stream where we crossed the Duck Hole? Well, on our next trip we'd take my little toboggan and saw and go over there. No one could resist the temptation to do a little fishing at that spot winter or summer. With the aid of the sharp toothed saw, we'd cut ourselves a big block out of that frozen stream. Next, with the aid of the blade, we'd slide the ice cake over the slippery steel and onto the sled. With two of us it would be a cinch to skid it back to camp where we'd deposit the ice chunk into a large, preheated iron kettle. All that would be left to do was to wait until the ice melted and the fish began swimming around in the kettle. Then we could pick out just the trout we wanted for a winter fish fry.

Richard was a storehouse of information regarding the old days in his territory of the Adirondack Mountains. His stories provide valuable information about an area we can become familiar with only by hiking through.

Those were certainly good remembrances. I never did get married, just didn't feel it would be fair to a woman. I knew I could never separate myself from all the mountain wandering.

When the state finally destroyed my cabin, I felt as if I had lost an old friend who had served me well in comfort and joy. The Duck Hole country held so many great memories. Now, in my current health, the only way I ever envision I could ever go back would be if my ashes were scattered there. For sure, that was where I spent the happiest days of my life. I wouldn't need a lot of fancy words to send me off. Returning would be my greatest joy. I'd just like someone to whisper a few words. The wind will pick up the news that I have returned and carry the edict down the valley and up the mountain slopes. Home is the hunter.

The Ever Enchanting Hanging Spear Falls

Following a nostalgic evening of conversation with Noah at Singing Pines, Noah and Richard's interest in the old days revived old feelings. Both knew one can never truly go home, but Richard expressed his interest to revisit their favorite haunts: Duck Hole, Cold River, Big Dam and Seward Pond.

Taken together, all Richard's trips into the wilderness in the 1930's, '40's and early '50's hit hard at his heart; yet he was a realist. When it was time to move on in his life, the freedom and adventure he had spent at Cold River occupied a blue-ribbon chapter in his biography.

Wisdom grows with experience, a fact clearly illustrated when, after hearing Richard say he was going to return to the Cold River country, Noah expressed his desire to go along if only "he were a year younger."

In Richard's story, "The Ever Enchanting Hanging Spear Falls," his perspective is that of a mature man whose's spirit remains unbroken although it had been ten years since he had gone back in the deep woods. That's what is classic about Richard "Red" Smith.

It was a beautiful autumn day with fleecy white clouds drifting aimlessly, appearing as flocks of sheep in heavenly pastures, ever changing in shape, with whisper-soft breezes herding them across the deep blue sky. Majestic Whiteface Mountain was dressed in a purple cloak of filmy mist, eagles soared on thermal updrafts close to their nests on rugged spines of granite splendor. I cherished this picture forever in my memory.

I watched the eagles' effortless flight, their long glides to the shimmering waters of Lake Placid far below, and their return with food for their hungry nesting broods, I couldn't help the envy I felt, even as I marveled at their mastery of the skies.

In my dreamy musings, I recalled a turtle from a nearby pond once had similar thoughts of flying and, being of an inventive nature, had coaxed a pair of Canada geese into his plans of flying. By grasping a sturdy stick in their bills, he would secure a strong bite on its center and would soon be flying! All went well as the geese took off from the pond, the turtle swinging delightfully between his two cooperative friends. What a great invention he thought, as he flew through the sky. His dream had come true; he was indeed flying! He was overcome with joy. But as with most inventions, a certain amount of "bugs" have to be worked out. An inquisitive eagle flew near for a closer look at this strange new sight and asked who had thought of such a clever plan? The selfish turtle not wanting to share any of the praise, opened his mouth and said, "I did!" R.I.P.

The following morning, the rising sun found me motoring along the Adirondack Lodge road toward Heart Lake. I scanned the panoramic view for glimpses of Indian Pass and of Royal Mount Marcy, and of the ancient "Tahawus," the cloud splitter of old Indian legends. He sat adorned in ermine clouds, appearing as courtly robes, with the smaller surrounding peaks paying homage to their gentle king, all clustered closely around the feet of this giant ruler of the Adirondack skies.

I had never planned to return to my Cold River haunts following an investigative trip just after the November 1950 storm and another when "Operation Blow-Down" ended.

The storm left thousands of acres of broken and twisted soft and hardwood trees hung up on each other or laying crisscrossed on the forest floor. They resembled a giant's game of jackstraws on a gameboard the size of the Adirondack Park. Not only was the scene immediately following the storm disheartening to view, but it also created an unprecedented fire hazard. Trees were laid high off the ground where they would dry out without decaying. The massive tangle created an impassable barrier to firefighters.

A salvage job was the only practical solution. Logger's, under contract, entered private and state owned land removing any wood that would still bring them a profit. It did make the land more accessible for firefighters and reduced the threat of fire. But in the wake of the operations, an eyesore was left, an ugly forest scene of unmerchantable timber, brush and litter.

It was during the removal operations that one of Noah's cabins was brought out to be reassembled as a display in the new Adirondack Museum at Blue Mountain Lake. Noah was happy that someone felt there was historical value in his hermitage. Where he was practical, I had a twinge of sentimentally when I stood on top of Cold River Hill and viewed the results of "Operation Blow-Down." It wasn't the same place that I once knew and never would be again.

Yet, here I was years later swinging carefree along the Indian Pass Trail. I was embarking on an extended outing. My route resembled a beeline, a zig, a zag, and a wide arc.

Nearing the crest of the steep rugged Indian Pass, a warm gentle rain began falling causing a ground hugging fog. It blotted out the trail completely, drawing a misty curtain which blocked my view of the towering wall of Wallface, a rock cliff that hung majestically above the deep ravine where Indian Pass Brook headed southward toward Henderson Lake.

While I waited for the fog to clear, a flock of Canada geese came winging, through hardly above tree level, so close I could hear the frantic beating of their wings. I was sure the wise old leader had been through the pass many times before, using the cliffs as a sounding board with the radar effect echoing their "honking," keeping them on course through the rugged pass. Shortly after, as if by magic, the fog dispersed. Far below glistened the waters of Preston Ponds where I was sure the geese were feeding.

The drizzle had now stopped. The fog still hung in selected little patches above perpetual ice filled crevices which, while the rain was falling, had generated the instant fog. When it stopped, the temperature rose quickly stopping the process. Nature's thermostat!

With the noon sun overhead, I decided to swing over to the MacIntire Mountain Range to visit Hanging Spear Falls. It would be an excellent destination to eat lunch, but I was unsure of its location having never been there before. I had located it on the map, however, and was sure I could find it by first picking up the waters of Calamity Brook that ran parallel with the Flowed Lands Trail and then bushwhacking through the pass south of Calamity Mountain to the Opalescent Trail. While route searching over the mountainous terrain, the stillness of the forest gave forth fluttering vibrations, which could easily have been caused by restless, probing mountain breezes caressing mossy rock ledges and mountain gorges. Yet each time I heard these forest sounds, they seemed clearer, and to be coming from a definite direction. Many of these most encouraging sounds turned out to be tiny wayward rivulets, half-heartedly trying to make great waterfall "noises," sliding gleefully down slanted slabs of broken granite.

Vibrations of the forest are hard to explain. One senses them only by having acute hearing and keen eyesight, and they often go unnoticed by the unskilled in woodcraft. A trembling leaf, when not a breath of air is stirring, or a fern frond bending on the side of a mossy ledge, pulsating in one definite direction, caused by the softest whisper of a current of air generated by an unknown energy source. This particular day it had been caused, I was sure, by falling water. By placing my hand on exposed tree roots and granite boulders, I could feel a minute shaking, but only in roots facing in one definite direction. The granites outcrops had almost the same sensation on sides facing the same direction the roots revealed.

At the time I thought perhaps, in a dreamy sort of way, this mysterious energy source was created by the spirits of long departed old time guides still roaming the mountains. Or perhaps I had unknowingly entered the cathedral mountain hideaway of God, pausing a moment to rest from His seemingly hopeless task of keeping on an even keel His troubled world. Surely it was a most beautiful place, with rising columns all around me in a silent tapestry, so peaceful and serene.

A jumbled mass of ledges were thickly and elegantly dressed in hanging moss, waving ferns and pretty infant evergreens. From the distant expanse of the forest came the unmistakable muffled sounds of falling water. I knew at last "Hanging Spear" was near at hand. My hastening footsteps brought me in sight of the churning frothy pool below the silver thread of falling water leaping in wild frenzy, not unlike a witches cauldron, overflowing with noisy thundering excitement, magic and mystery!

It was as if I was the first ever to look upon it! Not a twig seemed out of place! A minute column of water separate from the main fall appeared as a flashing silver ribbon, its gleeful murmurings identical to those heard far above on the sloping mountainside. Its familiar wayward actions expanding, changing, enhancing the beauty of "Hanging Spear."

All this wondrous display of changing colors amid the sparkling sunlight made me feel as guilty as the little boy caught with his hand in the cookie jar. I felt as though I had opened the door of Mother Nature's wardrobe and was gazing spellbound at her bridal veil made of the finest, fluttering, silvery lace!

Ah! "Hanging Spear!" What a wonderfully descriptive name for this lovely waterfall attired in the lasting beauty of flashing, spraying, cool crystal water. The person naming it must surely have had the inspiration of a poet.

As I ate a very late lunch near the fall's refreshing spray, its singing voice made new exciting verses in an autumn lullaby expressly for my ears. Some surrounding giant yellow birch and maple trees were already beginning to dress in the early colors of fall; they soon would be fabulously rich in gold and crimson, nodding quietly, as if catching a noonday nap before the long sleep of winter.

Reluctantly leaving the captivating company of the falls, I said good-bye as if I would never see them again.

Hiking north toward one of the Flowed Land shelters, while I was well out of range of hearing the falls, I imagined I heard an imploring, pleading voice repeat, "Come back, come back!" My cheeks, for many miles, remained mysteriously damp until I finally realized the lingering dampness was not caused by the fall's refreshing spray—I was under the spell of its magic.

Hiking along a winding trail the following day, first toward the bridge over Indian Pass Brook and then the distant Preston Ponds chain, I approached Duck Hole in the deepening shadows of early evening. I was greeted by the talk of a hundred Canada geese. I had little doubt the same flock heard in the fog of Indian Pass yesterday morning, now floated contentedly on the shimmering waters.

Sitting before the campfire after a fine evening meal, I relaxed in peace, listening to the enchanting sound of the forest.

A cricket in the woodpile, promising a fine new day, a final lonely cry of a loon, a pair of owls calling to each other on a forested ridge—I recorded, in memory, the end of a perfect day and drifted into the contented world of sleep.

High above in a starlit sky the moon was shining, lighting the massive Santanoni Mountain Range, looming in bold relief, eternally guarding the vast Cold River wilderness—the focus of my next day's jaunt. In the stillness of the night, all that was heard was the restless waters of the Duck Hole, spilling over the dam in a ceaseless flow on its endless journey to the distant sea. Surely, I soundly slept in a perfect setting where everlasting dreams are made, and life joyously acknowledged.

The Chubb

Richard wanted to paddle his beloved Chubb River one last time. This story tells of that accomplishment.

Last night I slept a deep and dream-filled sleep. I dreamed I was rowing down the Chubb River in the company of a lad. He had the same interests as I did at his age. He was influenced by the mountain men of the Old West. His greatest ambition was to follow in their footsteps. I saw the lad yet I never really focused on his looks. He was excited. He told me his father had given him a deer hide. He told me how he used a Sears and Roebuck tanning kit he bought and paid for with money earned from trapping muskrat, to process the hide into a buckskin vest and pants, moccasins and a knife sheath. The sheath would hold a skinning blade he would fashion using horn for the handle.

We were sharing an adventure in the wilds; he was a scout for Kit Carson and Jim Bridger. Me? Only at the end of my dream—as we hauled the plank-bottom boat out of the water at the end of the day, did I figure it out.

Many times I had thought we were similar. Sitting at the helm, he'd point excitedly across a water-filled marsh. The warm, bright afternoon sun made his red hair even more brilliant. I squinted to cut down on the reflection of the rays that bounced off the slow moving brown water. The combination of distant mountains and primeval marshland made me feel as if I were in an ancient land of lush vegetation, providing habitat for a wide variety of birds, fish, amphibians, reptiles and small mammals.

We talked of trapping and solitude. The sun's heat penetrated our cotton clothing, warming our skin. We both basked in its calming effect, letting our arms hang over the side of the boat, and skimming our fingers in the water. Those simple pleasures enhanced the flavor of the setting much like the calling of an owl does on a still winter's night.

At the end of the voyage we landed at the take-out, a short portage from Averyville Road. As I disembarked, I concentrated to avoid having my right foot slip off a landing rock into the black muck along the shore-line. Attempting to balance my weight with a wooden paddle, I pushed with my left leg, then tried steadying myself. The side of the boat tipped, the gunwale slanted downward close to the surface of the water and then rocked back as I stood up. "There!" I exclaimed to my mate out loud. "That was the cat's pajamas."

But the lad was gone. I was alone. I glanced nostalgically at the river flowing by. In the mainstream, white streamers of bubbles whizzed around a boulder, while lily pads with yellow flowers decorated a protective cove. Sun danced off of the surface of the water. It was then my dream made sense. I was that young lad.

No wonder there had not been a clear distinction between the two

characters in my dream! The boy was a young version of me. He thirteen, I seventy-three years of age. The winding water of the tranquil
Chubb River and its many pleasant scenes were not a distant memory.

*I was as excited as Richard was on this morning. Not only would I be
helping my friend obtain a much wanted goal, but it also gave me an
opportunity to be with him on the trail.*

I ate breakfast in front of the window, I always enjoyed looking out.
The thermometer indicated it had been a typical late autumn night. Morning songbirds whistled. A thin layer of frost brushed the cooler surfaces
with a dusting of white; at 8 a.m. the shady areas still retained most of the
nighttime coating. A great cobweb, woven between nearby shrubs, was
revealed only because of the dew that clung to the fine threads of the
insect's trap. I watched the maze warm in the eastern exposure. How
rapidly, I noted, the sun's rays converted the heavy dew into vapor and
sent it skyward. Today would be supreme, I thought. The combination of
warm daytime temperatures, a deep blue, cloudless sky and browning colors of late fall, could not be better for the adventure I was about to repeat
after sixty years.

"Woo, whoooo." The call was coming from my driveway. I knew
immediately it was Jay. He had picked up the old habit Noah Rondeau
and I began long ago.

The next sound I heard was the screen door on my porch snapping
shut. Before I was able to push away from the table, my escort for the day
had already entered the house, crossed the living room and was stepping
up the landing that lead to the kitchen and bedroom section of my Handsome Hill cabin. "The top of the morning to you, Jay." He had a smile as
wide as Texas when I met him in the narrow hallway. "You're a mite
earlier than I expected."

"The Chubb River is awaiting us, Rich," he responded as we grasped
each others hand in a hardy clasp of friendship.

A half hour later we were padding down the narrow foot-trail that
lead from the state's Averyville Road parking lot to the edge of the river
of my youth. I led, carrying the paddles. Jay latched the daypacks to the
thwarts and eased the canoe overhead. I had all I could do to convince my
legs to pick themselves up over the hemlock tree that had fallen across the
portage. I thought I had recovered sufficiently from an earlier hospitalization, but a reoccurring hip problem reminded me I was not a "spring

chicken," even though I possessed the will.

It wasn't my fleetness of foot that allowed me to reach the put-in first. The downed tree and a few twists in the trail just slowed my porter up more. I heard a metal clank or two behind me and knew immediately just about where Jay was along the trail. Mother Nature had several well-placed trees along the footpath that had been knocked a few times by canoeists who carried vessels overhead as they blindly plodded forward.

While I waited, admiring the beauty of this shallow but wide portion of the river, I experienced a flashback. There by the placid drifting water was a rock that reminded me of the stepping stone in last night's dream. Rock, I know what you are doing here and I know where I am heading!

For long periods of time Richard and I would paddle and drift. There was no need for much conversation. The sounds of nature and water dripping off our paddles were contentment.

The light fog of the morning had burned off by the time we placed the canoe in the water. Once our craft was loaded, we shoved off into the main current and nosed upstream. The first laps of the paddles reminded me of what I knew would lay ahead. The turns and twists would be like ribbon candy—oxbows, lush vegetation and marshland. Long river grass that pointed downstream, washed by the current, lay prostrate on the surface of the water. There would be dead falls in the first section, I was sure of that. Berry brambles and tag alders, twisting and tangled, would choke at the river's edge. Beyond the low sphagnum shoreline, dense conifer forests would wrap the Chubb in a protective shield from the rest of the world. I looked forward to the vintage gold of the tamaracks in late autumn. Half-submerged logs and water soaked, rotting stumps would be like beacons that mark the shallows along a canal. Soft, tall, browning grass would offer inviting places just to pull up to, and to sit along the bank to watch the river flow by.

On the higher section, above the rapids, the sight of the second still-water will make my heart cry with joy. In the distance, to the west, will be the high summits of the forested Sawtooth Range. Farther beyond and to the south will be the divide between the Sawtooths and Street and Nye Mountains. There the Chubb tumbles through a high mountain pass into a primitive morass—a quagmire so extensive that it is unequaled in few other Adirondack scenes. And beaver dams? There will be many to pull over.

This wasn't another dream. This was the first place, during my youth, where I had experienced wilderness adventure and I was returning. I felt more alive than I had in a very long time. This was real. Once again I was on the Chubb.

I was happy to be the porter. I was surprised to encounter so many beaver dams to pull over or drag around on the upstream voyage.

Sixty years ago I had rowed this same river in a crude boat I had fashioned out of used lumber. It was a heavy craft for my age. I remember that well. My original plan was to push it over sapling poles that would act as rollers. Every few minutes I would need to skirt the spent rollers in front in order to keep moving forward. Lucky for me that Hank, a farmer who lived next door, came by when he did. If he hadn't offered to help, I might still be attempting to launch that boat!

While watertight, it was not sleek, nor an example of fine construction and beauty. But the vessel did serve me well and the narrow, flat-bottom design provided plenty of space for my traps and supplies. I poled more than I ever rowed, but when I did pull at the oars I always sat looking forward. I thought it was rather peculiar people would travel with their back toward the direction of travel. I likened it to someone backing blindly into the unknown. I knew where I had just been. I didn't need to be reminded of the scenery I'd left behind.

Sighting familiar landmarks, Richard would work into a story of times past. His remembrances like that of Running Fox and Moon Flower, the two Native Americans he met once near Paint Bed Notch. I chided him, in a respectful manner, that perhaps the story might be more dream than fact. He politely replied, "Truth is sometimes hard to believe, but the only dreaming done was the higher state of consciousness Running Fox called upon to focus on an important search site."

I don't believe Jay and I had traveled more than half a mile before we entered a bend in the river that looked very familiar. Rounding the far end of the upstream side I was greeted with a rush of memories. I wouldn't have thought it to be true, but the water had preserved some of the spruce and hemlock stumps that I'd placed traps on so long ago. Projecting slightly above the water line they had recently been occupied by mammals who had left calling cards—fresh droppings. Farther on, across the floodplain which had seen several hard frosts by this time of year, loomed the dark silhouette of a dragon pine tree, standing higher than the other conifers in the forest whose roots are delicately anchored in the quaggy sphagnum moss.

I knew where I was heading and anticipated what would come next. Several times we edged the canoe over the remnants of old beaver dams with little difficulty. And then the private camp I had mentioned came into view. I had hunted with a local police officer from the camp which is also the last marking of human activity along the river. Beyond it lay the High Peaks Wilderness Area.

Soon after passing the primitive scene of camp, meadow and forest land, the river narrowed. We were approaching a fine scenic section but were first halted until we decided how to circumvent a persnickety new beaver dam. Forging around it was not possible because of the configuration of the mucky shoreline. Our only solution was to disembark, gingerly clamor up the well-engineered, five foot barrier of woven sticks, then haul the canoe up and over with the tow line.

As I balanced myself with a paddle atop the narrow perimeter wall of the dam, I remarked to my younger companion that the old tom cat he'd dragged along hadn't planned on getting his paws wet on this trip. He was so thoughtful of my concern, knowing full well the pool of water on the upriver side of the dam was well over each of our heads, that he calmly reassured me we were going to be very careful. His wife had issued a warning that morning, "Be careful of the curves." I kidded him about what kind of curves she had meant. He responded that it surely wasn't the bend in the river we had just negotiated. Then he added as we crawled carefully into the canoe, "You don't have to worry about this dam on the way back, Richard. There's enough water flowing over it so I can leap with the old tom cat over the edge." I nodded my head as I gave him a thumbs up sign. It meant, "Oh lordy, I can't wait."

Entering another scenic passageway, we paddled slowly and in short time reached the rapids and carry. They marked the divide between the first and second levels of water. Normally I'm a quiet man, but I found I was beside myself with excitement. This wilderness setting was once my home. As we continued up river passing wooded shoreline, I talked about the day I met Moon Flower's father.

When we looped eastward and entered the Chubb River Marsh and entered my old neighborhood, I was renewed. "You see there, yonder on that far ridge? That's where I built my first cabin. I hunted, trapped and lived the entire winter of 1939 up there." What strange feelings surged through my senses. I had lived fully that winter and following spring. And, I had detached myself from mainstream living. I was following a plan, one designed to experience the liberty from conforming malcontent, something my old hermit friend, Noah referred to as "civilization's discontent." The wilderness area gave me the sensation of being totally embodied in a garden of nature. Noah philosophized that all humans, sometime in their lives experience a desire to seek out some form of primitive unification with the natural world they live within. "Most folks are friendly," he'd illustrate when talking about people in general, "but they're also frustrated, too busy. Their world moves too fast. And it's far too complicated for my own good! Back here, at Cold River, I feel free of man's restrictions. I can play my fiddle, dance a jig in the moonlight—if I've a mind to—and never once have to answer to anyone but myself."

We bent with the channel as it snaked into a tight, narrow, inverted S-curve. Then, as we swung out of the twists, the slope of Peacock Mountain rose to our left. In the distance, the high slopes of Street and Nye Mountains made a wide panoramic vista that is impossible to ever ignore. I knew as I eyed the High Peaks that my day must shortly come to an end.

Pointing to a steel gray beaver lodge, I suggested we beach and sit atop. The aging lodge would make a stately throne for this aging man. The sun had reached its zenith. The day was pleasant and warm. I was inoculated by the sounds and sights. Truly the Chubb River seemed ageless. I found that, as in my youth, I had heard today the full-throated melody of the song birds. Splashes ahead and behind told me the wildlife still remained active. Great herons swooped down, stood erect in the shallows waiting for an unsuspecting frog and then launched themselves into the air off to visit another site and find another meal. A beaver's head poked above water. It paddled silently, little ripples of waves issued behind, indicating its forward motion. Then, with a slap of its tail, it dove below the tannic surface. Everything was as it had always been. I was grateful the river is protected. It will outlast my life on Earth. That's good. Others will come and enjoy what I have always held dear to my heart. They'll experience the same pleasure I have renewed within me today. It's a sensitive language, this environment.

For a long, very long time we just sat quietly. Jay knew it was to be my last visit. Then, knowing we had to retrace our route before nightfall I opened my mouth. "I'm ready to leave." My voice worked! I didn't sense a bit of letdown. I had soaked up the sights of a favorite place on

Earth. For a day I'd given myself over to inner, sensitive human feelings. I did not think beyond the day until we returned to Handsome Hill. Sitting in the driveway, we talked, and with our conversation returned the routine feeling of home and hearth.

It was half past seven in the evening when Jay pulled out to return home. We had enjoyed two good trips together this fall. Jay's choice had been to spend a day during peak foliage at "Singing Pines," my camp and abode that my long time Adirondack hermit friend, Noah John Rondeau, called home during the last years of his life. I had greatly appreciated the opportunity given to me to renew my connection with the Chubb River.

It had been a simple pleasure. But sharing the experience with someone else who could also enjoy it made it more fulfilling. As the season advances and colder weather replaces the fleeting beauty autumn brings each year, I know I'll adjust to life's routine of less out-of-door activity. I will pick up the evening newspaper and read about man's failings and jealousies. Neighbors will talk of petty irritations. There's so much that hampers and thwarts our brief lives. Thankful I am for the opportunities to look at what is really meaningful in life. To me it is and always has been, spending time in nature.

Richard's Last Verse

*As Richard and I sat on top of an old beaver lodge watching the waters
of the Upper Chubb flow by, the old woodsman recited this poem to me.*

So vivid in memory are those precious moments
I have but to close my eyes to relive once again
those wondrous days in the wilderness.
Where still I pray the stately wolf
and mountain lion creep.
Where once I slept on balsam beds.
Where once the flashing speckled trout
caused me to leap and shout.
Where once I learned what happiness
and life were all about.
Where once I gazed with rapture,
watching sleepy spruces nod.
Where high upon the mountain top,
I paused to thank and speak to God.

Richard Smith
1919 - 1993

Epilogue

Rondeau and Smith, Cold River Camp
Tuesday, May 17, 1939

Frost last night: Fished Cold River. 9 fish.
Afternoon: Cut and hauled wood.
Drank hermit sling with a hermit.
Evening: Supper in Cold River dining room.
Much atmosphere.

An Earlier Time

I lay awake thinking about the good-hearted habits of Noah and of the many neighborhood adults who shared time with me. They broadened my knowledge and accepted me in their lives when I was growing up.

Hank and his wife, Mabel, were two of the kindest next door neighbors a child could have had. Childless themselves, they encouraged the neighborhood children to visit often. I appreciated my visitations with them.

They were good role models and treated me like a son. Hank enjoyed a good laugh even if it was at his own expense. He was also a terrific story teller. He tried to encourage me to remember some of the old stories he told, telling me that some day when all the old timers are gone, I'd be able to carry on some of the traditional stories passed down to him. I wasn't masterful but I did enjoy spinning yarns. Several high school English teachers told me they enjoyed reading the tales I wrote in my composition book. Many of those class assignments were in part due to Hank's telling.

The one characteristic that most identified Hank was his entertaining way of saying "He-gal" whenever he wanted to cuss or when reacting to a surprising situation.

Once, when our cows produced too much milk for our consumption, my chum, Bill, and I decided to make butter. If we could earn twelve cents for each two-pound brick, it would provide some pin money for the picture show on Saturdays. As we were mixing the buttermilk, the by-product of butter, with hog feed, I thought of a trick we could play on old Hank. He had recently purchased a cow and had been making a lot of his beautiful Jersey. The following day was Sunday, a perfect time to play a joke on him, for we generally visited at breakfast time. Ever since my mother had died, I looked forward to sharing some meals with them. Mabel was a good cook. The next morning Bill and I wrapped a brick of butter—it was our donation toward breakfast—and disguised a large canning jar of buttermilk. As we followed my well-worn dogtrot to Hank and Mabel's yard, we reviewed our scheme. We were going to pour the buttermilk into the milk pitcher Mabel always had on the table.

Their kitchen table was always set the same—a calico cloth spread over a wide pine-plank harvest table, with a large pitcher of cold, fresh milk with glasses placed in the center. Upon our arrival we told Mabel our plans before Hank came in from the barn.

When we sat down to eat Hank filled his glass, tipped it back and gulped half its contents before he realized it wasn't fresh milk. With great surprise, he exclaimed, "He-gal, this is buttermilk! How come?"

Bill chimed in, "Hank, you must have pushed the wrong button when you milked that amazing new cow. Didn't you notice the buttons on its rump? There's three of them. One's for plain milk, then there's one for buttermilk and another for chocolate."

Mabel couldn't contain her laughter. As she cracked up we joined in as Hank nodded his head from side to side saying, "He-gal, I never know what you boys will think of next."

Chronicles are Pushed Aside

Although I gravitated away from woods life, I never left my mountains except for a short stint in the army. Like native trout, I found it hard to survive in new waters.

Following my return from military service in the late 1940's, I took on a career of camp caretaker for a number of places around Lake Placid. My sunup to sundown work schedule pushed most thoughts of the carefree wilderness life I once followed into a recess in my memory. Cherished recollections of my early years, following high school graduation, were like old photographs—respectable snapshots, in focus and well composed, but stored in an album that is seldom opened. Most thoughts of yesteryear remained tucked away until I received a letter from my old friend, Tony Okie.

Tony Writes

I had not heard from Tony in more than twenty years. After high school graduation we parted company. Tony joined the military. For a few years, I followed my heart's desire to live in the woods. In 1959, Tony had retired from the military and moved to California where he was embarking on a new career selling insurance. He reminisced about our growing up together and asked about the path my life took. I was delighted to answer his questions and described my days of living in the wilderness—the most noteworthy part of my life.

A Younger Generation Become Interested
in their Old Neighbor

My early experiences in the woods took on a different perspective as the years passed. People would ask me so many questions about things that I had always considered commonplace. "Tell us about Cold River in the early days when you lived at Duck Hole? "You knew Noah for thirty-two years. What was he like?" "What did you and Noah do back at his hermitage?" "Has Singing Pines changed much since Noah lived there?" "What woodcraft skills did Noah teach you?" Gradually I realized they were genuinely interested in my past experiences and how lucky I was to have known Noah and have him take me under his wing.

Writing: A Commonplace Method of
Communication in my Day

During high school I had found I enjoyed writing. My English teachers were supportive and encouraged me to always write for my personal enjoyment. I did. I kept a journal. To a generation that is involved with electronic forms of communication, that might sound outdated, but I am happy with being labeled just that. I have never even owned a phone.

After Tony wrote me, I once again began writing. My journals served as a memory; my stories were long narratives, in friendly letter form, to Tony. A few years later, I began corresponding with Doctor Latimer's son. He was interested in our mutual friend, Noah.

I found letter writing to be therapeutic—most of mine, done during the winter. My caretaking responsibilities are at a minimum during that season. As old age began to catch up with me, I found the winter wind-chill factory that turns out new products to freeze unprotected ears and noses, and the nighttime temperature that can drop to forty degrees below zero, to be too unpleasant to venture out-of-doors. I enjoy spending more time in my snug cabin on Handsome Hill along River Road.

My Old Hermit Friend Has a Book Written About Him

Following Noah's death in 1967, Maitland DeSormo decided to write the biography, *Noah John Rondeau, Adirondack Hermit.* I was one of many whom he contacted. Noah had willed me many personal items: rifles, several journals, photograph albums, poems, a scrapbook, hand tied fishing flies and his autographed metal briefcase. I shared some of those things with Mr. DeSormo, but I took offense when he made reference to Noah being an "old buck" and a "delightful hippie hermit." I am sure he meant no disrespect, but I did feel my old, respected friend—the bearded hermit of Cold River—deserved more. Noah was an icon to many. He was The Hermit of Cold River. But, to his closest friends, he was simply a personable individual whom we felt very much attached to. It was in that light—a human level—that I wrote about my contact with him to my friends, Tony and Dr. Latimer.

Adirondack Life's Helping Hand

I never dreamed anything would come of the letters I wrote Tony, but to my surprise, years later, he shared some of them with Jeff Kelly, then editor of *Adirondack Life* magazine, who suggested my tales would be of interest to his magazine's readers. Subsequently, in 1985, six stories in the form of letters to Tony appeared under the heading *A Woodsman Writes.*

Jeff told me my stories were well received. Recognition that I contributed in some small way to local history as well as to the enjoyment of others was more than I expected. The stories also brought DeSormo back to my door. His call was twofold. He offered to buy the Rondeau items I owned, and he told me about a man he knew whose interests in the outdoors were similar to mine; he had agreed to inquire to see if I would meet and talk with him about Noah. I told him, "No thanks," to both inquiries.

I never considered that time had healed our falling out—although it occurred over twenty years ago. Nevertheless DeSormo was persistent. He showed up on my doorstep two years later to ask if I had changed my mind about selling Noah's possessions. I hadn't. He then mentioned the continued interest of a fellow down on Tug Hill who still wanted to meet me. His continued nudging made me curious so I relented, I said it would be fine by me if he gave him my address. He'd have to write since I didn't own a phone.

An Interested Man

In 1989 I was in my mid-seventies. I was secure. I had my circle of friends. Old, close friends of decades. I was comfortable. Little did I think that at my age, especially since I was more reserved than most people, that I was about to widen my friendship once again.

Shortly after DeSormo's visit, a letter of introduction arrived commending me on my *Adirondack Life* articles and requesting my help regarding my close association with Noah. The inquirer was straight forward. He wanted to produce a manuscript illustrating life at Cold River. The book would include a combination of many of Noah's friends experiences with Noah, photographs, poems, and journal entries—none of which had been published. I thought my friend Noah, grand old woodsman that he was, would have approved. Borrowing one of Noah's sayings I replied that I was recovering from a hospitalization, but that he was welcome to come up and talk. "I am as well as could be expected, but wearing out."

Although not inclined to mix with people, I immediately liked this fellow. I thought him honest and sincere. He wanted to portray Noah's life accurately. That was most important to me; so I supported him. I didn't want Noah to turn into some mythical folk hero.

For three and a half years I have corresponded—sometimes as often as three times a week—with Jay O'Hern. He travels to Lake Placid when he can. We've grown close and I consider him a true friend. I made every effort to put down my remembrances. The passage of years has buried some details, but the most important experiences have remained with me, thanks in part to my journals.

Historical Reflection

I have enjoyed recalling what has been important to me. When Noah and I stopped and set down the heavy packs of staples we lugged from Shattuck Clearing along the trail, there was no need for conversation. We just leaned back against a tree, smoked our pipes, and watched Cold River flow by as it had for thousands of years, the leaping amber water singing its lullaby of song. We were perfectly content. There was no need to talk.

Those times of contentment would be hard for anyone to convey. Noah and my footprints of yesterday will surely be overlapped by modern

hiking boots as backpackers continue to explore the wooded territory surrounding the Cold River.

A Surprise

To my great surprise, while on a canoe trip with Jay, he pointed out
that our letter writing and conversations had given him so much information that he proposed developing two manuscripts. He had plenty of information for his original idea about Noah. What I wasn't prepared to
hear was his concept for the second. "It will be about you and your stories, Rich," he said. To think me, an old woodsman being published. The
thought made me laugh.

Life's Downhill Pull

I am truly grateful to have lived when times were less hectic. When
a creel of fish could be caught in a few enjoyable hours. When the air was
cleaner and life was at a slower pace. Life's onward trail once smooth and
sunny all too soon turns tough, strewn with windfalls—the pitfalls of life.
By the grace of God I made it to the crest. I saw panoramic vistas, and a
pleasant valley below complete with towering pines and fresh clean
brooks.

The spring has left my step and my pack is much heavier now as I
continue down the trail toward the last sunset of tomorrow. I savor each
sunrise and think back to the time during my younger years when I care-
freely descended down a winding mountain slope, feeling as if I had the
world by the tail. I enjoyed seeing the rebirth of Nature's wildflowers and
the return of Her troupe of songbirds that hopped about on freshly painted
shades of forest green; then, I had not yet learned to fully appreciate how
meaningful beauty was. But, I was lucky. I met an ace woodsman in my
youth. He was my friend, a hermit-friend, who lived in Cold River Valley. I placed a great deal of trust and confidence in him. He taught me
many tricks of the trade of becoming skilled in woodcraft. And, in the
process, much of Noah John Rondeau's philosophy rubbed off on my outlook. Yes, my time was well spent among my beloved Adirondack Mountains.

I had a few feeds of venison this fall, just enough to keep the memory of earlier meals at Cold River City strong. There isn't much happening these days on River Road. Now and then a car passes pursued by a bored-to-death dog. My birdfeeders have become the most active place around my cabin. Bluejays screaming shrilly, "Thief! Thief!" Downy woodpeckers and nuthatches join the parade.

Postscript

When the balmy days of September had faded, giving way once more to light snow and thin ice in the water bucket, I suggested to Richard this would be a good time to begin thinking about next year's trip. Our scheme was to come up with a journey we'd both enjoy taking the following fall. I suggested a horseback ride into Duck Hole. The trek sounded good in theory he told me, but he might lack the strength. His bone cancer was claiming more of his stamina, although he hadn't lost his spirit of adventure. Promising not to toss away the suggestion, he emphasized he would like to return to Duck Hole. He enjoyed the idea of once again experiencing a bit of the enchantment, seeing the sights and hearing the sounds of his old stomping grounds.

To announce Christmas, his seasonal "Letter to Santa" arrived in a greeting card. It was a tradition he revived, for our amusement, that first began with Noah. In a notation, he mentioned he hadn't cast aside my suggested trip, but hinted the other option of an aerial flight pragmatically was a sounder plan. Where once his youth overcame any and all obstacles, the flight might be an interesting way to see old familiar places from a different perspective.

In the decade following the destructive "Big Blow" of November 1950, an interior ranger station was built at Duck Hole. The caretaker took a deep interest in the care of the terrain surrounding the pond. Richard had visited the site, finding it ridiculously tamed. "It wasn't natural; there was no wilderness look." He felt the state's concept of managing wilderness resembled what a groundskeeper would do at a golf course. He recalled reading in the newspaper that the Conservation Department had released 40,000 trout in the waters of Duck Hole. "That foolish act prompted a ride up to Singing Pines the next evening to see Noah. I knew he would appreciate hearing about such nonsense."

"Oh yes, that must mean our great Governor Rockefeller must be coming for a wilderness experience," wisecracked Noah who had a twinkle in his eye. "I must go out and spread the news to my friends, the otters. They will want to learn of this good fortune." Whereupon he stepped out the front door, swung around back to the firepit, pulled a sheet of birch bark from the tinder box and rolled it into a megaphone. Lifting to his mouth he harked, "Hear Ye! Hear Ye all otters of Cold River Valley. The Conversation Department in their great wisdom has released 40,000 trout for your dining banquet. Come one, come all, there will be enough to go around. If not, the department will probably replenish the supply at a moment's notice. I know you will be pleased to hear this bit of new. Hooray! Hooray! Cheers for the American Conversation Department." It was a scream.

The governor was, soon after, helicoptered to the interior ranger's station. It was his habit to use the headquarters as his home base from which he would ride horseback on bridle paths he helped establish. His favorite destination was the lean-to and stable along the south side of the Cold River. From there it was a short bushwhack to the river and the famed "Black Hole"—the boulder strewn section of the wild, scenic river.

Richard was an interesting storyteller, and so it came as no surprise that in March he related an event that included a parable. "I recall in the fall of 1965, I was at Singing Pines helping Noah with his end-of-the-season gardening projects. The crisp autumn morning was stroking the fine strings of our desires into a frenzy. I thought it would be nice if my old friend and I could hit the trail once again, so I asked him if he was keen about taking a day to go deer hunting with me. Very matter of factly Noah responded, 'Richard, my dear friend, I hate to disappoint you. If I was one year younger, you would have to run to catch up with me. As it is I would only slow you down. The enthusiasm is with me still, all that's lacking is the physical will.' Now, I'll end my scribble as the old washerwoman said and hang my 'close' on this line." I grasped the intended meaning: Richard's health had deteriorated.

The next few months saw Richard's once long letters drop away. His frequent hospitalizations were for longer periods and once home he was very weak and unstable. I reminded him of the old days, borrowing events he had told me from his treasure chest of unforgettable stories, "threads on the loom of time" he liked to say. He had a favorite poem he once placed by two favorite sweet, cool springs near Duck Hole. I told him I would plan on making the trip back to his favorite wilds for him, and photograph the area. He would once again appreciate the natural beauty since all of the man-made structures had been removed. Slowly, as man's marks on the environment faded, the land he knew as a wilderness was once again returning. While I was there I planned to place a copy of his poem by the spring that was closest to where his cabin used to be.

The words, while simple, reminded him he was still capable of dreaming of the freedom he had experienced when lingering in the woods:

> Pause fellow hiker
> Drink your fill of fine brew
>   from nature's still.
> It's cool.
> It's pure and refreshing.
> Of its praises you will sing.
> Best of all it's always free.
> Pause fellow hiker—
> Enjoy it with me.
>
> Richard Smith, 1941

Richard never wanted to entirely retire from his last caretaking job. Each day of employment was a joy to him. "Every morning as I went to work by motorboat," he wrote, "old Whiteface was in view greeting me as she has for a lifetime. Ageless as the galaxy, timeless as infinity. Gloriously attired in her ever changing wardrobe of light. Enchanting lady of royal bearing poised as if about to make an entrance into a grand ballroom. Dignified. Grand and admired."

A few years ago he constructed a gazebo for his employer's wife on a small point of land jutting out into the lake. From one direction it looked over Lake Placid toward Whiteface, so close and friendly. In the opposite direction old Marcy, Algonquin and Avalanche Pass could be seen. "I'm surrounded by my old friends, the mountains. I relax in the little building and enjoy, with a little envy, their timeless, enduring beauty. Their eternal existence. Only the mountains seem strong enough to withstand the ravages of progress. The mountains will always be a part of me."

A few snowdrop bulbs, cold hardy alpine plants, continue to push their heads through the forest duff around the base of a small erratic where once a woodsman used to hang his hat. The warming rays of the sun absorbed by ancient minerals radiate heat energy that melts the winter's snow crust in the shape of an irregular ring around the stone's base. First planted by Richard as a sign that would signify the coming of springtime, their tiny petals, clusters of white blooms, display both the beauty and resilience of nature. With the ground still cold and blanketed with several feet of wet corn snow, the flowers are now a perennial memorial in front of an Adirondack headstone.

Eight miles downriver Richard's old hermit friend's Town Hall has long since disintegrated. A slight depression in the earth is all that marks the site of many of "Quack's" most memorable life experiences.

Descendants of Richard's pet Willie the weasel and a younger generation of chipmunks that once used to rob Noah's flower seeds both scamper over the leafy forest floor. The earth, in all its regenerative powers will, under a new spring canopy of ash, beech, birch, maple, balsam, and spruce, take back the woodsman.

A Home Coming

At the base of a tree
overlooking the meadows that once comprised Cold River flow
in sight of Seymour, Seward, Donaldson and Emmons Mountains,
Richard's ashes were mixed with Adirondack duff,
pebbles and water from Cold River,
sprigs of balsam and spruce,
a piece of rusted ironware and chips of Noah's crockery.
The hunter has returned.

Words from Crane Mountain, his favorite poem by Jeanne Robert Foster were spoken.

"When darkness should be my home,
Eternal mountain, do not leave my heart;
Remain with me in my sleep,
In my dreams, in my resurrection."

Deer hunting season
October 1993

Bibliography

UNPUBLISHED SOURCES

Rondeau, Noah John. Journals for 1939, 1943, 1944, 1949 and 1950; scrapbooks and personal photo albums of Rondeau, now property of the Adirondack Museum, Blue Mountain Lake, NY.

Rondeau, Noah John. "The Barefoot Girl," a poem, used by permission of the North Elba-Lake Placid Historical Society.

Correspondence from Richard Smith to William J. O'Hern.

Correspondence from Richard Smith to C.V. Latimer, Jr., M.D.

Correspondence from Richard Smith to Anthony Okie.

PUBLISHED SOURCES

Anderson, Donald Jack. *Goodbye Mountain Man*. Published by the author, Commercial Printing Company, New Castle, PA, 1976.

Anderson, Donald Jack. *Trapping with Great Trappers*. Swiftwater, PA.: Summit House Publishers, 1979.

Halpern, Daniel, ed. *On Nature*. New York, NY.: Antaeus, 1986.

Jamieson, Paul. *Adirondack Canoe Waters: North Flow*. Glens Falls, NY: The Adirondack Mountain Club, 1981.

Verner, William K. "Reviewed by William K. Verner." *The Living Wilderness*, Spring, 1971.

Wilson, Kenneth A. "Return to Rondeau's Hermitage." *Adirondack Life*, Vol. 5, Number 4, Fall, 1974.

Wood, Richard. *Narratives of Trapping Life: Stories of the Trail and Trapline*, _____, 1924.